# CHOPPER

Firsthand Accounts of Helicopter Warfare,
World War II to Iraq

# CHOPPER

*Robert F. Dorr*

BERKLEY BOOKS, NEW YORK

THE BERKLEY PUBLISHING GROUP
Published by the Penguin Group
Penguin Group (USA) Inc.
375 Hudson Street, New York, New York 10014, USA
Penguin Group (Canada), 10 Alcorn Avenue, Toronto, Ontario M4V 3B2, Canada (a division of Pearson Penguin Canada Inc.)
Penguin Books Ltd., 80 Strand, London WC2R 0RL, England
Penguin Group Ireland, 25 St. Stephen's Green, Dublin 2, Ireland (a division of Penguin Books Ltd.)
Penguin Group (Australia), 250 Camberwell Road, Camberwell, Victoria 3124, Australia (a division of Pearson Australia Group Pty. Ltd.)
Penguin Books India Pvt. Ltd. 11 Community Centre, Panchsheel Park, New Delhi—110 017, India
Penguin Group (NZ), Cnr. Airborne and Rosedale Roads, Albany, Auckland 1310, New Zealand (a division of Pearson New Zealand Ltd.)
Penguin Books (South Africa) (Pty.) Ltd., 24 Sturdee Avenue, Rosebank, Johannesburg 2196, South Africa

Penguin Books Ltd., Registered Offices: 80 Strand, London, WC2R 0RL, England

This book is an original publication of the Berkley Publishing Group.

Copyright © 2005 by Bill Fawcett and Associates
Cover design by Richard Hasselberger
Text design by Stacy Irwin.

First edition: July 2005

Library of Congress Cataloging-in-Publication Data

Dorr, Robert F.
    Chopper : firsthand accounts of helicopter warfare World War II to Iraq / Robert F. Dorr.
      p. cm.
    ISBN 0-425-20273-9
      1. Military helicopters—United States.    2. Helicopter pilots—United States—Biography.
3. Flight crews—United States—Biography.    4. Air warfare.    I. Title.

    UG1223.D676 2005
    358. 4'183—dc22

                                                                    2005041164

PRINTED IN THE UNITED STATES OF AMERICA

10   9   8   7   6   5   4   3   2   1

# Author's Note

These first-person accounts of American helicopter pilots and crews in combat are the result of seventy-seven interviews and several flights aboard helicopters completed in 2003 and 2004. Any errors are the fault of the author. However, this book would have been impossible without the help of many.

The following combat veterans were interviewed for this book: David Althoff, Rod Barber, John Birch, John Caldwell, Jim Cardoso, Piet Cilliers, LeRoy Cook, Mark Daley, "F-117 pilot" (name withheld), Bruce Dallas, Charles Field, Chad Franks, Doug Froling, John Gaskin, Eric Giacchino, Thomas Galvin, Ron Gatewood, Ernesto Gomez, Carter Harman, Bob Harrison, Michael T. "Ghandi" Healy, Jeffrey M. "Huey" Hewlett, Robert Kelley, David "Doc" Kinsey, Richard C. Kirkland, Lee Komich, Kevin Kuginskie, Donald P. McMahon, David L. McMichael, Leonard Martinez, Jacob M. Matt, Paul Mercandetti, Andrew H. Mills, Frank Moreno, Mike Novosel, Mike Novosel, Jr., James T. O'Kelley, Jim Phelan, Hal Salem, Joseph Scholle, Roland Speckman, Dale Stovall, Craig H. Streeter, Frank Sturgeon, Robert Towles, Tom Trask, William R. Weber, Darrel Whitcomb, Kenneth Ray Whitley, Paul Winkel, and Matt Ziegler.

The following people also provided interviews and assistance for this book: Allen A. Atwood, William Bartsch, Chuck Gaskin, Hill Goodspeed, Michael Haas, Katy Hadduck, Joseph G. Handelman, Alex Harman, Joseph G. Handelman Bruce Harman, Robert Hewson, M. J. Kasiuba, Sean Kelley, Geoff LeBaron, Robert Shane, John "Slats" Slattery, and Norman Taylor.

I also want to thank Herb Mason, a historian at Air Force Special Operations Command; Bill Fawcett; and Tom Colgan.

A brief passage from *Dustoff: The Memoir of an Army Aviation,* by Michael J. Novosel (Novato, CA: Presidio Press, 1999) in Chapter Thirteen is quoted with permission of the author. A few sentences in the Michael J. Novosel, Jr., interview were adapted with permission from the Army's own magazine, *Soldiers.*

Some veterans interviewed for this volume have written their own books. Novosel's *Dustoff* and *The Rescue of Bat 21,* by Darrel Whitcomb (Annapolis, MD: Naval Institute Press, 1999), are important reading for those interested in helicopters in combat. *War Pilot: True Tales of Combat and Adventure,* by Richard C. Kirkland (New York: Random House, 1999) is a collection of tales about both airplanes and helicopters.

—Robert F. Dorr
  Oakton, Virginia

# Chapter 1

## Behind the Lines in Burma

## What Happened

They called it a "whirlybird" or an "eggbeater"—words not used today. Few pilots had seen one. A handful of young military men went to the Sikorsky factory in Stratford, Connecticut, to learn to maintain and fly the YR-4B, and then, without missing a beat, they took it halfway around the world to Burma. One of the men said he felt more like a guinea pig than a pioneer.

Among them were pilot 2nd Lt. Carter Harman and mechanic Sgt. Jim Phelan. In Burma, they joined the 1st Air Commando Group, a maverick band of type A–independent thinkers who weren't much for military discipline or the chain of command, but who looked at the ugly, ungainly flying machine and thought they might be able to do something with it.

The chance to test the new machine came when Tech. Sgt. Ed Hladovcak, the intrepid sergeant-pilot known as Murphy ("Do you see anybody around here who knows how to pronounce Hladovcak?") crashed in an L-1 Vigilant liaison plane, along with three British soldiers whose names no one ever wrote down.

**Second Lieutenant Carter Harman**
**April 20–26, 1944**
**Sikorsky YR-4A Helicopter**
**43-28247**
**First Air Commando Group**
**Aberdeen, Burma**

Previously unpublished photo of Carter Harman as a first lieutenant in 1944. He completed his Army service as a captain the following year.

*Carter Harman*

Hladovcak and the trio of His Majesty's soldiers were miles behind Japanese lines, deep in the jungles of Burma. Another liaison plane, an L-5 Sentinel, pinpointed their location but could not land in vegetated terrain crisscrossed by paddy fields. Second Lt. Carter Harman was 500 miles away in India when Hladovcak went down and he received the message: "Send the eggbeater in." The R-4 would have to carry extra gas and would be able to lift only one survivor at a time, but Harman impressed one observer as "cool and serious" when he took off to attempt the rescue. Harman eventually saved all four Allied soldiers, one at a time, in his unorthodox flying machine. "It didn't faze him a bit," remembered mechanic Phelan, even though the rescue ended with a getaway that proved to be an anticlimax.

**JIM PHELAN** It was very hot in Burma. Consequently, you didn't have the horsepower you did in cooler weather. The heat was a problem. Originally, we had four R-4s in the 1st Air Commando Group and three of those cracked up one way or the other.

In those days, nobody had heard of any helicopter, our R-4 or any other. I was at the Aberdeen base that we had set up for the invasion of Burma and everybody wondered what this thing called the R-4 would do. It had just a 175-horsepower engine, and nobody was quite sure. Carter Harman went off down to the front lines with it, and it worked.

**CARTER HARMAN** Everybody saw immediately that Air Commandos were upstarts who answered to no one but their own boss. When the 1st Air Commando Group arrived in the China-Burma-India Theater, it was like a bunch of cowboys bursting into the parlor and smashing your Aunt Mae's dainty little tea saucers.

Independent, untidy, at times arrogant, and commanded by a mere colonel who answered only to Washington—Philip "Flip" Cochran, the real-life model for Terry and the Pirates—the Air Commandos became the personal air force of Brigadier Orde C. Wingate, the unorthodox British commander in the CBI. Their tools were the P-51A Mustang fighter, B-25 Mitchell bombers packing a 75-mm cannon in the nose, the L-5 Sentinel liaison aircraft, the Waco CG-4A glider, and, of course, the trusty C-47 Skytrain.

Their strangest tool was a box-shaped gadget known as an egg-beater, or sometimes a helicopter, the R-4, built by Sikorsky and shipped to Burma in 1944. One onlooker described the R-4 as "a flying shoebox with windows."

The Air Commandos, known originally as "Project 9," were conceived as a one-of-a-kind outfit to fight only during the 1944 dry season. Their job was to support Wingate's "Chindit" long-range raiding parties, named after a legendary winged stone lion. With 528 men and 348 aircraft, Cochran and air ace Lt. Col. (later Maj. Gen.) John R. Allison wreaked havoc with Japanese forces, giving the Allies an edge in a campaign that had stagnated for two years.

On March 5, 1944, they launched Operation Thursday, using C-47s and CG-4A gliders to haul Chindits behind Japanese lines. More than 100 C-47s, each pulling two gliders, hauled 2,500 troops 260 miles to a drop zone scouted by Cochran in a P-51A and dubbed "Broadway." Contrary to all wisdom, much of the flying was done in darkness with no lights or radios and the C-47 pilots used almost two-thirds of their fuel on the outbound leg. Some returned to base with less than forty gallons. In twenty-four hours, troops secured a landing field, making the gliders unnecessary. The Japanese never again saw success in the region.

2nd Lt. Carter Harman (standing, left), with another pilot and ground crew members, in front of the Sikorsky YR-4B helicopter at Lalaghat, India, in about January 1945, eight months after Harman's famous rescue. The other pilot (standing, right) is 1st Lt. Frank Peterson. Crew chief Sgt. James Phelan is in the front row, far right.

*U. S. Air Force*

Instead of going away when the season ended, the group expanded to become the 1st Air Commando Division. Learning of a new aerial gadget being tested in the United States, the Commandos tested their political leverage in Washington by requesting four Sikorsky YR-4B helicopters. The boxy R-4 was challenged by the high, hot conditions of Burma, but the Commandos pulled off history's first combat helicopter rescue.

Upstarts who would have failed a white-glove inspection were the norm among the Air Commandos. "Irreverent?" said Col. Fleming Johnson, an Air Commando veteran. "Hell, we were damn near insubordinate half the time. We wouldn't have shined on anybody's parade ground. We weren't good at snapping salutes or saying, 'sir.' And Regular Army officers didn't understand that we were different." In fact, Cochran, Alison, Johnson, and the other Air Commandos were more than different: They were the point of the spear.

**JIM PHELAN** The funny thing is, the first R-4 almost didn't make it to Burma.

On February 4, 1944, we departed the Sikorsky plant at Bridgeport-Stratford with the first R-4 dismantled and packed aboard a C-46 Commando transport. We got as far as Baltimore and cracked up.

We went off the end of the runway, through a field, and into a ditch. I was thrown around inside the C-46. There was a hellacious noise. Nobody got hurt. They removed the helicopter and brought it to a hangar at Baltimore. We fixed the helicopter and replaced its landing gear. After that, they repaired the C-46. They moved the C-46 to a new base for a test hop, and I caught up with them at the new base.

We had a couple more emergency stops, one in Charlotte, North Carolina, and one someplace else. We finally got to Homestead, Florida. We paused there and then flew on to South America. After that we flew from Brazil over to Ascension Island, and then over to South Africa. We went across Africa and found ourselves in Egypt, where we flew across the Suez Canal and eventually reached Karachi, India.

When we got to Karachi, I had a problem with their water. It was dysentery. I got sick and had to go into the hospital for three days. While I was hospitalized, the C-46 took off. So the R-4 went on without me. After three days or so, I followed.

The orders from Gen. Henry H. "Hap" Arnold gave a very high priority to anyone connected with the 1st Air Commando Group. Arnold was the boss in Washington and when you had orders from him you were treated kind of special. So I easily got a flight from Karachi, supposedly to Calcutta. But we landed someplace in between. I was under the mistaken impression the place was the base I was going to, so I got off—but it was the wrong base. It was a British base.

I was stuck there for about ten days. Then, I took a train to Calcutta and got to the airbase there. I caught up with the other guys at Dum Dum Airport in Calcutta and they told me the helicopter was already at the Air Commando base. At this point, I got aboard a C-47 Skytrain and was flown to a destination that was short of the Air Commando base up there in Assam by about fifty, sixty miles. At that point, Carter

Harman, who was the pilot of my helicopter, came and picked me up in a single-engine UC-64 Norseman and flew me to the Air Commando base at Lalaghat. I arrived on April 18, 1943.

On April 21, the L-1 Vigilant with Murph and three others on board was shot down. They wanted Carter. They wanted him to go into Japanese territory. Carter took the helicopter and flew it to Aberdeen, the base we had inside Burma.

I was nearby but not directly involved in Carter's rescue attempt. You might ask how I got there, so far from home. That's easy. I was drafted into the Air Corps. They sent me to school in Boston to become an aircraft mechanic. Then they sent me to a base in Indiana to work on twin-engine Beechcrafts. They put out a call for people to work on helicopters, and since I came from Stratford, I knew all about helicopters. At least I thought I did.

**ED HLADOVCAK**  Maybe the L-1 had been flying too low. Who was to say? The Vultee L-1 Vigilant was a sturdy aircraft used for operations behind Japanese lines. It had performed well picking up three wounded British soldiers and had been making its way back toward friendly troops when the Japanese opened fire. The date was April 21, 1944.

The L-1, piloted by a distinctly un-Irish "Murphy," took serious hits. Probably no pilot could have prevented the crash landing that followed. The L-1 went down in a rice paddy. An embankment caught the plane's fixed landing gear and snapped it off, ending any prospect of that particular L-1 ever flying again.

Murphy and the three Brits crawled, thrashed, and climbed until they were deep inside jungle foliage about half a mile from the wrecked plane. For some hours, it seemed there was no one friendly in the area. Murphy and the Brits hunkered down, watching as Japanese soldiers arrived at the wreckage of the L-1, secured the crash site, and fanned out. As the day progressed and the heat became more insufferable, the voices of patrolling Japanese came closer. Their uniform leggings were visible through the undergrowth.

If anyone could have looked down at this, they would have thought, "What a mess."

When a helicopter had to rescue the pilot of a crashed liaison airplane—Carter Harman's YR-4B picking up pilot Ed "Murphy" Hladovcak and his passengers from a crashed Vultee L-1 Vigilant like the one shown here—the event was a look into the future. Within a decade, helicopters began to replace liaison aircraft for rescue duties. Today, the military no longer uses an aircraft like the L-1.

*Consolidated Vultee*

---

In mid-afternoon, one of the 1st Air Commando Group's smaller L 5 Sentinel liaison planes flew overhead and dropped a note. The message referred to the sharp slope behind Murph. It read: "Move Up Mountain. Japs Nearby."

It was never clear whether the Japanese had pilfered the crashed L-1 yet. In the crashed plane's tiny cargo hold were three Japanese ceremonial swords Murphy had picked up from a battlefield in a souvenir hunt. If the Japanese found those swords first and captured Hladovcak, there was going to be hell to pay.

**CARTER HARMAN** Yes, I was that second lieutenant who flew the first-ever helicopter rescue mission. How did I find myself in Burma at the controls of a YR-4B helicopter trying to pick up Murphy and assisted by crew chief Jim Phelan? I guess it happened because, unlike Jim, I didn't get drafted.

I grew up in New Jersey. When the war started, there was a lot of drafting going on. A lot of us were thinking, "Hey, maybe I don't want to be drafted because I'll be in the infantry without rank." I was a journalist before the war. I reported on music for the *New York Times*. More important, when the war started I had already done some flying, which seemed like a sure reason not to be in the infantry. I had logged time in a Piper Cub and a Waco biplane.

So instead of being drafted, I joined the Army Air Corps and went to Texas. I was in flying class 43-C and after getting those silver wings I became an instructor in biplane trainers.

The helicopter thing was a volunteer thing. Someone said, "You want to volunteer?" I said, "Yes." I knew what a helicopter was, but not much about it. They were fairly new. I went to the Sikorsky plant at Bridgeport to learn about the R-4 helicopter. In fact, one reason I volunteered was Bridgeport was close to home.

I realized that I had a good thing. There was a small group of us, three pilots and half a dozen crew chiefs and others, including Jim Phelan, and this new gadget called a helicopter was pretty interesting. Sikorsky acted as a training school and graduated the first class of Army Air Forces helicopter pilots in October or November 1943. The pilots were myself, 1st Lt. John Beeson, 1st Lt. Burt C. Powell, 1st Lt. Frank M. Turney, and Capt. Jack Beighle.

We were the first Army service pilots of helicopters, although a handful of test pilots may have come before us. Sikorsky's great civilian engineering test pilot Jimmy Viner, among others, taught us to fly this new type of aerial machine. Because helicopter development was taking place slowly, one or two of these officers was reassigned to fighter training.

In October 1943, instructed by Viner, I became the seventh Army pilot ever to solo a helicopter.

Beighle didn't go overseas. He went to Wright Field in Ohio to help with helicopter development, then returned to Sikorsky. He assisted Viner during the first helicopter hoist rescue on November 29, 1945—after the war—when they pulled survivors from a grounded oil barge in Long Island Sound near Fairfield, Connecticut. That event is often

With a B-25 Mitchell bomber in the background, mechanics assemble an R-4 helicopter at Lalaghat, India (not in Burma, as a caption from the era suggests). This is the helicopter that was flown on a rescue mission by Frank Peterson and Irvin Steiner in January 1945, making it the second helicopter—after Carter Harman's—to achieve a combat rescue.

*U. S. Air Force*

called a "first," but it happened seventeen months after I flew the first combat rescue mission. Beighle later became a longtime employee at Sikorsky and helped develop newer and better helicopters over many years until his retirement in 1969.

There's another rescue that sometimes is cited as the first. On January 26, 1945, Capt. Frank Peterson flew an R-4 to evacuate a wounded weather observer, Pvt. Howard Ross, from a 4,700-foot mountain ridge in the Naga hills of Burma. Peterson flew with a copilot, 1st Lt. (later Lt. Col.) Irvin Steiner. That was a very early helicopter success, but it came eight months after I flew the first such mission.

The assignment to India and Burma was special. The 1st Air Commando Group had all kinds of airplanes, every kind there was. On March 16, 1944, I arrived at Lalaghat, India, in a C-46 Commando transport carrying a YR-4B helicopter as cargo.

Our plans to assemble a team ran into trouble from the start. One author once compared the arrival of the 1st Air Commando Wing in Burma as having the impact of "a brick thrown through a stain-glass window." We got there after the commandos were set up and operating, but our arrival ran into tribulations and tragedy.

Our mechanics assembled the helicopter outdoors in the heat and grit at Lalaghat, with few tools and no equipment. Tragically, on the first flight of a helicopter in India on March 21, 1944, the YR-4B crashed, killing Powell—the first man to die in a U.S. helicopter in a combat zone.

More helicopters arrived almost immediately, accompanied by helicopter pilot John Beeson. But Beeson went out to fly a conventional support mission in a C-46 transport and was wounded in the hip by ground fire. This meant that from the beginning of April 1944, I was the only qualified helicopter pilot in the China-Burma-India Combat Theater.

On about April 21, 1944, Air Commando boss Cochran sent radio instructions for me to proceed with a helicopter to Taro in northern Burma. I was about to learn about the big trouble that L-1 liaison Murphy had gotten into. But first, I had to fill a tall order to get to my destination. Taro was 600 miles from Lalaghat, way beyond the YR-4B's usual range of 100 miles.

I was very much aware that our YR-4B helicopter came with a canvas-covered stretcher that could be attached to the side of the aircraft to carry a litter patient. To prepare the helicopter for what was going to be a marathon journey, I threw four jerry cans of extra fuel in the unused copilot's seat (there was no one in India or Burma who could serve as a copilot, and the weight of another crew member wasn't going to be helpful, anyway) and I put the litter stretcher behind the seats. Then, I took off to cover the first leg of the flight to Taro. That meant climbing above mountain peaks that loomed to 5,000 feet—in theory, the ceiling of the YR-4B—and visually navigating to Dimapur. I landed safely at Dimapur and filled the gas tanks from my own jerry cans before beginning the second leg of the trip, aiming for Jorhat. That was a bomber base where our boys were flying B-24 Liberators.

This trip was solo. The helicopter was primitive by today's standards, but I was comfortable being alone with it. I didn't know much about the population of the region, though, except that there were plenty of Japanese troops, so I felt some apprehension about who might be shooting at whom. Also, there was some puzzlement. I was undertaking this solo travel without much of an idea as to why.

I stayed overnight at Jorhat and the next day flew on to Taro with a brief refueling stop at Ledo. But when I reached the destination where

World War II helicopter pilots Irvin Steiner (left) and Frank Peterson with the C-54 Skymaster transport that transported them and their YR-4B helicopter to Burma in January 1945.

*U. S. Army*

they wanted me, Taro, I still didn't know why I was there. "It's time for a break," I told one of the soldiers. I went for a dip in a mountain stream and tried to wash my clothes as best I could. I was still wearing the summer khakis I'd brought from halfway around the world.

That's when a radio message came from the 1st Air Commando Group base in Burma known as Aberdeen, a temporary airstrip deep inside Japanese territory. The base was home to L-1 Vigilant and L-5 Sentinel liaison airplanes piloted by sergeant-pilots like Murphy and used for air rescues. Survivors who were brought to Aberdeen via L-1 or L-5 were transferred to larger aircraft for evacuation to India. It was all being done under the noses of the Japanese.

The message consisted of four words: "Send the Eggbeater Immediately." They wanted me to proceed from Taro to Aberdeen, which was 125 miles to the south—again, a distance beyond the limited range of the YR-4B.

It took me until April 25 to reach Aberdeen. It was a difficult flight. Previously, I had been stopping to refuel from jerry cans I was carrying. At Taro, mechanics installed an extra fuel tank borrowed from an L-5 inside the fuselage of my helicopter, but still I would have to set down whenever I wanted to transfer fuel, so this last leg might be an overnight trek. I didn't know it yet, but Aberdeen-based L-5s were pinpointing Hladovcak's location on the ground. Since they knew the "eggbeater" was on the way, the Commandos were planning to use me and the YR-4B for the pickup.

**ED HLADOVCAK** On April 24, a strange series of sounds cracked in the air. It was gunfire, or was it? How difficult could it be for the Japanese to find one exhausted, hungry American sergeant-pilot and three injured British soldiers? But the sounds came and went. If there were Japanese troops behind that green foliage, they did not appear.

The next day, the three British soldiers were much worse. Their wounds were becoming infected. The heat refused to subside. There were insects everywhere, especially mosquitoes, known to carry a virulent strain of malaria.

**CARTER HARMAN** When I landed at the Air Commando base at Aberdeen, I believe it was early morning on April 25, 1944. The information was that the four downed men led by Hladovcak were holding out in the jungle and had not been found by Japanese troops, but it was unclear how long that could continue. L-5 Sentinels were dropping supplies and messages to Hladovcak, aiming at a white parachute he had draped across the rice paddy, but that brilliant white cloak was probably going to make him highly visible to the Japanese, too.

They dropped a message to Murphy telling the sergeant-pilot about a spot where a liaison plane could pick up Hladovcak and the three British soldiers. It was a sandbar on a river nearby. British commandos had secured a small sector of the bank, enough space for an L-1 or L-5 to land. At Aberdeen, they knew now that none of the four men could reach the riverbank on his own power. They believed, however, that I could get into the clearing where the men were waiting and that my YR-4B could lift them to the riverbank, where the liaison planes could take over. Since I could only carry one of the men at a time, I would have to make four round trips. Helicopters were still new, of course, and we were still learning that they did not like hot weather. Needless to say, they also did not like Japanese soldiers, and my YR-4B was exceedingly vulnerable to any kind of gunfire.

I wondered about the largely unproven 200-hp Warner piston en-

A second wave of helicopter rescues in Burma became possible when this Sikorsky YR-4B was transported from Wright Field, Ohio, to Myitkyina, Burma, in January 1945 for operations by pilots Frank Peterson and Irv Steiner. In the background is an L-5 Sentinel aircraft also used for behind-the-lines rescues.

*U. S. Army*

gine that powered the YR-4B. It had reliability problems. I was going to have to push engine and helicopter to the limit to make the pickups in this weather.

I flew from Aberdeen to the sandbar riverbank, where I made the rendezvous with an L-5 Sentinel. Then, we took off together and the L-5 led me to the clearing where Hladovcak and the three British were struggling to stay alive. I did not see any Japanese troops but was told they were all around us. I wondered if the engine and helicopter would hold together trying to pull off a job that was more rigorous than anything they had been designed for.

They told me later that Hladovcak went crazy when he saw my eggbeater arriving. He had, of course, never seen a helicopter before. I was pushing the YR-4B to the limit when I set down in the clearing in a swirl of flying dust and pieces of greenery. Murphy loaded the most seriously injured British soldier aboard. The YR-4B strained, vibrated, and took off. I was able to make it to the sandbar where a liaison plane flew him to safety.

I hauled out a second British soldier, still wondering if my engine and aircraft might fail on me, still searching the jungle canopy for Japanese troops. We reached the riverbank and that's when everything went wrong.

The Warner engine seized on me. There was a clunking sound and a lot of vapor around the engine. It had overheated on me and it wasn't going to start. I was going to have to spend the night on the sandbar. I didn't see how our luck could hold out much longer, and I wondered if that was the night the Japanese would overrun Hladovcak and the remaining British soldier.

It was a long, lonely night, and the liaison-pilot guys warned me we might have weather problems on top of everything else the next day. When morning came, there was some low cover but nothing to prevent flying, if the engine would only start. It did. I was able to pick up the third British soldier and get him to safety. Murphy was now alone—and, he said later, very lonely—in the clearing in the jungle.

The details of the anticlimactic final rescue are still a little vague, but I remember that Murphy held out alone near his crash site and that I was able to go in again in the YR-4B. As I approached him, soldiers broke out of the treeline about 1,000 feet from him, some with their rifles held in the air. "It's too late," I thought. "After all this work, it's too late." Later, Hladovcak told me he was shouting out loud about Japanese troops bearing down on him.

I got there first. Hladovcak climbed on board. I put the aircraft into a hover. Now, the troops swarmed directly beneath us and for a moment the YR-4B threatened to seize again. The helicopter sank back toward the jungle. Then, I was able to get the YR-4B to full power and we climbed away from those men with rifles.

I took Hladovcak all the way back to Aberdeen. When we got there, we were told that the troops who'd swarmed beneath my helicopter were, in fact, friendly Chindit troops who had been intent on rescuing Murphy. There were Japanese nearby, but I never actually saw them. When I bounded off the ground with Murphy on board, we were escaping from our own guys.

I spent several more weeks with the 1st Air Commando Group and retrieving several people who needed rescuing. Then, the last R-4 helicopter was damaged beyond repair. But in early 1945, another helicopter became available.

# Sikorsky R-4 Helicopter

Recently, a visitor to the Air Force Museum in Dayton, Ohio, looked at the first operational United States military helicopter and remarked that it looked like "a flying shoebox with windows."

The Sikorsky YR-4B Hoverfly was not elegant or graceful, but it was a practical machine that introduced helicopter flying to the Army Air Forces (AAF), predecessor of today's U. S. Air Force.

The museum's web site tells us that the original military model of this helicopter, the XR-4, was developed from the famous experimental VS-300 helicopter, invented by Igor Sikorsky and publicly demonstrated in 1940. The XR-4 made its initial flight on January 13, 1942.

Shortly after first taking to the air, the square-shaped XR-4 flew from Sikorsky's Stratford, Connecticut, plant to the Army's test center at Wright Field, Ohio. This trip of about 350 miles was one of the world's first long-distance helicopter cross-country flights.

## Vought-Sikorsky YR-4B Hoverfly (VS-316A)

Type: One- or two-seat combat rescue and general utility helicopter

Power: One 200-hp Warner R-550-1 or -3 Super Scarab seven-cylinder air-cooled radial piston engine driving a three-bladed, 38-ft (11.6 m) main rotor

Performance: Maximum speed, 75 mph (120 km/h), cruising speed 60 mph (96 km/h); climb to 8,000 ft (2440 m), 45 min.; service ceiling 8,000 ft (2438 m); range, 100 mi (161 km), combat radius est. 50 mi (80 km)

Weights: Empty, 2,020 lb (917 kg); normal takeoff weight 2,200 lb (997 kg); gross weight, 2,535 lb (1151 kg)

Dimensions: Main rotor diameter 38 ft (11.6 m); length overall, rotors turning, 48 ft 1 in (14.65 m); fuselage length 35 ft 5 in (10.8 m); height, 12 ft 5 in (3.80 m); tail rotor diameter 7 ft 8 in (.230 m); wheel track, 10 ft (3.05 m); main rotor disc area est. 1,134 sq ft (114 sq m)

Armament: None

Crew: One pilot or one pilot plus medical technician

First flight: January 14, 1942

2nd Lt. Carter Harman hovers in ship no. 42-28247, the YR-4B that became the first helicopter to arrive in a combat zone and the first to fly a combat mission. The location is Lalaghat, India, en route to Burma, in March 1943.

*U. S. Air Force*

The YR-4B model was powered by a 180-horsepower Warner R-550-1/-3 pistol radial engine driving a thirty-eight-foot main rotor. The helicopter was capable of a maximum speed of just seventy-five miles per hour and had a range of 130 miles.

The AAF acquired 130 R-4 helicopters of various models, of which 20 were transferred to the Coast Guard and 45 to Great Britain.

Three YR-4Bs went to 1st Air Commando Group in Burma in 1944. The Y prefix meant the helicopter had a "service test" mission, which was a peculiar way to refer to going into combat. The group, a predecessor of today's special operations units, carried off history's first helicopter combat mission, with 2nd Lt. Carter Harman at the controls of a YR-4B. Flying sixty miles behind enemy lines, Harman made a series of pickups that saved three British soldiers and a downed American pilot.

Group commander Col. Philip G. "Flip" Cochran wrote, "Today the 'egg-beater' went into action and the damn thing acted like it had good sense."

The Harman helicopter rescue "was quite an accomplishment," said retired Col. Michael Haas, author of *Apollo's Warriors,* a book about special operations forces. "The YR-4B was aluminum and canvas. It could be deathtrap in the wrong hands, when flown properly it performed well. The Burma rescue was the first United States operational rescue by a helicopter and it really opened a lot of eyes."

In what amounted to a second wave of helicopter activity in Burma, an R-4B was rushed to the combat zone in January 1945. Five pilots were down in the jungle behind Japanese lines, where L-5 liaison planes could not land. Pilots Capt. Frank Peterson and 1st Lt. Irvin Steiner, maintenance officer 1st Lt. Paul Shoemacher, and three mechanics made the trip from Wright Field, Ohio, to Myitkyina, Burma, in a C-54 Skymaster that carried their R-4B. "In Myitkyina we were attached to an Air Jungle Rescue unit that flew small aircraft and a B-25 Mitchell medium bomber for search, rescue, and drop sorties," said Shoemacher.

"Peterson was the ranking member of our flight test crew and had the most helicopter experience; he elected to be the rescue pilot when an American soldier at a weather station in the Naga hills, Pvt. Ross, had been accidentally wounded and needed hospitalization. Peterson and Steiner flew the YR-4B to a strip about sixty miles from the weather station and refueled. They took off easily and, flying low over the jungle, they were difficult to track by the faster L-5s that were forced to circle above them.

"In the YR-4B with no radio, mirrors were used to flash their location. Climbing above 5,000 feet through the passes in the craggy hills was barely possible. Peterson made the final leg alone, following the L-5s over the dense Naga jungle to a small clearing on the crest of a razorback ridge." With enormous difficulty, Peterson picked up Pvt. Ross and saved his life by flying him to safety.

An R-4B also reached the Pacific island of Saipan before fighting ended in August 1945, but it's believed that rescues in Burma were the only combat actions by the Hoverfly. In the postwar years, newer helicopters quickly replaced R-4s. In 1948, the Air Force dropped the "R" (for rotorcraft) designation and replaced it with "H" (for helicopter), so the R-4 became the H-4. A beautiful example of this pioneering helicopter is on display at the Air Force Museum.

# Chapter 2

## Into the Breech in Korea

### What Happened

Nothing. That's what was supposed to happen that day.

First Lieutenant Charles H. Field was the pilot of the 3rd Air Rescue Squadron's "standby" H-5 at Seoul's YoiDo airfield, known to troops as K-16, on April 30, 1951. Field was notified that a South African F-51 Mustang pilot, Lt. Piet Cilliers, had been shot down near Sariwon, North Korea, about seventy miles behind the lines. Celliers belonged to South Africa's No. 2 "Cheetah" Squadron, a component of the United States Air Force's 18th Fighter Bomber Wing.

Field and Air Force medical corpsman Spellman E. Patterson took off to attempt a rescue. At this juncture, the recently independent U. S. Air Force still used Army-style ranks; Corporal Patterson and his fellow medics were forerunners of today's pararescue jumpers, or PJs.

When Field's helicopter arrived at the scene of the Mustang shootdown, Chinese troops were directing small-arms fire at Celliers, who hiked to the top of a ridge but then sustained a bullet wound in the leg. Mustangs led by Col. William P. McBride, 18th wing commander, relieved Cilliers' wingman Guy Peterson and began strafing the Chinese troops while those troops closed in on the pilot from two directions.

**First Lt. Charles H. Field**
**April 30, 1951**
**Sikorsky H-5F Helicopter**
**Third Air Rescue Squadron**
**K-16 YoiDo Airfield, Seoul**

Standing in front of an H-5 helicopter, 1st Lt. Charles H. Field. Jr. receives an award from Maj. Klair E. Beck, commanding officer of the 3rd Air Rescue Squadron. The location is K-16 airfield, located on an island in the Han River south of Seoul.

*U. S. Air Force*

**PIET CILLIERS** I was an F-51D Mustang pilot with No. 2 "Cheetah" Squadron of the South African Air Force, which operated in the Korean War as a component of the U. S. Air Force's 18th Fighter-Bomber Wing. We South Africans are proud of our service in Korea and were proud to fight shoulder-to-shoulder with the Americans.

Our squadron arrived in South Korea at the end of 1950. We were based at the southern tip of Korea in a place called Chinhae.

On the morning of the April 30, 1951, I led a formation of four Mustang aircraft. I briefed the other pilots to attack a railway line north of Seoul and then to attack targets of opportunity.

After attacking a railway bridge, we split into pairs and I decided to go to a place called Sinmac, a staging post between the North Korean capital of Pyongyang and the bomb line, which was to the south on the outskirts of Seoul. We were about 100 miles behind enemy lines. Sinmac was where "Commie" vehicles and supplies were placed under camouflage during daylight hours before proceeding south at night. It was therefore well defended by flak.

When I arrived there, I stupidly did not take the necessary precautionary actions to avoid the flak. Flying at 500 feet, I was hit by medium antiaircraft fire.

The Mustang started burning almost immediately. I had to make a quick exit. I jettisoned the canopy. But then the fire came into the cockpit.

Things began to get a bit desperate (and hot), so I pushed the stick forward with the idea of ejecting myself, but my speed was too high and I only got halfway out with my legs stuck in the cockpit. The aircraft was descending fairly rapidly. I managed to kick myself free and immediately on clearing the aircraft, opened the parachute. I recall being stuck on the side of the aircraft. I was not afraid; I thought that I would soon be meeting up with a good friend of mine who had been killed a few weeks earlier.

As the chute opened, my aircraft hit the ground.

I was in the chute for not more than ten seconds. Perhaps at the time it was an advantage because the Commies were unable to track my descent for long.

When I hit the ground I released the chute harness and moved away as quickly as possible. I, however, had a wound in my leg and a broken bone so I could not move very far. On a slight rise where water had washed out the soil at the side of a paddy field, I managed to find a suitable place to hide.

**CHARLIE FIELD** Cilliers did not have a radio. When I took off in that shaky, clattering H-5 with my medic, Corporal Spellman Patterson, crouched behind me, we had some communication with our airfield, but none with the pilot on the ground. The terrain in Korea is rugged and mountainous. Winters there are harsh. There was still snow on the ground. The weather, as usual, was tricky, and the intelligence guy had explained it to me in plain English: "The whole goddamn Chinese army

H-5 pilots like Charlie Field did not always operate from fancy paved airfields. This Air Force Sikorsky H-5G of Field's 3rd Air Rescue Squadron is flying from an open field near Suwon, Korea, in 1951.

*U. S. Air Force*

is swarming through the hills up there, so it would be a good idea for you to watch out for yourself."

The H-5 helicopter was revolutionary for its era. A few years later, the Navy version became well known to Americans when Mickey Rooney brought one into a Korean rice paddy in a failed attempt to rescue William Holden in the movie version of James Michener's *The Bridges at Toko-Ri*. It's a slim helicopter, sitting on tricycle landing gear (in the Korean War version) with a 450-horsepower Pratt & Whitney engine with a forty-nine-foot, three-bladed rotor. Our maintainers usually had to work on it out-of-doors. Helicopters were very much underpowered in those days, so although the H-5 was a very good and reliable aircraft, I never felt for a moment that I had too much power. I also didn't have any excess lifting capacity. If we were going to travel any distance or reach any height, three was going to be a crowd: Two crew members plus one survivor was going to be just about all this aircraft could handle. A military press release of the era called the H-5 "slow, unarmed, and vulnerable."

The H-5 was also hampered by other limitations that cut down on its effectiveness. It wasn't equipped for safe operation at night, or in heavy rain, icing conditions, or high winds. The fuselage leaked like a sieve. It really was not an instrument aircraft, either, so we were pretty much limited to visual flying. There was no armor, no armament.

So how the hell did I get here, crossing over the Main Line of

Resistance, heading into "the whole goddamn Chinese army" in a vulnerable and somewhat primitive helicopter?

I was born in 1926 in Atlanta. I was in high school when the United States entered World War II. In Forest High School in Atlanta, they came around and gave us a test to see if we could get into the Army Air Corps. That was in September 1943. After we passed the test they said, "Don't sign up for the draft because you're already in the Army."

I signed up in July 1944. They sent me to basic training at Keesler Army Air Field, Mississippi.

They gave us tests. A perfect score was 999, which qualified you for pilot, navigator, and bombardier training. I passed and became part of the OLT program ("on-the-line trainee"). We wore the aviation cadet patch on our sleeve and had regular enlisted ranks; I went from private to private first class.

They sent me next to Craig Field, Selma, Alabama. I arrived in October 1944. At Craig, a good old guy asked me one day if I would like to do some flying. I got to carry mail in the back seat of an AT-6 from Craig to Eglin; I got a little stick time in the back of an AT-6. The first time I tried a barrel roll, the instructor said, "If you were an aviation cadet, I'd give you a B." This was a holding school for going to preflight. It dawned on them that we were never going to get to preflight because things were stretched manpower-wise, so we ended up doing housekeeping detail. When V. E. Day was declared, they disbanded the OLT trainee program. They offered to sign me up for the inactive reserve. So I was a private first class in the Army when they gave me an honorable discharge at Maxwell Field, Alabama, in November 1945, just a few months after the end of World War II.

I was back home in Atlanta waiting to get into Georgia Tech, which was scheduled for March 1946; I had a part-time job and ran into a flying program out at the local airport in Atlanta. They guaranteed you a private license for $325. Doing part-time jobs, I took this training in a super-dooper Piper J-3 Cub. We had three hours of dual and fifteen hours of solo, so I got my private ticket in January 1946. I couldn't afford much pleasure flying, though, because it cost four dollars an hour to fly that J-3 Cub solo. If you took dual instruction, as I did to get checked out at night, it was seven dollars an hour, which was almost totally out of reach. I soloed in January 1946 without a radio, using light signals at the Atlanta Municipal Airport, the same location as Atlanta-Hartsfield. I did a deal with somebody to arrange a flight in a Ryan PT-22 primary trainer, which was a sleek, silver machine. I also got stick time in the Fairchild PT-19. They were all open cockpit. There were no luxuries in those days.

I wanted to fly and was accepted as an aviation cadet in 1947, just before the Air Force became an independent service branch in September of that year. In training, I flew the AT-6 Texan single-engine and B-25 Mitchell twin-engine trainers. My class graduated at Barksdale Air Force Base near Shreveport, Louisiana, on October 8, 1948. I married Frances Beauchamp who was an Air Force flight nurse. We have two sons. And in 1950, as a fresh new Air Force pilot with a fresh new blue uniform, I was for the first time introduced to the Sikorsky H-5.

## Crash at the MASH

I made my first flight in an H-5 in June 1950, the month the Korean War began. It was a completely strange situation to me because I had no idea what a helicopter was, and this was the first time I ever saw one. You're supposed to learn how to come straight off the ground and come to a three-foot hover, so you're on a cushion of air circulating through the rotor system. You don't learn that immediately. As you go forward off that bubble, you dip the nose and add power. When you get about 15 mph forward speed, you go through transitional lift. Then, the aircraft smoothes out and flies real nice. It was mainly a matter of getting a feel for the thing. It was not a simple thing to learn to fly a helicopter. It took me eleven, twelve, thirteen hours of dual training before I could solo that little jewel.

The pilot sits up there in the nose. In training, we had the H-5D model, which had a buffer wheel up on the nose instead of a nose wheel. They put a second set of controls in the back seat for the dual controls for the instructor. New classes started every five weeks; my instructor for the first five weeks went off to Korea; my new instructor was just five weeks ahead of me. We'd start out hovering 360 to the left.

I'd try it from the front seat. He'd try it from the back seat. We learned all kinds of maneuvers. When we autorotated we weren't allowed to descend all the way to the ground.

Because of the war, I graduated two weeks early. They sent me to Camp Stoneman, California, to ship out to Korea.

I got to Japan in mid-October 1950. In last part of October, or maybe it was the first of November, I went to the airfield known as K-16, located on an island in the Han River south of Seoul. The airfield was near the suburban city of Yongdongpo, but we called it "Long Dong Po."

Before we could fly in combat, they told us to get some practice in the old H-5 and get warmed up. At this time, one of our outfits was up near the Yalu River and around Thanksgiving, here came the Chinese. I was sent to a spot called Jackson Air Strip forty miles north of Pyongyang to sit there all day waiting for a call for any medical or pickup they need. About three o'clock, they tell me to get back to Pyongyang to the MASH [Mobile Army Surgical Hospital] to move some troops out of there, to help evacuate.

On November 30, 1950, I prepared to take off for the purpose of evacuating my three crew chiefs as well as my helicopter and myself. The Chinese had intervened in the Korean War, friendly forces were falling back, and we were expecting the Chinese to retake Pyongyang momentarily. As we prepared for takeoff, there were four on board the helicopter, which was the absolute, absolute maximum load.

I took off from the MASH hospital at Pyongyang, and suddenly found myself trying to clear the two-story, brick school building where the hospital was. Somebody saw a big blue puff of smoke. Just when I was about to clear the building, that's when the engine quit. I did a 180-degree autorotation to land. When I tried to flare for a landing, my left landing gear went into a trench. There was a violent snapping sound. The helicopter rolled over on its side and came smashing to a halt.

Nobody was hurt. My pride was wounded, though. The pilot's seat was on the right side, the medic's on the left. When the other guys couldn't get out of the left side, they used my right shoulder to step on to get out. I have a black-and-white photo of that helicopter lying in

HARD ldg - Pongyang Nov.
By C. H. Fie

ENG. FAILURE

On November 30, 1950, with the Chinese army "swarming down the pike," as Charlie Field described it, Field attempted to take off from the Mobile Army Surgical Hospital at Pyongyang, the temporarily occupied capital of North Korea. Four men were aboard the H-5. The helicopter came to grief as shown in these views of the craft lying on its right side. Field said that only his pride was hurt.

*Charles Field*

front of the schoolhouse with one of the wheels broken off, most of the glass shattered, and dents in the fuselage. If we hadn't been in the North Korean capital at a time when the entire Chinese army was coming down the pike just north of us, it would have been practical to repair that helicopter. I don't think I could repair my pride.

While the Chinese attack pushed our forces back, we rotated around the various MASH hospitals and did routine stuff. One day a week, we were on call to pick up downed pilots. We called that "your day in the barrel." It's a nervous situation standing by for pilot pickup, but when they say, "Go," you become relaxed, you fly, and it's a pleasure to have something to do. You know it's going to be hot when you get there.

## Fighting in 1951

Around January 1, 1951, we still had three choppers that we were keeping at K-13 [Suwon airfield, twenty-five miles south of Seoul] but flying at K-16 [on the outskirts of Seoul] during the day. That morning, we rescued four British soldiers who were in a big battle northwest of Seoul. They told us the Chinese army was knocking at the city gates.

One of my flights was in the opposite direction of the front lines, to K-37 airfield near Taegu in the southwest corner of South Korea. The field, with its 2,500-foot dirt strip, was adjacent to a particularly nasty-looking mountain. That mountain was a story all to itself. When President Truman fired Gen. Douglas MacArthur, they flew Gen. Matthew B. Ridgway over to take command. They were flying him back at night and were trying to bring him in to the main airfield at Taegu, known as

K-2. Because of darkness, weather, and confusion, they brought Ridgway's transport down to the little strip at K-37 instead, because it had the brightest runway lights. They thought they were landing at K-2. Not being familiar with the area, they said, "We can take care of this." The tower at K-2 said, "We don't have you in sight." They landed on the better marked runway at K-37 by mistake, totally unaware of the peak of the mountain and narrowly missing it, maybe by only a few feet. That would have been a hell of a way for our new supreme commander to die. When they touched down they were embarrassed but at least Ridgway was alive. That's a little background on how people can be lucky.

In early 1951, the Chinese took Seoul. There was heavy fighting in and around the city and after it changed hands several times, we took Seoul back and kept it for the rest of the war. In spring 1951, one of our helicopter pilots got shot down near the Han River. He was not hurt seriously.

It was not long after that when I found myself scrambled into the air to attempt to pluck Piet Cilliers out of the hands of the Chinese.

**PIET CILLIERS** I joined the South African Air Force in 1945, shortly before the end of World War II. Our pilot training arrangement was known as the Empire Flying Training Scheme, under which British Royal Air Force and other Commonwealth pilots also were trained.

The training course began with initial flying in a De Havilland Tiger Moth biplane, carried out at No. 6 Air School at Potchestroom, South Africa. Next, I progressed to Senior Flying Training on a Harvard 11A, known in American jargon as an AT-6 Texan, at No. 22 Air School at Vereeniging, South Africa. During my flight training, No. 22 was closed down, so I finally qualified for my wings at Dunnottar, South Africa. I flew 32.55 hours on the Tiger Moth, and 170 on the Harvard. I qualified for my wings in the beginning of 1946, and was appointed to the rank of second lieutenant.

Not many Americans even remember that we South Africans fought side-by-side with you during the Korean War. Our No. 2 "Cheetah" Squadron functioned as part of the United States Air Force's 18th Fighter-

Bomber Group, flying F-51D Mustangs in the early part of the conflict and F-86 Sabres later on. When one group of our officers arrived in the combat zone, an American officer expressed surprise that we were all white. "We thought everybody in Africa was black," he said. Other Americans thought we talked funny, or had odd-looking uniforms, but we were very much a part of the effort and we sustained heavy casualties in the process.

I've already described my shootdown on a mission against Chinese ground forces. After I parachuted, my wingman descended to about 200 feet and started giving me cover. There was a considerable amount of antiaircraft and small arms fire going on all around me, and I was sure that my wingman would shortly be joining me on the ground as the shells were bursting on his tail just behind his aircraft. It was looking like I would soon see the inside of a Chinese prisoner-of-war camp.

**CHARLIE FIELD** Heading across the bombline into Chinese territory, I navigated visually and spotted smoke from the downed Mustang. That old H-5 shakes and bounces a lot, and you can feel the engine straining, but it was a crisp day and the smoke was just about the clearest marker you could possibly have.

I spotted the pilot's hand-held signal mirror. I also saw muzzle flashes from Chinese troops firing at my H-5.

**PIET CILLIERS** I was on the ground for about two-and-a-half hours and was worried that I would be outside the very limited range of the rescue helicopters. The thought that went through my mind was: *What was I to do when the gooks closed in on me?*

I couldn't make it back to friendly lines. My injured leg would not get me very far. Was I to attempt to fight it out with my .38 revolver, or just give myself up?

I was fortunate that there was full sunlight and I was able to use my signaling mirror to indicate my position to the covering aircraft. I had no other means of communicating, such as a radio. Those were very harrowing minutes.

After a while more aircraft joined to give me cover, and at one stage there must have been about fifteen aircraft. After a while an American pilot, Capt. Gerry Hoag, strafed something about 200 yards from me, and then I noticed about ten armed gooks creeping up on me. I had a few items that were supposed to help me if shot down, including a signal mirror, but I crawled over the ridge onto the top of the paddy field and used my signaling mirror as a shovel to dig a small ditch in the soil to get out of the line of fire.

Suddenly, a helicopter appeared from the east, approached me, and flew over and then away. With my mirror, I showed my position to the helicopter. It came past a second time without landing. When it came around for the third time I prepared to fire a signaling flare to indicate my position. This would have given away my position to the Chinese troops as well. The small-arms fire and ack-ack was increasing considerably.

That Chinese soldier stood fully erect and emptied the clip of his rifle at me in a continuous burst of fire.

**CHARLIE FIELD** I put the helicopter down on the ridge. Patterson scrambled out of the rear fuselage and assisted the downed pilot. Thanks to Patterson's heroic effort, we got him aboard the H-5 and saw a look of incredible relief on his face. I was increasing power and beginning to lift away from that miserable hilltop when a Chinese infantryman popped up in front of me.

**PIET CILLIERS** On the third run, the chopper landed next to me. I did not stand up for fear of being hit by small arms fire, so I crawled under the chopper to the open door on the far side. The crewman helped me in and the pilot increased power for takeoff. I learned later that a Chinese soldier was standing right in front of the nose of the helicopter spraying bullets at it.

**CHARLIE FIELD** Somehow, he missed me. By then, the rotors were grabbing air and we were pulling off. The H-5 rose in its traditional, nose-down attitude and suddenly I could see Chinese troops everywhere around us, closing in on our location.

The Mustang wing commander, McBride, was overhead and began orchestrating a strafing of the Chinese troops. McBride was functioning as the on-scene commander and his voice was booming in my earphones, calling K-16 to request a second helicopter "because the one we're escorting is smoking."

That's when I got on the radio and asked the colonel, "Who's smoking?"

"You are," McBride said.

## On Fire Aloft

Behind enemy lines or not, when I see smoke and fire, I'm ready to park. McBride told me again that I was burning. We had a rushed, nervous discussion about whether I should find a paddy field to land in, in hope more helicopters could be sent to pick us up. Another H-5 wasn't going to be able to lift the three of us plus its pilot and the Chinese troops seemed to be pretty close. I could see what looked like streaks of smoke but had no other sign within the helicopter of a fire. I told McBride we would continue.

**PIET CILLIERS** As we got airborne, I told the pilot that there was considerable ground fire and suggested he weave, not realizing that helicopters do not weave. The gooks that were creeping up on me opened fire on the helicopter.

After becoming airborne, I gave my .38 revolver to the crewman, but when Charlie informed me that the chopper was hit and with a chance of having to carry out a forced landing, I asked for my firearm to be returned. We fortunately made it to K-16 [Seoul] on a shoestring, leaking oil and with very little fuel left. The crewman got his .38 back.

**CHARLIE FIELD** The distance may have seemed relatively short, but that was one long helicopter trip. I managed to coax the H-5 back to our base at K-16 and they rushed the South African pilot, Cilliers, quickly to the medics. I learned later that he was evacuated to an American hospital ship in Pusan, and then flown to a British hospital in Kure, Japan. After recovering, he returned to South Africa.

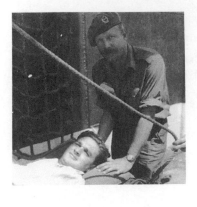

Shortly after being rescued by H-5 helicopter pilot Charlie Field in the midst of a swarm of Chinese troops, South African fighter pilot Piet Cilliers (in stretcher) is taken to medical aid.

*Piet Cilliers*

My H-5 helicopter was a mess. It hadn't been very pretty to begin with, but now it had smears from oil leaks and a bunch of dings. I learned on inspecting the H-5 that one of the Chinese rifle bullets had punctured a fitting on an oil return line. The smoke had come from burning oil rather than more dangerous aviation fuel.

I flew dozens of other missions in Korea, including one in which I rescued another South African Mustang pilot. They awarded me the Silver Star for the Cilliers rescue. I served a full career in the Air Force and retired as a major. I later did some civilian helicopter piloting as a flying game warden. Today, I live in Austin, Texas.

**PIET CILLIERS** I had the honor of meeting Charlie Field in 1995 when he joined a group of 18th Fighter Bomber Wing members who visited South Africa. I found him to be a grand chap with a great sense of humor. However, his strong Texas accent confused me a bit at times! If it were not for Charlie Field, I doubt I would be here today, and I am sure that that would apply to many of the downed aircrew that chopper pilots like Charlie rescued from under the gooks' noses in the Korean War. Today, I live in Capetown. I still have the signal mirror that brought me salvation from the H-5 helicopter, "and even some North Korean soil to go with it."

# H-5 Helicopter

During the Korean War, the Air Force's Sikorsky H-5 became the first helicopter used regularly for combat rescue missions. The H-5F and H-5G models used in Korea accommodated a single pilot and up to three men on a bench behind the pilot. It rarely carried all four, however, because every extra pound of weight was a huge burden on its engine and rotors. The H-5 had limited lifting capacity and short range.

Of 1,690 Air Force members shot down behind enemy lines in Korea, rescue forces saved 170, or 10 percent. The H-5 is credited with about two dozen of these, but veterans of the Korean conflict remember the figure as higher. Charles Field alone completed five rescues.

The H-5 came into existence because of the pioneering work of Igor Sikorsky, who designed his first helicopter in 1909. Sikorsky immigrated to the United States from Russia and by 1939 was constructing his first realistic helicopter in his capacity as engineering manager for

## Sikorsky H-5F (R-5F) Dragonfly (S-51)

**Type:** Two- to four-seat combat rescue and utility helicopter

**Powerplant:** One 450-hp Pratt & Whitney R-985-AN-1/5 Wasp Junior radial, fan-cooled pistol engine driving 49-ft (14.94-m), three-bladed main rotor

**Performance:** Maximum speed, 103 mph (166 km/h); cruising speed 75 mph (122 km/h); climb to 5,900 ft (1800 m), est. 7 min.; service ceiling 11,000 ft (3352 m); maximum duration est. 4 hours; range, est. 180 mi (305 km)

**Weights:** Empty, 8,788 lb (1820 kg); normal takeoff weight, 4,400 lb (1,995 kg); gross weight, 4,985 lb (2263 kg)

**Dimensions:** Main rotor diameter, 49 ft 0 in (14.94 m); length overall (rotors turning), 57 ft 1 in (17.40 m); fuselage length 40 ft 11 in (12.47 m); height, 12 ft 11 in (3.94 m), wheel track, 12 ft (3.60 m); main rotor disc area, 1,810 sq ft (168 sq m)

**Armament:** None

**Crew:** One pilot, one medic

**First flight:** August 18, 1943 (XR-5)

the Vought-Sikorsky Co. Sikorsky designed and built the VS-300 helicopter, which made its first tethered flight on September 14, 1939.

In spring 1941, the government awarded Sikorsky a contract to develop the VS-316A, a larger helicopter that became the military R-4. One of the early aircraft in this series, a YR-4B model, flew history's first combat rescue mission in Burma in 1944 (Chapter One). Sikorsky also developed the VS-316B, which was known in military jargon as the R-6 but which never saw combat. The "R" for rotorcraft was changed to "H" for helicopter in July 1948, making Sikorsky's best known aircraft at that time the H-4, H-5, and H-6.

Long before that, the Sikorsky built the craft it called the VS-337. The military called it the R-5, a name that would be changed later to H-5. The helicopter made its first flight at the Sikorsky plant in Bridgeport, Connecticut, on August 18, 1943. Early production of sixty-four aircraft in this series gave the Army Air Forces—which became an independent service branch, the United States Air Force, in September 1947—four more XR-5s, twenty-six YR-5As, and thirty-four R-5As. The R-5A had litter carriers on each side of the fuselage and was used by the Air Rescue Service.

Sikorsky then built twenty-one R-5Ds (H-5Ds), which were modified from R-5A airframes and had nosewheel landing gear, a rescue hoist, and an auxiliary fuel tank. These were followed by five R-5Es (H-5Es) with dual pilot controls. Sikorsky also built a four-seat civilian version of the H-5, known as the model S-51, one of which was used by Rep. Lyndon B. Johnson (D-Texas) to campaign for reelection in Texas in 1948. Sikorsky also built a Navy and Marine Corps model, the HO3S-1. Finally, on the eve of the Korean War, the company began building the H-5F, H-5G, and H-5H models that were flown in combat by pilots like Charles Field.

# Chapter 3

# A Night Mission That Couldn't Happen

## What Happened

Richard Kirkland piloted the H-5 in Korea after flying with top aces in the P-38 Lightning fighter in the South Pacific in World War II. "Not everybody can claim to have gone from flying the most beautiful airplane ever built to flying one that wasn't so pretty," Kirkland remembers.

In the winter of 1953, Kirkland was supporting the 8055th Mobile Army Surgical Hospital, the real-life equivalent of the hospital in the movie and television series "M*A*S*H." Kirkland and other helicopter pilots lived in pyramidal GI tents within easy running distance of the helicopter landing pad. When they weren't flying—exactly as depicted in the TV show—they were partying. But they never forgot the phone in the pilots' tent. It was a direct landline to the aid stations along the battle front.

One of Kirkland's fellow partiers was MASH surgeon Dr. Sam Gilfand, nicknamed "Hawkeye" for his accuracy with a blade. He was the real-life inspiration for a future movie and television character. He was also a prankster. And he was noticeably not in attendance that evening when Kirkland, detachment commander Chuck Enderton, several pilots,

**Captain Richard C. Kirkland**
**Winter 1953**
**Sikorsky H-5G Helicopter**
**2157th Air Rescue Squadron**
**K-16 YoiDo Airfield, Seoul, Korea**

1st Lt. (later Maj.) Richard Kirkland with the H-5 helicopter he flew in the Korean War.

*U. S. Air Force*

and nurses were beginning a "M*A*S*H"-style party—and the phone rang.

"One of my men has been shot in the stomach. He's too badly wounded to be moved by ambulance. He's got to be picked by chopper or he's going to die."

Kirkland was sure he recognized Gilfand's voice. No real Army lieutenant would call on the phone after dark. The H-5 didn't fly after dark.

Kirkland was skilled at spotting a practical joke.

"A gut-shot soldier?" Kirkland smiled. "Sure, I'll come and rescue your soldier." Kirkland held the phone in one hand, trying to mix a martini with the other. He didn't feel he could sustain the joke. "That's a great joke, Hawkeye. But we're having a party and I'm ready to mix a martini, so—"

At that moment, surgeon Hawkeye walked into Kirkland's tent with a nurse in tow. On the phone, the voice said, "Sir—"

It was not Gilfand's voice. It was not a joke.

"Holy shit!" Kirkland proclaimed. "Are you a real lieutenant at a real aid station?"

"Sir, I don't know what the hell you're talking about but I've got a soldier here who's going to die if he can't be evacuated tonight, now—"

Kirkland wasn't supposed to fly at night. In fact, the H-5 wasn't meant to fly at night, ever. It had no navigation lights. It had no instrument lights. Although Kirkland was now an experienced helicopter pilot, he had never flown an H-5 at night, not in peacetime, not in training, never.

Moreover, night flying was against regulations.

"I'll come and get him," Kirkland said.

"You can't do that," Enderton said. As detachment commander, he was Kirkland's boss. But Kirkland kept talking with the lieutenant and secured a promise that soldiers would illuminate the aid station with truck headlights.

"The gooks will see that, won't they?"

"Sir, the station is down in a gully. We're hoping the lights can be turned on without Chinese troops seeing them." The lieutenant at the aid station was clearly under enormous pressure.

"This is real," Kirkland said to Enderton. Before Enderton, who was his superior, could stop him, Kirkland headed out of the tent. He knew he couldn't attempt the rescue alone. He went to find a medic to volunteer to accompany him.

**RICHARD KIRKLAND** A recommendation to award me a Distinguished Service Cross went into File 13 because I broke too many rules that night. My commander told me my situation was a toss-up between the nation's second-highest award for valor and a general court-martial.

The mission was to evacuate a wounded soldier from the front lines to the MASH. There was a big catch. The catch was, it had to be done at night.

Sikorsky H-5 of the type flown by Richard Kirkland takes off carrying two external patient litters slung on either side of the fuselage. Kirkland's 3rd Air Rescue Group eventually received the larger H-19 and also operated the SA-16 Albatross amphibian in background.

*U.S. Air Force*

In my squadron, I'm the only one who flew a night mission during the time I was there. I was piloting an H-5 with my enlisted medic, Roger, in the backseat. Sadly, I no longer remember Roger's full name.

We did a bunch of things that weren't by the book, including flying the rickety H-5 at night and landing within shooting distance of the North Koreans. Remember, our helicopters have zero light, no light whatever, not even on the instrument panel. In an H-5, you've got to watch your tach or you're in deep trouble. You've got to use throttle to keep your revolutions per minute (rpm) where it's supposed to be. So I needed Roger to come along on the mission and lean over my shoulder to shine his flashlight on my tachometer whether the North Koreans were going to shoot at us or not. There were no interior lights in the H-5, no instrument lights, nothing like that. It was going to take Roger's flashlight to enable me to see the way. Roger wrapped masking tape around the bulb so the flashlight created only a very narrow beam, which we hoped the Chinese wouldn't see. More important, we needed to prevent glare that would give me vertigo, which would kill us faster than any Chinese infantrymen.

None of our precautions could prevent the Chinese from seeing our exhaust. The H-5 sent a tongue of fire licking back into the night from its exhaust stack, and that was a good aiming point for any enemy with a gun.

I also needed Roger to help with the casualty. The idea of administering medical help while in flight was still new then. But we had been told this soldier was in very bad shape and needed immediate help.

## Flying in the Dark

The helicopter flight to the battalion aid station was relatively short, but navigation at night was a difficult challenge. Korea is mountainous, and this region was lined with canyons. Roger had been happy to volunteer—those crazy young medics were the forerunners of the pararescue jumpers who made such a mark in the Air Force in later years—but the cramped interior of our little H-5 was not intended for him to shine a flashlight over my shoulder.

The topography in Korea was what made it possible for a helicopter to fly right into the jaws of the enemy and rescue a patient without getting shot down. There are deep canyons between the bare mountain ridges that run down the length of the Korean peninsula, all the way from Siberia. You find a good canyon—that's one where the Chinese don't have an infantry division—and you can fly straight up to the front with the terrain masking you. If you get in the wrong canyon, you'll have the gooks shooting at you from all directions.

So with Roger shining the light on my tach instrument, I weaved through the canyons, flying our helicopter in locations where no fixed-wing airplane would have been able to go.

That night, I knew which canyons were safe for us, but there was still a huge danger of flying into terrain in the darkness. So I kept the helicopter high enough to clear the ridgelines, hoping that I would find the battalion aid station. Once I was approaching, the lieutenant would hear me coming and turn on the truck lights. But the Chinese would hear me coming, too, wouldn't they?

I was wondering the danger posed by Chinese troops and weapons lurking in those mountains when I suddenly realized that I was lost.

**CHARLIE FIELD** One of our guys was killed after he rescued somebody up near the Yalu and made the mistake of allowing night to fall before he got home. They gave him the Distinguished Service Cross, but that don't help when you're six feet under. I stayed out after dark on a mission in my H-5 one night and they told me I would have to wipe that forty-five minutes of flying time off my record, because it was a violation of the rules. We didn't even have exterior running lights on those H-5s.

**RICHARD KIRKLAND** Lost, at night. Over enemy territory in Korea. I don't remember my life flashing in front of me during that H-5 flight to the Korean front in a moonless black night—but it probably should have. I had already been in one war. Maybe I was pushing the odds.

In the Korean War, I flew sixty-nine combat missions in H-5s and H-19s. My outfit was the 2157th Air Rescue Squadron, 3rd Air Rescue Group, which was credited with saving 10,000 lives in medical evacuation missions, 9,000 of which were done by helicopters.

We also supported the Army's famous MASHes. My squadron was divided into seven elements with four to eight pilots in each, and we were all over the map, but we spent a period of time servicing the 8055th MASH near Uijongbu with our H-5s. The toughest duty of all was on a small island off the coast of North Korea, Cho-do, which was far behind enemy lines. There was an intelligence listening post and a rescue detachment at Cho-do. We would rotate up there for two to three weeks at a time, knowing that we were within just a few miles of North Korean and Chinese forces.

I didn't start out to be in the Korean War. I came on active duty on August 28, 1942, and graduated with Flying Class 43-F in June 1943. I went to the Southwest Pacific to join the 9th Fighter Squadron, 49th Fighter Group, in combat in New Guinea and the Philippines, beginning in October 1943. I flew sixty-one combat missions in the P-38 Lightning and forty-two combat missions in the P-47 Thunderbolt. Many of these were escort and fighter sweep missions.

I flew the sleek, powerful P-38 in combat with some of America's great aces, including Major Richard I. Bong, our all-time top ace with forty aerial victories. I was in a slew of dogfights myself, and got credit for shooting down one Japanese Zero fighter, although I actually believe I got two. I also flew a combat sorties with Charles Lindbergh, when he was advising P-38 pilots on how to conserve fuel on long-

Capt. (later Maj.) Richard C. Kirkland (left) with the Sikorsky H-19 that replaced his H-5 in Korea. The others are Lt. Bill Tuttle and Tech Sgt. R. T. Hanke.

*Sikorsky*

range missions over those vast waters. Lindbergh got a Zero, too, although it isn't listed officially anywhere.

My aerial victory came when my flight of four P-38s flew into a swarm of Zeros during a sweep over Manokwari, on the north coast of New Guinea. The Japanese fighters started with the advantage of higher altitude and came swarming down on us in a head-on pass.

That wasn't smart. With its heavy nose 20-mm cannon and four .50-cal machine guns on the nose centerline, the P-38 Lightning is a formidable enemy from dead ahead. Nevertheless, our two aerial formations rushed into each other, converging at more than a thousand miles per hour, both sides firing furiously. This midair merger quickly became a madhouse, with P-38s and Zeros careening in all directions. Now, the Zeros had a better chance to take advantage of their extreme maneuverability during a close-quarters fight.

I saw a Zero pop in front of me. I fired a burst but, not surprisingly, he whipped into a tight turn. He was now shooting at me, but his tracers were vaulting overhead. I turned into him and he broke off. I swung back into my climb and discovered that my wingman was missing. "Red Two! Red Two, get back in formation!" I shouted.

My earphones were silent. I looked around. That shavetail second lieutenant was nowhere in sight. A moment later, his voice: "Get 'em off! Get these Zeros off my tail!" I stood my Lightning vertically on its fifty-two-foot wing, looked down, and saw my guy in a dive with two Zeros closing in behind him.

I didn't have time to get into the fight. The only chance to help my wingman was to attempt a tactic I'd tried once before without success. I dipped the nose and fired a long burst—shooting from much too far. Somehow, the unbelievable happened. My tracers fell between my wingmen and the pursuing Zeros and one of the Japanese fighters took hits and rolled out of control, smoking.

## Going Into Helicopters

I made the difficult decision to remain in uniform during the lean years after the war. During the immediate postwar years, there were opportunities to fly just about everything. My logbook includes the B-17, C-47, C-82, OA-10, BT-13, T-6, L-5, and L-13. In later years in the rotary wing world, I flew the H-5, H-19, H-21, and H-43.

In 1949, the Air Force decided to send me to helicopter school. Helicopters were new then. A lot of people didn't know much about how they worked. They were still being called whirlybirds and eggbeaters, terms that are no longer used today.

School was at Connally Air Force Base, Texas, where we trained in H-5s. I think my World War II buddies, who flew with me in the mighty P-38 Lightning, would have razzed me mercilessly about flying an eggbeater.

The H-5 was known as the R-5 until July 1948. It was a direct descendent of the World War II R-4. It looks so primitive when we look at it today, with its slender fuselage, cramped interior, and limited space for fuel and payload. The 450-horsepower Pratt & Whitney R-985 engine and the three-bladed main rotor gave it sufficient power for many missions, but nobody ever accused the H-5 of being overpowered.

On February 14, 1950, I was spending Valentine's Day as duty officer of the 8th Air Rescue Squadron at McChord Air Force Base, Washington, when a high-ranking Strategic Air Command officer showed up and ordered me to get everybody on duty. He said that a B-36 bomber had been lost in the wintry weather not far from our base.

What he didn't say, what I learned later, was that it had atomic bombs on board.

The snow and ice conditions and the low-hanging clouds weren't going to permit a thorough air search, so I suggested using our H-5 to shuttle ground rescue people to a likely point in the mountains where we thought the bomber was down. Helicopters were still very new to most folks in the military, and carrying three passengers at a time in the H-5 was stretching this helicopter's capacity to the limit, but we hauled the ground rescue teams successfully. We embarked on a search-and-rescue strategy that seemed to make sense, spent several days fighting the frigid weather searching for the B-36—and found nothing.

We searched the west side of the Cascades just across the border in Canada. Everything we knew about where the B-36 had gone down told us the bomber was there. When the weather improved, I took my H-5 to a place called Surf Inlet, Canada, landed on the pier there, and spent three weeks searching from the air—and, still, found nothing. Over time, ground rescue teams supported by our helicopters found all but five of the B-36 crew and brought them to safety, but we never found the bomber itself.

The B-36, then the largest airplane in the world, was returning from Alaska when it crashed. The aircrew abandoned the aircraft when severe icing plus an engine fire endangered the crew. Five out of seventeen who parachuted lost their lives. I learned later that official documents show the bomb on board, weighing 11,000 lbs worth of Mark IV "Fat Man" plutonium bomb, similar to the weapon dropped on Nagasaki, was jettisoned over the Pacific and detonated at about 1,000 feet prior to the crew bailing out. There were four spare detonators and the "suitcase" for a Mark IV device in the wreckage, suggesting the nuclear device on board lacked its plutonium warhead. For reasons that remain largely a mystery even today, the B-36 was nowhere near the location identified by radar trackings and other information. This was only the second time in history that a giant B-36 had crashed, and we were looking for it in the wrong place.

The B-36 was eventually found deep in the interior wilderness of Canada's British Columbia, far from where it was supposed to be.

When our duty at Surf Inlet was finished, I was flying home with two passengers when my H-5 started vibrating, then lost its tail rotor.

When the tail rotor comes off, the fuselage wants to turn around in a direction opposite that of the main rotor. You lose control right quick when that happens. I had two passengers and I shouted, "We're going in!" Fortunately, we were only a short distance off the water and I landed on what appeared to be the surface.

Instead of breaking up and sinking, the helicopter simply came to a halt. I had landed on a shoal. To my surprise, we were only in two or three feet of water at low tide. The bad news was, the tides shift by up to eighteen feet so it was only a matter of time when the helicopter was submerged.

I found a length of rope in the fuselage and persuaded my two passengers to wrap the rope around the tail boom. While they tugged on the rope to prevent the fuselage from counter-rotating, I applied just enough power to leapfrog the H-5 from the shoal to the shore. We actually saved that helicopter; it was picked up by a barge and taken back to McChord.

## Atomic Tests

When war began in Korea, I was sure my P-38 Lightning experience would put me back in fighters and into combat. But I didn't get a fighter assignment and I didn't go to Korea, not then. In my next job, I was still a helicopter pilot, now part of a classified task force that supported the atomic bomb tests at Eniwetok in the Pacific in 1950 and 1951. We had two H-5s. Our job was to shuttle nuclear scientists and government bigwigs from one island to another while the tests went on.

Most participants in the tests traveled by boat. There were hundreds of them, but only a few really important folk became regular passengers on our H-5s. We wore special badges that identified us as having the special "Q" clearance, way above top secret, that went only to those working on atomic weapons.

Despite being cleared for the information, I didn't understand at first what they were doing in this atoll of thirty small islands. They were building tall steel towers at several locations. Finally, one scientist said to me, "We're going to put a device on top of this tower and detonate it."

"A device? Is that like an atomic bomb?"

"Exactly. Except that we won't drop it."

They said this would enable them to measure the yield. The way I saw it, they should have known how big the explosion was going to be *before* they set it off.

I sat through the detonation of a nuclear device, an experience almost too awesome to describe, and flew scientists with geiger counters afterward. There was a whole series of blasts during that year I spent on a Pacific atoll. One of them was the first hydrogen bomb. "We have now built a bomb more powerful than all the bombs dropped in World War II," a scientist told me.

I just looked at him.

"But don't worry," he added. "It's so powerful it will never be used."

After my exile out there in the Pacific, I eventually got the expected orders to Korea. And I was in Korea in those final months of the Korean War in 1953—when I found myself flying into enemy territory in an attempt to rescue a wounded soldier at night. "Never fly at night," they had told me in helicopter school.

## Night Rescue

My breath was forming clouds in front of my face. It was brutally cold inside the H-5 cockpit. The controls were sluggish but the helicopter was staying in the air. Unfortunately, the peaks and shows in the darkness below had gotten jumbled. I was trying to look at a map to identify the right canyon in the moving orb of light from Roger's flashlight. I had gloves on—no choice—and the heater was blasting air at my knees, but I had gotten disoriented and there was no sign of the battalion aid station. Fortunately, so far at least, the Chinese seemed not to have noticed me, either.

If you didn't know which canyons were friendly and which weren't, you were going to get killed out here. We were given an intelligence briefing every day that covered movement by ground troops on both sides, but it wasn't so easy to recognize a given ridge or canyon in the dark. For others, Korea was described as a battle of hills—Pork Chop Hill, Old Baldy, Heartbreak Ridge—but for every peak there was a dip, and for every ridgeline there was a canyon where an H-5 could be safe. Or not.

I had my teeth clenched and was praying that the lieutenant at the aid station would hear me coming and turn the lights on. I climbed to an altitude where I could see in the starlight, told Roger we wouldn't need that disconcerting flashlight, and pointed us toward a river bend that looked like a promising spot. But it simply wasn't working. I simply couldn't figure out where we were—and in the H-5, both fuel and time were extremely limited. I was willing to endanger myself, but I had to think of Roger. His adventurous spirit wasn't a good reason to risk his life unnecessarily.

"I'm going to turn back," I said to Roger—and then I saw the truck lights come on. They were straight ahead, under our noses, as if I'd been on a beeline toward them.

The truck lights gave me an excellent spatial reference and that meant I wasn't likely to get vertigo, so I told Roger to illuminate my instrument panel again. I began a steep, controlled approach, looking about furiously for possible enemy fire—and flew right into the top of a tree.

It wasn't much of a tree and there wasn't much foliage on it, so although there was some clattering and banging, there wasn't much damage. It had actually been quite a feat colliding with this tree: There were almost no trees in those bare ridges and canyons.

The H-5 settled on its gear and came to a halt, rotor turning, and I let out a gasp. I pulled the clutch-engagement lever and allowed the rotor blades to keep turning. I pushed the sliding door open and Roger bounded out. Suddenly, American soldiers in full combat gear were helping Roger with the wounded man. They were led by a gaunt, unshaven lieutenant who wore exhaustion and pain on his face, but who also had a humanity about him. He came up to the helicopter and looked in at me.

"When you ran into that tree, I thought for sure you were going down," the battered lieutenant said to me.

"You may have saved this man's life, captain. I can promise you, we could not have kept him alive till daybreak."

It the glare of headlights, I shook the lieutenant's hand. "Let's get him out of here," I said, not certain the H-5 was going to take off. "Do you know where the gooks are?"

"I'm sorry to tell you, captain. They're right over there." He pointed to a ridge perhaps a thousand feet from the aid station. "Get out of here now, sir, okay?"

I looked at him.

"Don't worry."

## Getting out Alive

When we finally had our wounded soldier in the litter pod and were ready to get out of there, it wasn't nearly soon enough. "Here we go, Roger!" I told the medic. I twisted the motorcycle-like grip on the H-5 as far as it would go and pulled in full power. The helicopter bucked, then separated from the ground and lifted into the black Korean night.

That was when the whole mission went to hell. Glowing red golf balls whipped through the air around us. It was coming from all directions. The H-5 wasn't especially nimble with three men on board and there wasn't much I could do to dodge this torrent of flying steel. I held full power, felt lift bringing us skyward, and bit my lip while the Chinese threw everything they had at us.

They had a perfect visual target with the six-foot plume of fire that streamed back from my exhaust stack. I could hear the sound of lead and steel thunking into the fuselage. The controls began to feel strange and the helicopter began to disintegrate around me.

I was losing power. The helicopter started to sink.

"Roger!" I said. "The flashlight!" I lowered the collective. The narrow beam of yellow shined on the panel and my tachometer told me that rpm were falling. I pushed the collective to the limit for a burst of power and was sent lurching upward in my seat, restrained by my shoulder straps. The flashlight careened across the cockpit as the H-5 dipped.

It was supposed to dip before the excess power took hold and that's what happened. We didn't collide with the ground. Instead, we were almost stationary in midair as the H-5 struggled to claw for lift.

Abruptly, the Chinese abruptly stopped shooting. I don't know why. Suddenly, I felt I was hanging, then creeping slowly forward, at the bottom of an inkwell. After taking so many hits, it would not have surprised me if the helicopter had suddenly disintegrated and fallen into bits and pieces around us.

Instead, the H-5 lurched and moved forward. We were flying. We were going to continue flying, at least for awhile.

## Struggling to Get Home

Roger retrieved the flashlight. I scanned my instruments. The rpm looked good. Fuel was low. Temperatures looked okay. Enough rounds had hit the H-5 to transform it into Swiss cheese, but after objecting to the problem with rpm the H-5 was now docile and was flying properly. One thing about those early choppers: When they didn't like what was going on, they'd let you know. They would shake like a Labrador retriever stepping out of a pond.

I'm at a total loss to know why the shooting stopped just when they should have blasted us out of the sky. I got my bearings and turned south. Later, I learned that the battle-weary lieutenant was on the landline phone to Enderton at the MASH, telling them we were coming. They were ready for us. They rushed the badly wounded soldier into surgery where Hawkeye attended his wounds. He was right on the brink, but he survived. I never learned his name.

Later in my Air Force career, I was project officer on the Kaman HH-43 Huskie helicopter (Chapter Nine). After I retired in June 1963, I spent twenty-eight years with Hughes Helicopter in Culver City, California, and Mesa, Arizona. I have had the good fortune to tell about my flying experiences in several articles and books of my own, including *Tales of a Helicopter Pilot.*

These are additional views of H-5G helicopters like those flown by Richard Kirkland.

*U. S. Air Force*

# H-5G Helicopter

The H-5G flown by Capt. Richard Kirkland was the final version of the H-5 to be used in the Korean War and had only minor differences from the H-5F model flown by 1st Lt. Charles Field (Chapter 2). Like the H-5F, the H-5G accommodated a single pilot and up to three men on a

## Sikorsky H-5G Dragonfly (S-51)

**Type:** Two- to four-seat combat rescue and utility helicopter

**Powerplant:** One 450-hp Pratt & Whitney R-985-AN-5B Wasp Junior radial, fan-cooled pistol engine driving 49-ft (14.94-m), three-bladed main rotor

**Performance:** Maximum speed, 103 mph (166 km/h); cruising speed 75 mph (122 km/h); climb to 7,000 ft (2133 m), 8 min; service ceiling 12,400 ft (3779 m); maximum duration est. 4 hours 30 min; range, est. 200 mi (320 km)

**Weights:** Empty, 8,788 lb (1820 kg); loaded 4,985 lb (2263 kg)

**Dimensions:** Main rotor diameter 49 ft 0 in (14.94 m); length overall (rotors turning) 57 ft 1 in (17.40 m); fuselage length 40 ft 11 in (12.47 m); height 12 ft 11 in (3.94 m)

**Armament:** None

**Crew:** One pilot, one medic

**First flight:** February 16, 1946 (S-51)

bench behind the pilot. It was a primitive flying machine in many ways. It smelled of canvas, rubber, and oil leaks. It wheezed and shuddered. But it was a solid aircraft and it performed many successful rescues.

The H-5 set records from the time it arrived in Korea. On October 10, 1950, an H-5 picked up a downed British pilot, and a physician serving as flight medic administered blood plasma during the return flight. H-5 pilot 1st Lt David C. Daniels and physician Capt. John C. Shumate pulled the downed pilot from his aircraft, carried him 200 yards to the helicopter, and administered the transfusion after takeoff. Daniels and Shumate were awarded the Silver Star.

Even with the minor improvements that went into the H-5G model, the H-5 wasn't the ideal helicopter for combat in Korea. The Korean peninsula has the full extreme of seasons and is covered with mountain peaks. No helicopter performs well in the "high and hot" conditions that prevail in the Korean summer. But winter is worse. Lubricant can freeze. Engines can seize. At the very time it should have been performing better in cold temperatures, the H-5 suffered most from its inherent center-of-gravity problems, which pilots sometimes solved by carrying a five-gallon Jerry can filled with sand and shifting the can's location, as appropriate, to cope with weight and balance changes.

# Chapter 4

## Perilous Pickup in the Yellow Sea

### What Happened

For half a century, John Caldwell wondered if he would ever again see the F-84G Thunderjet pilot he rescued during the Korean War.

Retired Lt. Col. Caldwell, seventy-eight, of Goliad, Texas, was a helicopter pilot who flew the Sikorsky H-19A at Cho-do Island off the coast of North Korea. The island of Cho-do was in the Yellow Sea far north of the 38th Parallel, tucked into the "armpit" created where North Korea met China. A little-known secret was that Americans operated from this island, far behind the front lines, throughout the Korean War.

On May 25, 1953, Caldwell's helicopter was sent out on a risky mission to try to rescue a fighter pilot down in the Yellow Sea. Caldwell was copilot. The pilot of the helicopter was Major James L. "Jim" Blackburn, "the coolest man under fire I've ever known," said Caldwell, "He was one tough son of a bitch."

Caldwell and Blackburn were the only men who could help the downed pilot.

By radio, the helicopter pilots learned that an F-84G had gone down in the chilly waters of the Yellow Sea. The pilot had parachuted into the mouth of a river emptying into the sea from North Korea. An

**Captain John Caldwell**
**May 25, 1953**
**Sikorsky H-19A Helicopter**
**51-3873**
**2157th Air Rescue Squadron**
**Cho-do Island, Korea**

Wearing the "poopie suit" meant to increase survival prospects in the frigid Yellow Sea as well as the mustache popular among crews, Capt. John Caldwell prepares for an H-19 helicopter mission on the island of Cho-do, off the coast of North Korea.

*John Caldwell*

SA-16 Albatross amphibian was unable to make a water landing to rescue the downed flyer because of sandbars in the area and enemy gunfire coming from shore a mile away.

"This was my first H-19 mission from our alert position at Cho-do," Caldwell said. "My earlier missions had been flown along the front lines in the older H-5 helicopter. On this mission, Blackburn was supervising, observing, and grading me."

The Albatross guided Caldwell's H-19 toward the downed F-84 pilot, and then withdrew. "He had already stretched his limited remaining fuel by waiting for us as long as he did. We appreciated his careful pointing out the location of the pilot, and informing us of the fact that he was being fired upon from the shore.

"When we spotted [the downed pilot], we rushed in with our hoist sling extended. With absolutely minimum hover time, we plucked him neatly from his dinghy, or one-man raft, and headed out to sea with the fighter pilot still dangling ten or twelve feet below our chopper. By now, we, too, were becoming dangerously low on fuel."

Until now, this had been as routine as any rescue could be near enemy territory under hostile fire. The third crew member of the H-19, a medical technician, pulled the pilot inside and checked him over. He was uninjured. But the medical technician—below and behind the two helicopter pilots—looked out his open doorway and suddenly had a change of tone:

"Sir, there is a bent-wing airplane heading our way and it's not one of our F-86s!" The medic meant to say "swept-wing."

### Who's Who

Major Jim Blackburn, H-19 helicopter pilot
Capt. John Caldwell, H-19 helicopter copilot
Name unknown, H-19 flight medic
2nd Lt. John Gaskin, F-84G Thunderjet pilot
Capt. Perse Gaskins, F-84G Thunderjet flight leader
1st Lt. Randy Presley, F-84G Thunderjet pilot

Caldwell made a right turn, peered out, and saw a MiG-15 jet fighter approaching—one of the few times an enemy MiG engaged a helicopter over the open sea.

At the time, Caldwell did not know the name of the F-84G pilot he had rescued—Second Lt. John Gaskin.

With a MiG on his tail, one of the few times in Korea when a MiG closed in on a helicopter, Caldwell experienced a very obvious reaction: "In that instant, I became the smelliest helicopter pilot in the United States Air Force."

Caldwell did not know what would happen next. Though they had picked up Gaskin, Caldwell didn't know whether he and his helicopter crew would be able to save Gaskin's life after all, now that the MiG was closing in.

And Caldwell could not possibly have known that he and his fellow helicopter pilots would save John Gaskin's life a second time, fifty years later in a new century.

**RANDY PRESLEY** John Gaskin spent most of his life as the typical country doctor in the small town of Locust, North Carolina. He's what you think about when you see a Norman Rockwell painting of the country doctor, a relic of an America that doesn't exist any longer. All of that came later, of course. His life as a small-town medical practitioner, even his attendance at medical school, came long after the Korean conflict. In the final months of the Korean War in 1953, Gaskin

On a stateside assignment, Capt. John Caldwell poses in front of an H-19 helicopter.

*John Caldwell*

was one of my fellow F-84G Thunderjet fighter-bomber pilots at Taegu, Korea.

Although Gaskin was a class ahead of me in flight school, somehow I arrived at K-2, as we called Taegu Air Base, before him. He flew my wing when I was an element leader on my missions number twenty and twenty-one. I got in fifty-five missions before the shooting stopped [on July 27, 1953] and Gaskin got thirty-five. John bailed out on Memorial Day, May 25, 1953. That was the same day I lost one of my best friends, Ralph B. Miller, known as R.B., who was with me all the way from basic flight training at Bainbridge, Georgia, to K-2. There wasn't supposed to be any flak but the sky was full and R.B. must have been centered, as nobody saw him go in or a parachute.

I think John and I both thought, at some point, that we wanted to be among the glamour boys who flew the sleek, swept-wing F-86 Sabre in air-to-air combat against the MiG-15. Those guys had a war that prompted one of their wing commanders to call them young Sir Galahads. They went north to fight and shoot down the enemy. They became aces. They became the stuff of novels and movies. In contrast, nobody ever made a movie about us Thunderjet pilots dropping bombs on people. But if you want to know the truth, the airplane and the mission grew on me, and I'm sure the same happened to John Gaskin. Our mission was more dangerous and less glamorous, but it produced results.

As for the F-84G Thunderjet, it was a heavy airplane. It was very stable, a great gun platform. It inherited a lot of its traits from the P-47 Thunderbolt of World War II, which was built by the same company, Republic Aviation. It was a Mach .82 airplane, so it wasn't really that fast. A lot of my classmates were flying F-86s and trying to be heroes by shooting down MiGs, but we actually flew a whole lot more combat in the F-84. There were a lot more people shooting at you from the ground than there were shooting at you in the air.

I wasn't on the same flight with John the day he was shot down. It could have happened to any of us.

**JOHN GASKIN** I was a very young fighter pilot in the Korean War. I graduated from Flying Class 52-F, pinned on my wings, and went straight into the F-84G Thunderjet.

The Eighty-Four was a robust and powerful fighter-bomber that could haul all kinds of bombs and rockets. It was also armed with six .50-caliber machine guns. It was a straight-winged jet in an era when the air-to-air action was being fought by F-86 Sabres and MiG-15s with swept wings. With a maximum speed of about 600 miles per hour, we were a little slower than the Sabre or the MiG. We thought our air-to-ground mission was more important, though.

I eventually flew thirty-five combat missions in Korea with the 428th Fighter-Bomber Squadron, a part of the 58th Fighter-Bomber Wing, stationed at Taegu Air Base, Korea.

My flight leader was Capt. Perse L. Gaskins—different spelling, no relation—of Jacksonville, Florida, and some imaginative public information officer got the brilliant idea of calling us the "Gaskin-Gaskins team." No, we weren't related, but fate brought us together on one mission when we strapped into our F-84s, taxied out, and took off to head north toward the 38th Parallel and beyond.

It was my fifth combat mission. They sent us to attack a Communist rail supply line between Sinanju and Pyongyang. I was rolling in on my bomb run when there was this snap-snap-snap as shells thunked into the fuselage of my F-84. Perse noticed the trouble, sent the remainder of our flight home—some without dropping their bombs—and pulled up beside me. "I'll be right here at your side," Perse said. Gaskin and

Gaskins turned away from the target and headed west toward the Yellow Sea.

The drill was, if you got hit you were supposed to figure out whether you could limp home. If that wouldn't work, you would try to get near the island of Cho-do and hope our air rescue guys could pick you up.

Smoke was accumulating on my floorboards. I was feeling a vibration that wasn't supposed to be part of flying an F-84. I was losing altitude fast, and there was still a big swath of North Korea right in front of my nose. I was having visions of becoming a prisoner of war.

After what seemed like an eternity, with Perse Gaskins right beside me, we reached the open water. I was falling faster now, my altitude now down to 2,500 feet. Gaskins and I discussed whether I should bail, and his voice started getting scratchy in my earphones. At that point, we knew that air rescue had been alerted but we had no clue whether anyone was nearby to help us. I had wondered about sharks. Years later, I was told there were no sharks in the Yellow Sea, but that was no comfort then.

Suddenly, a sheet of fire swept over my F-84. "Get out of there now, John!" Gaskins's voice boomed.

What about rescue? What about sharks? It was getting hot inside the cockpit and my oxygen mask wasn't protecting me completely from the crud in the air in the canopy. My hand was poised over the handle.

"John, get the *fuck* out of there *now*!"

I jettisoned my canopy.

I ejected.

Gaskins orbited overhead with North Korean shore batteries pounding away at him. God bless him, he was below minimums on fuel and he was radioing a fix on my position. I did not know it then, of course, but he was in radio contact with an H-19A helicopter piloted by two guys whose names, I now know, were Blackburn and Caldwell.

Low on fuel, Gaskins was force to leave the scene. But first, he threw out a package of sea marking due to help Air Rescue locate me.

When my parachute snapped open, I had lost my sidearm and my shoes. We had to be close to the island of Cho-do, where we had rescue forces located in the enemy's backyard, but I didn't see any island. I was hanging from that parachute for only seconds when I went into the water.

**JOHN CALDWELL** Being a helicopter pilot on the island of Cho-do was not quite everybody's cup of tea.

Very few people knew it, but throughout the war we had small numbers of Americans on two islands in the Yellow Sea that were far behind enemy lines. Paengnyong-do, which we usually called P-Y-do or K-53, was right on the 38th Parallel and remains part of South Korea even today, although it's far north of today's demilitarized zone. Cho-do was much farther north, right up near the top of the Korean peninsula. Throughout the war, we had listening posts and rescue forces on both islands. Both islands were so close to North Korea that we could see the enemy coast, shimmering off in the distance. On days when the winds were right, the islands were within artillery range of North Korea. We were shelled regularly. This was not a very healthy location for a helicopter that was defenseless and vulnerable.

On Cho-do, we were using an older model of the H-19 than we'd flown during flight training in the United States. The Air Force had two models of the H-19, A and B models. The H-19A model, the one we had in Korea, had the same engine as the T-6 Texan trainer. The B model had a lot more horsepower, which we dearly needed and didn't have. When a new pilot arrived in our squadron, we had to retrain him in the A model, which was very different from the B and was much harder to fly. This was the trend throughout Korea: They gave us better junk in the field while the better helicopters were back home at the training ground.

To keep our helicopters operating and to keep our morale up so far from friendly forces and so deep in the enemy's backyard, we had the good fortune to have real leaders. One was Major (later Col.) William McDonald, the operations officer of the 2157th Air Rescue Squadron, the man who organized all this and made it happen. Another was my pilot on the day of that rescue, Tom Blackburn.

The word "RESCUE" partly obscured by an open cargo door, Capt. John Caldwell's H-19 helicopter flies over the island of Cho-do, off the coast of North Korea.

*Stuart Kennedy*

You have to keep in mind that at Cho-do we didn't have a lot to work with. Electricity? Running water? You've got to be kidding.

## Conditions on Cho-do

We had three tents and a bunker. The bunker was a makeshift place to seek cover. It consisted of sandbags on top of a cave, with the entrance reinforced with fifty-five-gallon drums filled with sand. We were occasionally shelled from the mainland when wind and visibility permitted, and that's where we hid.

There were two permanent installations, the radar site and our helicopter outfit. At the radar site, they looked for MiGs and other enemy air activity and relayed the information to our side. They also had language intercept guys who monitored enemy air activity. They were living pretty well over there with Quonset huts, generators, and some refrigeration. Sometimes they shared their refrigerated food with us.

As for us helicopter guys, we had three tents, one each for our flight crews, mechanics, and Korean supporters. We had no running water. We boiled all the water we drank.

There was no access to Cho-do by sea. You reached the island by landing a Gooney Bird [C-47] on the beach, only when the tide was out, or by helicopter. If you were flying a helicopter from South Korea, you would stop and refuel at Paengnyong-do en route. When the tide was out, or if the weather was bad, there was no way to get in or out of Cho-do.

2nd Lt. John Gaskin was on his fifth combat mission attacking a rail yard in North Korea when enemy gunfire crippled his plane and sent him crashing into the Yellow Sea.

*Chuck Gaskin*

We didn't even have fuel bladders on Cho-do. Our fuel was in five-gallon Jerry cans flown in by Gooney Birds.

There were just two helicopters on Cho-do. There wouldn't have been any way to support more than that. We were part of a much larger rescue apparatus that included H-5s, H-19s, and SA-16 Albatross twin-engined amphibians stationed at K-16 airport near Seoul and other places.

On the day F-84G pilot John Gaskin was shot down— I didn't know his name then, of course—our communications weren't working perfectly, but we did have an SA-16 amphibian in the air on alert. The problem was, Gaskin went down too close to the spot where the mouth of the Yalu River emptied into the Yellow Sea. The water there was too shallow for the SA-16 to land. It was going to be a helicopter or nothing.

**JOHN GASKIN** I was bobbing up and down in the water, struggling with my flotation device, when I realized that I wasn't alone. An SA-16 was circling in the sunlight about a mile from me. There were four swept-wing fighters higher up and for a moment I was afraid they would be MiGs—but they were F-86 Sabres. If I could just stay afloat, I figured, I might be okay.

The wind was pumped out of me and I was generating a lot of

adrenaline, and that's when I realized that the SA-16 was still circling. It had had plenty of time to touch down in the water and it wasn't doing so.

When I reached the height of a wave crest, splashing and thrashing, I looked around and realized that land was very close. I had been trying to get away from North Korea, out over the water, where the enemy wouldn't be able to interfere with a rescue. My F-84G hadn't gotten me quite far enough. My flight leader, Perse Gaskins, was heading home now and although I had friends overhead, I didn't know if the bad guys might be coming.

**JOHN CALDWELL** Blackburn and I were standing alert when Gaskin went down. With us was a medic whose name none of us remember today. Blackburn said, "It's your mission. Keep your hands on the controls." Blackburn and our medic were two of the gutsiest guys I ever knew.

The SA-16 spotted our F-84G pilot. I'll refer to him as John Gaskin from this point on, although I didn't know his name then. Gaskin had gone down in shallow water covered with sandbars, had popped open his one-man dingy, and was sitting in the dingy on top of a sandbar. When the SA-16 made a pass over his head, the guns on the ground opened up and stuff was flying through the air everywhere.

The SA-16 didn't set down to pick up Gaskin—not because of the enemy gunfire but because the water was too shallow. Moreover, the SA-16 was quickly running out of fuel, having been in the air circling since before Gaskin was hit.

At this point, we did not have Gaskin in sight from the helicopter. The SA-16 described where he was. This was fortunate because the URC-4 personal radio in Gaskin's possession wasn't transmitting.

In later years, when I was active with retirees in the Air Force Helicopter Pilots Association, I learned that handheld radios have been a problem in every war we fought. The technical knowledge to make a personal radio for a shot-down pilot was available long ago, but for some reason we have never made it happen. Survivors' radios failed in Korea, in Vietnam, and in Desert Storm. They're doing something about it nowadays, but the situation with survival radios is one of the big scandals in the military rescue business.

## Snatching the Survivor

With guidance from the SA-16 pilot before he turned for home, we spotted Gaskin sitting in his dingy. The humorous thing was, he was sitting on a sandbar, high and dry. It was colder than hell, even though it was May, so not being in the water was probably a good thing. I guess the water temperature was forty-five to fifty degrees.

When we started to descend in the H-19, we saw activity on the beach. The medic later said he saw bullets hitting the water around Gaskin.

We went in. The gunfire shifted toward us. I hovered overhead and our medic pulled Gaskin out of his dingy and into our fuselage. We were still pulling him up into the helicopter when I applied collective and started to get the hell out of there. The four F-86s that had been covering us went down and dropped napalm on the beach, and then cleared out of there. At the critical moment when we never needed help more, that's when our H-19 was the only aircraft in the sky.

Gaskin was wet. We took off our jackets and my boots and tried to make him comfortable. I was now wearing only socks to protect my feet and that was the last time I ever saw those boots. Gaskin did replace them forty-eight years later, however.

So here we were with our survivor on board, trying to get back to Cho-do alive. That's when the medic reported a "bent-wing" fighter on our tail. We were in the gunsight of an enemy MiG pilot boring down on us at about four times our speed. No wonder I had a reaction. We were in an unarmed chopper, with a maximum speed of only eighty [nautical miles per hour] at the mercy of the enemy MiG-15 jet.

What happened next was a rare moment that might have been gallantry—or, more plausibly, low fuel. The MiG dived at our helicopter, pulled up, did a snappy barrel roll, and climbed away to the north.

He didn't fire.

Did he recognize that we were attempting to save a human life? Or was he just low on fuel?

An F-84G Thunderjet fighter of John Gaskin's 58th Fighter Bomber Wing takes off from Taegu, South Korea, on a combat mission. Gaskin departed from his F-84G at low altitude over the Yellow Sea.

*U. S. Air Force*

I'll never know. Perhaps the pilot carried a bit of traditional chivalry aloft with him.

Still handling the controls with Blackburn looking over my shoulder, I set down at Cho-do. They unloaded Gaskin and put him on a C-47 Skytrain transport with a flight surgeon aboard. There was no problem about the Gooney Bird landing and taking off that day. They flew Gaskin back to his unit.

During the Korean War, we rescue pilots rarely learned whom we had rescued. Many years later, an author named Robert F. Dorr published a short article about my rescue flight and that was how I learned that the F-84G pilot was 2nd Lt. John Gaskin. He read the article and wanted to meet me. Forty-eight years after that rescue in the Yellow Sea, I contacted John Gaskin—now a retired country doctor with a long history of helping others, but also with a history of heart problems— and invited him to attend a reunion of helicopter pilots.

**RANDY PRESLEY** Long after the war, at about the time the helicopter pilots found John Gaskin and invited him to their reunion, I was in touch with him. He had flown thirty-five combat missions in all, thirty of them after being rescued, and we'd gotten to know each other well as F-84G pilots. During my visit, John and one of his sons and a grandson had gone to the movies to see *Pearl Harbor*, and I had a nice long visit with his second wife, Delores (Dee for short). John's first wife died sometime prior to 1986. We talked about John's health, which has been bad for years but he never let up. He'd had numerous angioplasties, hip replacements, bladder cancer in remission. I have newspaper articles about his retirement. He was the pinnacle of a country medical doctor. His medical work is known throughout the part of North Carolina where he lived.

**ROBERT F. DORR** In May 2001 at a reunion of the Air Force Helicopter Pilots Association in Biloxi, Mississippi, John Caldwell, John Gaskin, and I sat over coffee and talked about a long-ago war and a long-ago rescue. Accompanied by one of his three sons, Gaskin was in good spirits and had a great sense of humor.

You could see, however, that these men were serious. Gaskin knew he would be at the bottom of the Yellow Sea today had it not been for John Caldwell's H-19 crew. Caldwell knew that by rescuing an F-84G pilot he had given North Carolina a combat veteran who went to medical school, became the local doctor, and helped thousands of people over five decades while fighting his own history of heart problems.

**JOHN CALDWELL** In 1953, I asked the Air Force not to issue any publicity about the Gaskin rescue because I didn't want my wife, Judy, to know by picking up a newspaper and learning that I was up on an island near North Korea where people were shooting at me.

They published a story about the rescue and credited it to a different helicopter pilot. He wrote a "letter to the editor," said it wasn't him, and gave my name. That became a big, big news story—not the fact that we'd rescued someone, but the fact that a pilot had publicly refused to take credit for something he didn't do. The news made it into newspapers, radio, and television, and that's how Judy learned what I was doing in Korea.

In 2001, I said I didn't want any publicity then, either, but I reluctantly allowed Dorr to write a story that brought Gaskin and me together.

As part of our reunion in Biloxi that year, we took our group on a trip to the Stennis Space Center for a tour. We were getting out of the bus when John Gaskin suffered an abrupt heart attack and fell toward the pavement. His son caught him before he hit the ground, but he lost consciousness. My wife Judy, who is a nurse—yes, the same Judy, forty-eight years later—felt his pulse. John Gaskin had no pulse. He had begun to turn blue.

In wartime, a combination of circumstances had come together to make Gaskin one of those who lived rather than one who died. In peacetime, Gaskin again was affected by a succession of extraordinary circumstances.

With his son helping, one of the helicopter pilots in our association began giving John mouth-to-mouth.

By sheer luck, someone stepped out of the building in front of us with a portable defibrilator. By sheer luck, someone had a cell phone and dialed 911. And although we were thirty-five miles from the nearest town, by sheer luck an ambulance happened to be passing by at that time. It picked John up and took him to Slidell, Louisiana. And believe it or not, by sheer luck, the hospital he was taken to specializes in heart trauma.

We helicopter pilots saved John Gaskin's life a second time.

## H-19 Helicopter

The new helicopter taking shape on drawing boards at Sikorsky's Stratford, Connecticut, plant in the late 1940s was bigger than anything that had been attempted up to that time. It would carry more than just an extra crewman or a rescue litter. It would handle a payload of up to ten passengers, eight hospital litters, or 5,000 lb (2,267 kg) of freight in a large fuselage that sat on wheeled landing gear or on amphibious floats.

With its engine in the nose, mounted so that the drive shaft sloped up to the base of the rotor pylon, the new helicopter made good use of lightweight materials. The United States Air Force, seeing that the new helicopter would be able to fly missions up to a radius of 210 miles (338 km), ordered five test ships.

The military designation was YH-19, the Y prefix signifying a service-test mission. The first YH-19 (49-2012) completed its maiden flight on November 10, 1949.

The YH-19's 600-hp Pratt & Whitney R-1340 Wasp radial air-cooled piston engine was the same proven powerplant used in the North American T-6 Texan trainer. The engine was mounted at an angle in the nose of the fuselage, with the novel driveshaft arrangement already described. Large clamshell doors made maintenance easy. Maintainers could complete an engine change in two hours.

## Sikorsky H-19B Chickasaw (S-55)

**Type:** Two-place utility or search and rescue (SAR) helicopter driving three-blade 53-ft (16.15-m) main rotor

**Powerplant:** One 800-hp (682-kW) Wright R-1300-3 air-cooled, radial piston engine driving a 53-ft (16.15-m) three-bladed main rotor

**Performance:** Maximum speed 112 mph (180 km/h) at sea level; cruising speed 91 mph (146 km/h); service ceiling 28,000 ft (8534 m); range 360 miles (579 km); combat radius est. 100 mi (161 km); endurance est. 5 hrs 20 min

**Weights:** Empty 5,250 lb (2381 kg); normal takeoff weight, 6,200 lb (2812 kg); maximum takeoff 7,900 lb (3583 kg)

**Dimensions:** Main rotor diameter 53 ft (16.15 m); length overall, rotors turning, 56 ft 8-1/2 in (17.27 m); length 42 ft 3 in (12.88 m); height 13 ft 4 in (4.06 m); tail rotor diameter 8 ft 8 in (2.64 m); main rotor disc area 2,206 sq ft (209.94 sq m)

**Payload:** Ten to twelve armed troops or four hospital litters

**Armament:** None

**Crew:** Two pilots plus two

**First flight:** November 10, 1949 (YH-19)

In 1951, the Air Force ordered fifty production H-19As with two small fins forming an inverted V beneath the tail boom minor improvements over the YH-19 design. The Navy and Coast Guard ordered a version called the HO4S-1. Next came the H-19B version with a new powerplant, the 700-hp Wright R-1300-3. Two hundred seventy were built.

Two YH-19s joined the 3rd Air Rescue Squadron at Wolmi-do, Korea, on March 23, 1951, and participated in numerous rescues before one of the helicopters was transferred to CIA duties. There, in black paint and devoid of markings, it flew clandestine missions for the CIA. H-19A and H-19B models went to the 3rd and 2157th Air Rescue Squadrons in 1952. In its rescue role, the H-19 was equipped with a hydraulic hoist, mounted on the starboard fuselage just above the door. A number of combat rescues were achieved in Korea, including the celebrated save on April 12, 1952, of the ranking ace of the war, sixteen-kill Captain Joseph McConnell.

In Korea, Air Force and CIA H-19s dropped allied agents behind enemy lines and recovered them. Despite the helicopter's limited navigation suite, some of these missions were carried out at night. A dangerous cloak-and-dagger mission took place in summer 1952 when Capts. Joseph Cooper and Russell Winnegar of the 581st Resupply Squadron flew an H-19A into enemy territory with a small party of South Koreans to recover a crashed MiG-15 fighter. The MiG was the first to fall into allied hands and was evaluated by American scientists.

The 3rd Air Rescue Squadron had detachments scattered throughout Japan and Korea. By the time of the July 27, 1953, Korean armistice, the squadron had received over 1,000 personal citations—more than any other Air Force unit.

The Army introduced the H-19 long after the Air Force did, and the Coast Guard, Navy, and Marine Corps operated other versions of the helicopter. The H-19 was given the popular name "Chickasaw" by the Army when that service began naming helicopters for Native American nations in the late 1950s. During the Korean War era, these popular names were not yet in use.

# Chapter 5

## Marines in the Fray in Vietnam

### What Happened

Marines took to helicopters from the very beginning.

The Army was unprepared in Korea, played catch-up during the late 1950s and early 1960s, and then got it right in Vietnam.

The Marines had it right at the start. With help from the Navy, which handled procurement for the Corps, Marines were among the first to use choppers to rescue people in combat and to transport troops to and from the battlefield.

During the Korean fighting from 1950 to 1953, many Marines flew the HO3S-1, the same rickety craft known in Air Force jargon as the H-5 and piloted by Charles Field (Chapter Two) and Richard Kirkland (Chapter Three). Navy pilots flew it, too.

Navy squadron HU-1 at Lakehurst, New Jersey, soon followed by HU-2, trained Navy and Marine HO3S-1 pilots for search-and-rescue missions behind enemy lines during the Korean War.

To most Americans, the HO3S-1 helicopter escaped being totally unknown only because it was flown by Mickey Rooney in Hollywood's version of James Michener's novel *The Bridges at Toko-Ri*. In the film's

**Marine UH-34D pilots
1962-1967
Sikorsky UH-34D Sea Horse
HMH-362 "Archie's Angels"
Soc Trang, South Vietnam**

Capt. Ed Egan with UH-34D helicopter in Vietnam, 1967.

*Ed Egan*

climax, downed fighter pilot William Holden and HO3S-1 helicopter pilot Rooney die in a rice paddy in a realistic portrayal of a rescue that went wrong.

Real life was grimmer than the movies. On July 3, 1951, Lt. (j.g.) John M. Koelsch took off in an HO3S-1 helicopter belonging to HU-1 from the rescue ship LST-799 in Wonsan Harbor. Koelsch and crewman AM3 George M. Neal attempted to rescue Capt. James V. Wilkins, a Marine pilot shot down behind enemy lines thirty-five miles south of Wonsan.

Corsair fighters flew escort as Koelsch reached the rescue area. Because of solid clouds beneath him, he was forced to descend into harm's way without the Corsairs. He took his helicopter down in a perilous descent through clouds into mountainous terrain defended by Chinese infantrymen.

Under heavy fire, Koelsch persisted, hovered above Wilkins, and lowered a rescue sling. But a furious burst of gunfire tore into the helicopter and it plunged to earth.

Koelsch discovered that Wilkins's arms and legs were so severely burned that he was unable to walk. Koelsch and Neal fashioned a crude litter and carried the wounded Marine toward the coast. For nine incredible days, Koelsch's trio evaded Chinese troops but they were finally captured. As a prisoner of war, Koelsch continued his valorous actions and inspired fellow prisoners until he finally succumbed to dysentery

Before the Marines acquired the UH-34D, Navy and Marine pilots flew in Korea in the Sikorsky HO3S-1, the naval version of the Air Force's H-5 (chapters two and three). Doug Froling, a crewmember aboard the HO3S-1, called missions in the HO3S-1 "arduous."

*U. S. Navy*

and starvation in the hands of the enemy. He was awarded the Medal of Honor posthumously.

**DOUG FROLING** At the onset of the Korean War in June 1950, my outfit, Navy Helicopter Squadron One (HU-1), was based at Miramar, California, and had only a few HO3S-1s to serve the entire Pacific Fleet. At that time, the HO3S-1 was the only helicopter available with a hoist for rescuing downed pilots and other unfortunate military members who ended up in the water or stranded in enemy territory. This helicopter was new to the fleet and observers variously called it an "eggbeater" (large rotor blades to mix the air), a "dragonfly" (because of its shape), a "whirlybird" (because it occasionally lost direction), or even a "chopper" (because of the menacing sound of rotor blades that could do damage far beyond slicing through the air). In spite of those unflattering descriptions, those of us who flew in the machine had faith that we could perform our primary mission of rescuing others in the sea or in hostile territory.

## What Happened

While at sea heading toward the Korean War, Douglas G. Froling helped to rescue an F-4U Corsair pilot who launched from Froling's aircraft carrier near Hawaii.

"He went into the ocean instead of into the air," said Froling, seventy-three, of Seattle, Washington, a former aviation electrician second class and crew member of an HO3S-1 helicopter.

"I was working the hoist when we picked him up. We kept signaling him to get rid of his parachute first. Our little helicopter didn't have the power to lift both a wet pilot and a wet parachute."

Froling feels he had the Navy in him from the beginning. "I was born in Portland, Oregon, in 1930. With a war coming, my Dad, a World War I Navy veteran, sold his service station, moved to Seattle. He went to work building destroyers at Todd shipyards in 1941."

After high school, some college, and a job as a draftsman with Pacific Telephone, Froling "joined the Navy in 1950 to avoid the Army." It was the era of the draft. The Korean War began in June of that year.

"When I joined HU-1 at Miramar, California, in January 1951, there was a real mix of personnel, both officers and enlisted. Some were career Navy, some were World War II veterans recalled for Korea, and then there were us 'new kids.'"

In those days, a sailor with electrician and aircrew duty didn't go to technical school. Froling's training took place on the job, when helicopters were available.

After the rescue near Hawaii, Froling and his HU-1 crewmates spent seven months in Korean waters pulling plane guard duty aboard the USS *Philippine Sea* (CVA 47).

The Korean War often meant fighting the elements as well as North Korean and Chinese enemies. "I feared going down in those frigid winter waters more than I feared the bad guys," said retired Lt. Comdr. William Barron, seventy-seven, of Bay Point, California, pilot of the AD Skyraider attack plane. "At least, I knew I'd have a chance in my roomy airplane cockpit. Those guys in that frail helicopter took much greater risks than me."

Froling said that throughout his seven-month combat cruise, "My crew and I were constantly exhausted.

"The helicopter was the first aircraft launched in the a.m., and last put on the hangar deck in the p.m. After a full day on plane guard duty we did our required maintenance checks on the helo. And at times, we flew Navy mail runs to other ships in Task Force 77, and ferried people between ships as needed. On the days that our carrier was replenishing with bombs and other materials, we were kept busy moving people between ships.

"Our crew had no ready-room to lounge in," said Froling, "so we just hung out best we could near where the helicopter was parked, for instant duty if the helo was needed for some mission. I never learned to sleep sitting up like the others did. I think that we all slept constantly on the return cruise back to the United States."

HO3S-1 rescues behind enemy lines received some publicity, but the prosaic job of pulling plane guard duty is often ignored. To Froling, the HO3S-1 was "in many ways a throwback to the past. The main rotor blades were constructed like the wings of a First World War biplane, with a metal spar and wooden ribs covered with fabric. Still, that chopper and its crews rescued hundreds of downed pilots at sea, and worse, over enemy territory."

After his Korean War service, Froling returned to Seattle and the phone company, where he worked until retiring in 1983. He lives with his wife Patty, and is the father of three grown children.

**DOUG FROLING** It was a sparse beginning. Ten Navy and Marine helicopters were deployed to the Korean War effort by the end of 1950. The number of available Navy helicopters went way up in December 1950 when eight were airlifted from the sister squadron HU-2 based on the East Coast. On arrival at North Island, San Diego, California, they loaded the helicopters and their crews on the carrier USS *Valley Forge* (CV 45) for transportation to the Far East. By the end of 1952, my squadron alone had twenty-two helicopters deployed on aircraft carriers, battleships, cruisers, landing ship tanks (LSTs) and ashore on small Korean Islands. Navy helicopters rescued 317 military men over this period. The squadron lost twenty helicopters due to enemy gunfire and other crashes. Four pilots and their crewmen were captured and became POWs.

The Navy HO3S-1 flyers who were captured were: Lt. j.g. John Thornton, near Wonsan on March 31, 1951; Lt. j.g. John K. Koelsch, in a Korean mountain area, on July 3, 1951; and Lt. Edward C. Moore and Aviation Medicine Mate Duane Thorin, in another mountain area, on February 8, 1952. Koelsch gave his life and was awarded the Medal of Honor.

In my opinion, the HO3S-1 helicopter flown by the Navy was actually a throwback to World War I. The main rotor blades were constructed like those on a biplane with a metal spar and wooden ribs covered with fabric. A tech-rep from Sikorsky told me the only HO3S-1s that were equipped with metal blades began to reach the Marines only after the truce was signed in 1953.

It did not take long for the Marines to introduce a larger helicopter, the HRS-1, their equivalent of the Air Force H-19 flown by John Caldwell (Chapter Three). They had the HRS-1 in Korea two years before the Army did.

## Marines in Korea

On August 2, 1950, the Marine Corps purchased sixty HRS-1 helicopters, identical to the Air Force H-19A except for self-sealing fuel tanks. The first went to squadron HMX-1 on April 2, 1951. The first use of helicopters to carry combat troops to an objective was recorded on September 13, 1951, when HRS-1s of squadron HMS-161 hauled Marines across a seven-mile (11-km) contested zone to a Korean hilltop being assaulted by Chinese troops.

In twenty-eight sorties during what became known as Operation Windmill, the HRS-1 transported about 19,000 lb (8,618 kg) of supplies to a Marine battalion holding Hill 884 in eastern South Korea. The helicopters also evacuated eighty-four casualties. Similar action in

Operation Windmill II followed a few days later. Subsequently, in Operation Ripple during the summer of 1952, Marine HRS-1s quickly repositioned rocket launchers and firing crews before enemy artillery could locate the Marines' firing positions and return fire. Each HRS-1 lifted a single launcher, a launch crew, or twenty-two rockets.

Marines found the HRS-1 to be tough and durable. One helicopter returned to its base after losing eighteen inches of rotor blade in a collision with a tree. However, the Marines concluded that the helicopter was underpowered. In extreme heat and cold in Korea, the R-1340-57 engine came up with only 500 horsepower. On truly hot days, the helicopter was next to useless around Korea's jagged mountain peaks.

No dramatic change was offered in the HRS-2 model, which began to reach squadron HMR-161 in October 1952. This version was identical to the HRS-1 but for 3.5 degrees of downslope on its tailboom.

Like their Air Force counterparts, Marine Corps HRS helicopters performed numerous rescues of downed pilots. By the 1953 cease-fire, HMR-161 had accumulated 16,538 flight hours in the HRS-1/2 on 18,607 sorties. The helicopters were credited with 60,000 individual troop movements.

In post-Korea service, a Marine HRS-2 became the first helicopter to use the helipad at the Pentagon building on November 2, 1955. By then, the Marines were well along with development of a new helicopter that would serve them so well in Vietnam. It was called the HUS-1 at the time, and the UH-34D later. The official name was Sea Horse. Marines called it the "Dog."

## Marines in Vietnam

Before most Americans had heard of Vietnam, Marines knew it well. In 1962, Marine Heavy Helicopter squadron HMM-362, commanded by Lt. Col. Archie Clapp, arrived in Soc Trang in the Mekong Delta with 24 HUS-1 helicopters. Marines called the squadron "Archie's Angels" after its commander, but the name soon changed to the "Ugly Angels." When the Pentagon's system for assigning letters and numbers to aircraft was overhauled on October 1 of that year, the HUS-1, or "huss," was renamed the UH-34D.

**JERRY DOOLEY** It was a good thing Marines enjoyed a tradition of getting by without creature comforts. Soc Trang had just one building and one hangar left over from the French, plus a low, plaster barracks and a poorly maintained, 3,200-foot runway. We had to rebuild that entire place when we arrived, but our own supply line was thin and erratic, so we got by without a lot of typical pleasures. For a period, the head was a ditch in the ground with a wooden structure built over it.

Land is flat in the Delta. The flat marsh forests of the Mekong Delta offered little cover to helicopter crews or to the South Vietnamese troops who rode the UH-34D, much like a chariot, into battle. The lack of cover was a double-edged sword, of course—picture firing a machine gun from the air at men in black pajamas splashing across a flooded paddy field—but the Viet Cong were the ones who controlled the vegetated areas.

A few miles to the west of Soc Trang, across a flat expanse of marshes and canals, you came to the U Minh Forest, which for years was a stronghold for the various and sundry rebels who fought in that area, going back to the days the French fought in Indochina. The rumor was that the French once dropped an entire battalion in there and nobody came out alive. Our UH-34Ds hauled South Vietnamese troops all over the place, and there was no doubt that helicopters made a big, big difference, but the brass hats who planned operations didn't want to send any significant number of troops into the U Minh.

In the Mekong Delta, temperatures year-round were in the high 80s and 90s, with thunderstorms in the afternoon. That may not sound so sweltering, but it meant being drenched in sweat and parched in the throat all day long. It's primarily rice fields, so you have high temperature and humidity. That gives you a very high "density altitude"—a formula based on temperature and pressure—which is something helicopters don't like. No helicopter likes "high and hot," meaning high elevation and hot temperature, and in the density altitude conditions of the Delta, the UH-34D believed it higher and hotter than it really was. There were tremendous battles near Soc Trang, Can Tho, and Ca Nau, and while the UH-34D gave the South Vietnamese a new secret weapon, the climate conditions reduced its effectiveness: If you're lifting South Vietnamese troops, you can lift fewer troops because your useful

In the UH-34D flown by Marines in Vietnam, the two pilots sat up high, partially protected by the engine located in the nose below and ahead of them. Passengers occupied a compartment below and behind the pilots.

*Sikorsky*

payload is much less, possibly as much as 30 or 40 percent less. The good news is, that's not saltwater down there, so there were no corrosion issues, but it was always a challenge to keep the helicopters in operating condition.

Despite being a piston aircraft in a turbine era, the Dog was the right weapon at the right time. Before helicopters, the Viet Cong controlled everything. After helicopters arrived, South Vietnamese troops had the mobility to dislodge them. Because it offered an opportunity to arrive with the element of surprise, one South Vietnamese officer said that the UH-34D was going to enable his troops to turn the tide.

In the early days in Vietnam, what we were doing wasn't very high-tech. I carried a grease gun, otherwise known as an M-3A1 submachine gun when flying in the Mekong Delta. Several times, we came upon Viet Cong irregulars in canoes who were armed with M1 Garand rifles—retrieved from dead South Vietnamese—and, yes, with bows and arrows. I remember making repeated S-turns in a UH-34D, something that was difficult to do in almost any other helicopter, and blasting away with grease guns at the Viet Cong.

We were the first Marine helicopter squadron to enter Vietnam on Palm Sunday, April 9, 1962. We had been aboard USS *Princeton* as the ready force for some months and most of us were very happy to be ashore when we went into Soc Trang in the Mekong Delta. The Marine Corps named our deployment Operation Shu Fly. At the time, there were about 5,000 American "advisers" in South Vietnam. Defense Secretary Robert S. McNamara used the incorrect spelling of "advisors," and the press picked up on it.

Because of our advisory role, we Marine pilots had our photo portraits taken in civilian shirt and tie and were given civilian passports. Still, we flew in flight suits.

I really loved the people in Vietnam. Those that I saw were enthusiastic about us. They welcomed us. They wanted us. They supported us when we went into the "hot fire" area in War Zone D, north of Saigon. Needless to say, I had no idea in 1962 that the number of Americans in Vietnam would eventually reach more than half a million.

## North from the Delta

On one occasion, helicopters lifted South Vietnamese troops into an area of marsh fields and canals in the Mekong Delta, where they became caught up in a major battle with 400 Viet Cong. The foe seemed to be familiar with the local populace and with terrain features. A platoon of South Vietnamese became separated from the main force and found itself under attack. The platoon leader used a combination of flares, colored smoke, and hand signals to beckon a Marine UH-34D that brought fresh troops to exactly the right spot. The battle, which was near battalion size and was then one of the largest battles in the region, was deemed a victory for the South.

Soon after early fighting in the marshlands of the Delta, the Marines were moved farther north. From 1963 to 1969, they operated UH-34D helicopters at Da Nang, Chu Lai, Marble Mountain, and other locations familiar to Vietnam veterans.

The UH-34D was a tremendous improvement over the Korean War–era HRS-1 and it was built like a tank, but it was also a cantankerous flying machine that no one ever accused of being anything but ugly. Marines loved it without reservation.

**ED EGAN** Eccentricities? Those fat doughnut wheels stood out from her sides, created airborne drag, and detracted from a sleek look, but they provided great stability on the ground. Among those in my flight training class, nineteen out of thirty-seven were killed in action, so I guess we were entitled to have our thoughts about the helicopter. Sometimes it was gallows humor. When we had to take a leak, we called it wetting the tailwheel. In the UH-1E Huey, we usually wore our holstered .45 automatic over the groin to protect the family jewels, but in the UH-34D at least we knew we had that big engine up front which protected pilots up to about waist level. Pilots wore ceramic, three-quarter "bullet bouncers" that protected the trunk of the body.

I was a member of Marine squadron HMM-263, "Blue Eagles," in Vietnam in 1967. That was half a decade after the UH-34D first arrived in country. By then, the UH-34D was getting pretty old, but I guess you could call it "Old Reliable." We also called it "Old Ugly" and the "Dog." We had huge confidence in it.

In October 1967, my crew was tasked to extract a platoon of Marines who had gotten in over their heads and were engaged in a furious firefight with a superior force of North Vietnamese regulars. Under small arms fire from all directions, our seven UH-34Ds landed in a line in a rice paddy bordered by trees. The first six helicopters got off with their loads, but as the last in line, we waited for the final Marines to board. They were busy trying to disengage from the enemy, trading fire and grenades fifty yards away.

Of course, we try to avoid situations where the Viet Cong are right in front of us and are shooting at us. This time, we didn't avoid it. With the last nine Marines on board, we attempted liftoff, but the load of nine grunts and four crewmen was too much under the hot, humid conditions. There were limbs and branches jutting out near the paddy field and at one point someone cried on the intercom, "We're fighting in the trees!"

We pilots placed one wheel on a rice-paddy dike, lifted the other skyward, and ordered the crew chief out of the aircraft to drain fuel. He piled out along with the grunts. They started laying down fire at the Viet Cong coming across the paddy at us and he started trying, very rapidly, to find a way to get us out of there.

With rifles popping and bullets going over his head, the crew chief crawled under the UH-34D and opened a petcock valve while the copilot hit the fuel transfer switch. This allowed some fuel to spill out, reducing aircraft weight. We pilots then made a rolling takeoff with the one wheel helping to support the horizontal roll. It was too heavy to go straight up, so we flew it off like an airplane, that fat wheel rolling along the dike. Eventually, we developed enough translational lift to become airborne, although they were clipping treetops for a while.

This helicopter might look ugly to you but there's a lot of emotional attachment to it. It performed in the unlikeliest situations. One time, we were flying back from a mission from Con Thien over a narrow road called the North-South Trace. I was flying copilot with a pilot named Rick Rivers. We spotted somebody on the ground waving a poncho. We went down to help, took some hits from hostile fire, and flew so low we broke the main wheel off. We landed the aircraft on a pile of sandbags. Had the wheel not broken off, we'd have gone into a flat spin and died.

Among helicopters in combat in Vietnam, the UH-34D, alias the Dog, had a unique configuration. The 6-ft (1.82-m) height of its cargo/troop compartment meant that combat soldiers or Marines could stand fully erect while being transported. Soldiers or Marines could carry equipment, mortars, machine guns, food supplies, or ammunition. The generous size of the compartment made the UH-34D extremely flexible, but the configuration of the fuselage kept those in back isolated from those in front. The pilots could not leave their seats to go out back: Their feet were at the level of the head of a standing passenger.

**JOE SCOLLE** I flew the UH-34D in combat with squadron HMH-363, the "Red Lions." The UH-34D was the only Vietnam helicopter that could keep flying if the tail rotor was shot off. The large magnesium slab of the rear fuselage acted as a "sail" to offset rotor torque so long

Sikorsky UH-34D Sea Horse of squadron HMM-363 "Red Lions," Marine Aircraft Group Sixteen (MAG-16) en route to the assault ship USS *Iwo Jima* (LPH 2) off the coast of Vietnam, circa. February 1968.

*Joseph Scholle*

as air speed stayed above forty knots. Below that speed, you had to shut down the engine and autorotate in order to reach solid ground, but at least one UH-34D made it back to HMH-363's principal base, Marble Mountain, with crippling tail-rotor damage that would have caused a Huey or a Sea Knight to rotate itself into pieces.

There was no mission to which the H-34 was not assigned, from "Holy Helo" (delivering chaplains to conduct services) to emergency recon team extractions. Missions in the mountains west of the coastal plain were especially challenging since rotor and engine performance deteriorated quickly with altitude. Under these conditions an H-34 with any appreciable payload was operating at the edge of the envelope.

For many reasons, the most rewarding mission was medical evacuation, or medevac. It provided a lifesaving service to those fighting on the ground and sometimes to fellow helicopter crews who were down. There were a lot of nuances to doing this mission correctly. You wanted to land with the helo between the medevac and the source of enemy fire so as to shield those carrying the casualty to the chopper. You wanted to land as close to the medevac as possible to reduce the carrying task and exposure of the grunts to the Viet Cong. And of course when the help was available and the enemy was shooting, you wanted the escorting gunship to blow up the general part of the world from whence the fire came.

When the UH-34D went to war, the ground troops were South Vietnamese and the battle zone was in the Delta. But by 1965, the UH-34D was fighting everywhere in-country and the ground troops included

These are Marine UH-34D helicopters of squadron HMM-263 "Blue Eagles," at Marble Mountain, South Vietnam, circa. November 1966.

*Leonard Martinez*

fellow Marines, who arrived at Da Nang in April 1965. At many locations, such as the helicopter base at Marble Mountain, UH-34D helicopters operated from MA-2 matting, made of quarter-inch extruded aluminum with interlocking edges, similar to the pierced steel planking, or Marston Mat, of World War II. The MA-2 had a nonskid surface and no holes. Operations off the matting were excellent. Since there were no holes, Marines never had a foreign object damage (FOD) problem from dirt or stones coming up through the matting, and braking was excellent.

Ultimately, half a dozen Marine squadrons flew the Dog in Vietnam. They were HMMs 162 "Pineapples," 163 "Ridge Runners," 261 "Bulls," 263 "Blue Eagles," 361 "Tigers," 362 "Ugly Angels," 363 "Red Lions," and 365 "Clowns." Each had a small emblem unique to the squadron nickname painted on the helicopter. Little traditions are important to Marines, and it mattered a lot that each of these squadrons had its own history and heritage. Some of UH-34D squadrons spent brief tours of around four months in-country; others were there for two years or more.

Throughout the war, the United States Navy kept an amphibious assault ship off the coast of Vietnam, often the USS *Iwo Jima* (LPH 2) or the USS *Princeton* (LPH 5), with a battalion of ground troops trained for quick response to battlefield situations. UH-34D crews rotated duty aboard these flattops (*Princeton* was a converted Essex-class carrier) and savored the Navy food and bunks, far more comfortable than their hookahs in hot spots like Chu Lai and Con Thien.

This is a pair of Marine UH-34D helicopters of squadron HMM-364, "Purple Foxes," based at Da Nang, South Vietnam, and operating over Vietnamese terrain in April 1964.

*Warren Smith*

The Sikorsky S-58, as its builder called the H-34, was designed to meet the Navy's need for an antisubmarine aircraft, but most were built as assault helicopters for the Army and Marine Corps. Sikorsky built 1,821 altogether.

HMM squadrons in Vietnam reequipped with the Boeing CH-46A Sea Knight beginning in 1966. But the CH-46A suffered transmission problems that literally caused the tail of the aircraft to fall off. During the months spent solving this problem, UH-34Ds returned to service. When the Dogs finally flew their last mission with the Marines, many were turned over to the Vietnamese Army.

## UH-34D Sea Horse Helicopter

Today, Gerald Hail of Tulsa, Oklahoma, flies a Sikorsky UH-34D Sea Horse once operated by Marines in Vietnam. Hail proudly displays his ungainly aircraft at air shows and puts on demonstrations for the public. The big, brutish helicopter is a source of curiosity for those who do not remember ugly, pug-nosed, piston-driven helicopters; a reason for excitement when it carries out mock combat missions in front of awestruck crowds; and the basis for a tremendous outpouring of nostalgia whenever Vietnam-era Marines gather to look at it, kick its tires, tap their knuckles on its thin skin, and—if they're lucky—go for a memory-making ride in it.

They joke about it. The jokes reflect the maverick personalities of

A Marine UH-34D Sea Horse loading South Vietnamese troops at Chu Lai, South Vietnam, in December 1966.

*James T. O'Kelley*

# Sikorsky UH-34D Sea Horse (S-58)

**Type:** Four-place general-purpose helicopter

**Powerplant:** Wright R-1820-84 or -84B Cyclone 9-cylinder air-cooled radial engine rated at 1,525 hp at 2,800 rpm or 1,275 hp at 2,500 rpm driving four-bladed, 56-ft (17.06-m) rotors on fully articulated rotor heads

**Performance:** Maximum speed 120 mph (193 km/h) at sea level; cruising speed 98 mph (125 km/h); maximum rate of climb 1,100 ft (335 m) per minute at sea level; service ceiling 9,500 ft (2895 m); hovering ceiling with ground effect 4,900 ft (1493 m); hovering ceiling without ground effect 2,400 ft (740 m); range 225 miles (362 km)

**Weights:** Empty weight, 8,230 lb (3777 kg); gross weight 13,300 lb (6033 kg), useful load 5,070 lb (3000 kg)

**Dimensions:** Main rotor diameter 56 ft (17.06 m); length overall, rotors turning, 56 ft 8.5 in (17.27 m); fuselage length 46 ft 9 in (14.24 m); fuselage width 5 ft 8 in (17.26 m); tail rotor diameter 9 ft 6 in (2.90 m); cabin interior length 13 ft 3 in (4.03 m); cabin interior width 5 ft 3 in (1.60 m); cabin interior height 6 ft (1.82 m)

**Armament:** Door-mounted M60 or M1 machine gun

**Payload:** Up to 3,600 lb (1,888 kg) of personnel or equipment

**Crew:** Two pilots plus two

**First flight:** March 8, 1954 (prototype); September 20, 1954 (production)

the men. They say that if a Viet Cong mortar round doesn't get you, you may lose your footing on one of the parking apron oil slicks so familiar to those who remember how the UH-34D can drip. For that matter, you can survive the patch of oil on the tarmac and still kill yourself simply by falling from the top rung of the ladder leading up to the cockpit, which places you about nine feet off the ground. The UH-34D was squat and tall and worked well. Pretty it was not.

The UH-34D evokes nostalgia. It takes us back to an innocent era when John F. Kennedy sat in the White House and a handful of Americans fought as advisers in a sputtering brushfire war.

Marines like to compare the UH-34D to the Springfield .03 infantry rifle of World War II. Long after the Army had shifted to the prettier, more efficient M-1 Garand, Marines were still in combat with Springfields.

A 1,525-horsepower Wright R-1820-84/B Cyclone 9-cylinder air-cooled radial engine pulled the UH-34D through the air. The engine hung like a lead weight or, in the view of some, a welcome armor shield, in the helicopter's bulbous nose.

# Chapter 6

## The Battle of Ia Drang Valley

### What Happened

During four days of battle in South Vietnam's Ia Drang Valley in 1965, Army helicopter pilot Chief Warrant Officer Leland C. Komich made a dozen landings under fire to resupply embattled Americans and to rescue thirty-three, including twenty-six wounded. These helicopter sorties were voluntary and at great risk—in the words of another pilot, "in circumstances in which nobody in his right mind would have flown."

On November 14, 1965, Komich piloted a troop-lift UH-1D Huey to haul ammunition into Landing Zone Xray. There, First Cavalry Division troopers were surrounded and under attack from North Vietnamese soldiers, or NVA. It was the beginning of the Battle of Ia Drang Valley.

Komich was constantly engulfed in NVA gunfire. "Over the helicopter engine and rotor noise, it sounded a lot like popcorn, 'pop, pop, pop.' When the muzzle of a rifle was pointed directly at us, it made a sharper, cracking sound."

Another pilot described what happened to Komich at XRay: "Lifting off from LZ Xray, Komich's crew saw his wingman's Huey throw out bursts of smoke from its engine compartment. It had been hit by

**Chief Warrant Officer Lee Komich**
**November 14–17, 1965**
**Bell UH-1D Iroquois (Huey)**
**ORANGE 3**
**B Company, 229th Assault Helicopter**
**  Battalion, First Cavalry Division**
**Anh-Khe, South Vietnam**

CWO Lee Komich, who flew UH-1D Huey helicopters throughout the four-day Battle of Ia Drang Valley, at Landing Zone XRay and again at Landing Zone Albany.

*William Weber*

---

enemy fire and quickly made a crash landing just outside the battle perimeter in No Man's Land. Komich took the initiative to circle back and land under fire next to the smoking ship and to rescue its crew and all wounded being carried. He sat there, waiting, under enemy fire until all could be boarded."

Komich, quiet and serious, is a product of New England, born in Maine and raised in Massachusetts. He enlisted in 1960. He was a crew chief on H-19 helicopters in Germany before flight school.

Komich pinned on aviator's wings in 1964 and joined the 11th Air Assault Division at Fort Benning, Georgia. This was a test outfit, thrown together to refine and perfect a new way of fighting wars using a new kind of troop transport. After long months of hard training, in 1965, the 11th Air Assault changed names and took the identity of the 1st Cavalry Division. In Vietnam, cavalrymen carved an airfield out of the jungle at An Khe, the place they called "Golf Course."

These American soldiers were exceptionally well prepared. "You were pushed to the limit every day," Komich said of their training at Benning. "We once spent forty-five days in the field on a field problem. The training carried over to Vietnam very nicely. The first time I was in a 'hot' landing zone, I heard everybody shooting but thought, 'Jeez, that's the same sound you get in training with blanks.' But it was different when enemy rounds started opening up holes in the helicopter."

The battle at LZ Xray was a challenge even for well-prepared

This is Headquarters of the 229th Assault Helicopter Battalion at Anh-Khe, the "Golf Course," in South Vietnam.

*William Weber*

aviators. Once he'd rescued the downed helicopter's crew and wounded passengers, Komich decided he was needed back in the midst of the battle. He took the initiative to load his UH-1D with a fresh cargo of ammunition—bypassing the usual supply bureaucracy to get the job done—and flew back to the landing zone.

In the words of another pilot, "He went back into harm's way, circled trying to navigate through the smoke on the battlefield, and eventually landed with that much-needed ammo." Again, he picked up wounded Americans and hauled them out.

One soldier, borrowing the title of war movie, called the fight for Xray the "longest day." But the larger battle between American cavalry-men and NVA regulars lasted longer than a day. Four days later on November 17, 1965, at another surrounded spot in the jungle called Landing Zone Albany, Komich and other UH-1D pilots were tested again (Chapter Six). Komich retired from the Army in 1982. He lives in Alexandria, Virginia, and is employed as a pilot today, flying for a government contractor that handles emergency response to nuclear incidents.

**LEE KOMICH** Today, we know that Hal Moore's battalion came into contact with North Vietnamese regular troops in the Ia Drang Valley on November 14, 1965, and fought them over four days while being supported at landing zones Xray and Albany. Moore was the lieutenant

UH-1D Huey helicopters destroyed during the Battle of Ia Drang Valley.

*William Weber*

colonel (later a lieutenant general) later played by Mel Gibson in the film version of the battle, *We Were Soldiers*. Hollywood based the movie on the account written by Moore and Joseph L. Galloway.

I can't say we knew from the beginning that this would be the first major battle between the two sides, or that our helicopters would be pivotal in determining the outcome.

I don't think you can say enough about the helicopter we were flying. No other aircraft could have gotten us into Xray or Albany. I first saw the forerunner, the UH-1A Huey model, when I was in Germany as an enlisted crew chief on the H-19 in 1960. The Huey was so far advanced. I thought, "Wow." And it wasn't just my youthful enthusiasm. It really was advanced. Our older H-19 was a big, gangly thing with a huge bulbous nose. Maintainers spent all their time keeping seals in place and greasing it. The cabin would seat several people but if you actually put more than two or three, it lacked the power to fly. The UH-1A Huey showed up and, gee, you could put four or five troops in without any problem.

Most of us felt, however, that even the Huey series could use a little more power. That was the situation until we got to the H model (UH-1H), long after Ia Drang. When I was selected for flight training and left my enlisted duties behind, I got to fly the Huey but only in the final, or most advanced, part of flight school.

When they put it together, they did their homework. In my mind, the

## Who's Who

**Komich's helicopter (ORANGE 3):**

CWO Lee Komich, UH-1D Huey pilot (left seat)

CWO Chuck Nay, copilot (right seat) (morning, Nov. 14)

Capt. Paul Winkel, UH-1D copilot (right seat) (afternoon, Nov. 14)

Spec-5 Richard Smith, UH-1D crew chief/ gunner

Spec-4 Mickey Whittaker, UH-1D gunner

**Harper's helicopter (ORANGE 4):**

CWO Dallas Harper, UH-1D helicopter pilot (left seat)

WO2 Ken Faba, UH-1D copilot (right seat)

Crew chief/gunner, name unknown

Gunner, name unknown

**Others:**

William Weber, UH-1D crew chief

Huey compared with a Porsche. It was just so slick. The big difference was the turbine engine, which weighed a fraction of the old reciprocating engines but could produce 900 horsepower.

When I got to the Air Assault (meaning the 11th Air Assault Division forming at Fort Benning, Georgia, later to be reflagged as the 1st Cavalry Division) they said, "We're going to check you out in the B model (the UH-1B). I liked the helicopter a lot but it had its idiosyncrasies. It took that engine a long time to recover from idle. One of the other problems that we had at Fort Benning was, there were no filters for the engine. Without them, operating in the Georgia swamps, cottonseed and other debris would get in there and we started having compressor stalls. The joke was, you had to have a minimum of one compressor stall a week. Bell modified the Huey and put filters on it.

### Air Assault Division

The 11th Air Assault Division at Fort Benning was a new concept in warfare. We were going into battle in the helicopter the way soldiers had once gone on horseback. The helicopter was going to give us a new standard of mobility and flexibility.

Our division commander was Maj. Gen. (later, Lt. Gen.) Harry W. O. Kinnard. He refined training and tactics during months of hard work in the United States, and then took us to South Vietnam and led

Warrant Officer (later Major) Frank Moreno was another of the UH-1D Huey pilots who flew into Landing Zone XRay during the first days of the Battle of Ia Drang Valley.

*Frank Moreno*

us in battle. One of the battalion commanders was Lt. Col. (later, Lt. Gen.) Hal Moore. His battalion was the 1/7th, the same outfit once commanded by Gen. George Custer. We had a terrific team of Americans in the 11th Air Assault. We trained hard. We knew where we were going.

Before we left Benning, we received the UH-1D Huey models we would fly in Vietnam. Just before they sent us to Vietnam, they reflagged us as the 1st Cavalry Division (Air Assault). We wore the distinctive horse's head as our shoulder patch. In Moore's battalion, the 1/7th, instead of saying, "Yes, sir!" they said, "Garry Owen, sir!" maintaining the practice of identifying Custer's 7th Cavalry with the name of an old, Irish drinking song. Having flown the UH-1A in flight training and the UH-1B with the 11th Air Assault, I was now about to fly the UH-1D in combat with the First Cavalry Division.

In Vietnam, there were three basic Huey missions. Some Hueys were "slicks," plain transport ships, lacking external armament, used to shuttle troops around. Others were "gunships," armed with guns and rockets to provide fire support. And still others were "DUSTOFFs"—the medical evacuation Hueys that saved many American soldiers' lives.

More wounded men survived in Vietnam than in previous wars because of quick responses by Hueys. As we'll see, though, DUSTOFF wasn't a factor at Ia Drang.

As events propelled us toward the Battle of Ia Drang Valley, three top officers led our three helicopter companies in the First Cav's 229th Assault Helicopter Battalion. The commander of A Company was Major (later Col.) Bruce P. Crandall, who was played by actor Greg Kinnear in the *Soldiers* movie. Major Richard Rogers commanded my outfit, B Company. He was away when the Ia Drang battle began and his executive officer, Major David Carroll, was in charge. Major (later Col.) Willard M. Bennett, Jr., known as Will, commanded C Company.

In 1965, our division began operations at Anh-Khe, South Vietnam, nicknamed the Golf Course. For the first time in history, large numbers of soldiers were being carried into battle—and moved around, once the battle began—by air. The presence of the First Cav in the Vietnamese highlands changed the situation in that region, and the other side apparently made a decision to commit main-force regular troops from North Vietnam, known as NVA, for the first time.

Looking back today, it seems that all of this was preordained. A major fight was brewing. An American citizen army and an elite force of highly trained NVA regulars were preparing to clash in their first major battle. The week before the Battle of Ia Drang Valley began, *Newsweek* magazine began referring to the Vietnam conflict as "the Helicopter War."

Let me say a word about the NVA. I don't know whether it was individuals' discipline or if it was imposed upon them—I have no way to know—but the fact is, the North Vietnamese soldier would do things that it's highly unlikely American soldiers would do.

The North Vietnamese were masters at getting up into a tree or down into what we called a spider hole, which was just a hole in the ground, and they would stay there forever. When the opportunity came to snipe at their enemies, they would do that. One of our commanders thought he would have American troops try to do that. It didn't work. Americans lack the patience.

There are other stories about the North Vietnamese soldier. They seemed capable of functioning without difficulty in unbelievable heat, in thick foliage, and with leeches falling all over them. They were unflinching. They were very determined, dedicated. I suspect it was because within their society that's the way people are. One of our commanders tried to get American soldiers to fight in that manner and our troops weren't capable of it.

Their underground activities were extraordinary. We hit them on the Bong Son Plain where they had a facility that was three stories deep, all of it underground. I just can't imagine living underground like that. An amazing part about that is, we found the air shafts, oh, six to eight inches in diameter or something like that, and they were very well bored and they went down, oh, ten or twelve feet. I could be left in that rice paddy for a hundred years and be told, "All you have is a homemade entrenching tool. Dig a shaft twelve feet deep." And I wouldn't be able to do it. So we marveled about this. It turned out they were taking rabbits and putting them in open cages to test the air down there. Holy cow. Unbelievable.

## Ia Drang Battle

On the day before the Ia Drang battle began, I was at Plei Mi flying UH-1Ds. If memory serves, we had made a number of assaults that day. We didn't have crew rest policies in those days. We should have but we didn't. We just kept going and going, way beyond normal limits of endurance. I had flown thirty or forty straight days along with Dallas Harper, my buddy. We were told, tomorrow, take a day off. We were not too far from Pleiku, so we could go into town, buy some trinkets, drink some beer.

Early that morning, we were told troops were going into a landing zone and that we would be needed. That was Hal Moore's 2/7th Cavalry ("Second of the Seventh").

So off we went and the rest is history. We expected to carry two or three assaults into an LZ, and then fly back to Pleiku and head downtown for some relaxation. Instead, we began four days of constant operations, most of it in the middle of a big fight, four days without properly eating or sleeping while getting shot at.

At about 10:30 a.m. on November 14, 1965, UH-1—our Hueys of the 229th AHC—began landing cavalrymen of Moore's battalion at LZ XRay, on low ground beneath a peak called the Chu Pong massif. A subsequent wave of Hueys, including mine, returned with more troops at about 12:20 a.m. By then, one company of Moore's battalion, led by Capt. John D. Herren, was caught up in a point-blank firefight. Some of the fire was being directed at our helicopters.

At the time, we weren't keeping track of the exact time or duration of each lift. We were just too busy. The memories are indelible but the exact times are something we filled in later. I remember that one of our pilots, Robert Mason, who later wrote a best-selling book, *Chickenhawk*, wrote notes about everything and stuffed them into a shoebox. I thought, "What could he need that material for? Who could ever forget this stuff?" Many years later, Paul Winkel, West Point '56, a captain at Ia Drang, and later a retired colonel, reconstructed the time of day for each event at XRay.

I don't recall which lift it was, maybe our third or fourth trip into LZ XRay, when we started to take fire. That was not a big deal. It happened regularly. But then it started to get really bad. When you can hear the popping, when you can see muzzle flashes, that's when it's really, really bad.

When did I realize this was going to become a serious battle? Roger Bean, a young lieutenant who later became a three-star, was going into XRay when his UH-1D (callsign WHITE 2) took hits. Bean later said that an AK-47 round entered the back of his flight helmet, ripped along the side of his head, and came out the front, leaving blood spilling all over him and his copilot taking the controls to get them out of there. That's when I was certain things were not quite as nice as we'd hoped. I'd suspected this was coming and now I knew we were in a real fight.

One vivid memory I have from this: we were in a large formation heading toward the LZ at about 2:00 p.m. on November 14. I looked out and saw an A-1E Skyraider go into the trees and explode. There was no parachute. That was the Air Force A-1E that was attempting to fly close air support for Moore's battalion. I looked at Chuck Nay and said, "Did you see that?" Air Force pilot Capt. Paul T. McClellan was hit by enemy fire, or possibly damaged by his own ordnance, and went straight in. McClellan's name is on The Wall today, along with the cavalrymen we lost in the Ia Drang.

I don't have a good memory as to how many assaults we made that day. During the assault itself you were really busy flying the helicopter. Our company procedure was that both pilots would be on the controls in case one got hit. The anxiety goes up. I would rather hit a hot LZ than go back, sit down, and think about it. That day at XRay, it started to go bad and at one point they turned us away from an assault.

Capt. Ed W. "Too Tall" Freeman, piloting a Huey of Crandall's Company A, was functioning as second in command of a sixteen-helicopter lift unit when he learned that Moore was closing the LZ because of enemy gunfire.

Freeman went ahead to reinforce the embattled cavalrymen. According to a citation, Freeman flew "through a gauntlet of enemy fire time after time to deliver critically needed ammunition, water and medical supplies to the besieged battalion. The unit was almost out of ammunition and taking some of the heaviest casualties of the war while fighting off a relentlessly attacking, highly motivated, heavily armed, and vastly larger force of the North Vietnamese Army." Freeman evacuated wounded cavalrymen after DUSTOFF (medical evacuation) pilots refused due to the intense gunfire. Freeman made fourteen flights into LZ XRay, one flank of which was completely undefended, landing within 100 to 200 meters from the perimeter where NVA were attacking at point-blank range. His company commander, Crandall, received the second highest United States award, the Distinguished Service Cross. The awards were well deserved, but plenty of us were flying similar missions as the battle at XRay got hotter and hotter.

As for Freeman, he later told Gayle Alvarez of the Idaho Statesman newspaper that he was afraid during the relentless helicopter missions. Alvarez wrote, "He remembers nervously eating franks and beans and chain-smoking Vantage cigarettes. 'God knows how many. I smoked till I had a blister on my tongue.'"

## Trouble at XRay

As the battle grew, we made one of our many trips into LZ XRay with the intention of hauling in ammunition and hauling out wounded. At one point, as we were preparing to go into LZ XRay, Capt. Paul Winkel bounded out of his UH-1D, callsign ORANGE 1, and climbed into mine, replacing my copilot Chuck Nay. Our callsign was ORANGE 3. We headed toward XRay with a second helicopter piloted by my buddy, CWO Dallas H. Harper, and his copilot CWO2 Ken Faba. As we headed into the fight, I handled the controls and Winkel worked the maps and radios.

It was difficult for me to think that somebody out there really would kill me if he had the chance. That thought just wasn't there. But Paul said later he was keeping in mind that we were loaded with ammunition and just a single round from an NVA would turn us into a blazing torch followed by a dark clump of smoke in the open air high above XRay.

As far as formations go, when we started going back into the LZ, it was just two of us. It was Dallas Harper and me. Winkel was on the radio calling Moore (callsign TROJAN 6) to tell him that our flight (ORANGE 1) was coming in with ammunition. Capt. Vince Panzitta came on the radio from the battalion's command ship. He instructed us to turn left over the wreckage of the A-1E and then, when we picked up fire, to swing right ninety degrees to the center of the LZ. There was some fancy communicating between me, Paul, and Dallas as we tried to maneuver two helicopters, avoid NVA gunfire, and put down on LZ XRay without overshooting. It was repeatedly drilled into our heads that if we overshot, there would be nobody in sight but NVA. We went into the LZ and it was pretty apparent that it was an unfriendly place.

That's when the NVA began popping off at us. We touched down next to a marker panel. Our crew got rid of the ammunition every way they could, throwing it right and left. We were ready to get the hell out of there when Moore asked if we could take a couple of prisoners and some wounded. Winkel, on the radio, said yes.

You do not carry enemy prisoners of war and American wounded aboard the same aircraft, so we took the two captured NVA on my ship and they loaded three or four wounded cavalrymen on Dallas Harper's

Huey. The loading process took place amid quite a lot of noise because the battle was going on, right there. Everybody was trying to stay hunkered down. As soon as we'd gotten everybody, Winkel gave the signal and I got us out of there so fast we clipped a couple of tree branches on our way out.

That's when Dallas got shot down.

**PAUL WINKEL**  At the LZ, strapped in the seat looking through Plexiglas, I wondered. When the bullets came flying through the windshield, would it hurt for a long time?

The bullets didn't come, not through our windshield, not at that moment. We took off in echelon. I can still see the wingman's ship—Harper/Faba—just taking off in my mind's eye. Just as Komich pulled us off the ground, our crewchief, Richard Smith, yelled over the intercom: "Mr. Harper is on fire." At that point, from my seat in the right side, I turned to my left and over my left shoulder saw Harper's ship. Jets of gas or steam or oil or smoke—several, at least three or four—were streaming out the side of his engine, Harper's right side of his engine.

I suspect Dallas Harper took fire while he was at the LZ and we just didn't see it. He was lifting off "air assault" style in unison with our lead ship—Komich/Winkel—and we were echelon left. The smoke was pouring out the right side of Harper's engine. I saw this by turning around and looking over my left shoulder. At any rate, Lee swung around to our right and came back, intending to land next to Harper's ship, knowing full well that we could get shot down, too, while trying to help. Harper's aircraft was pouring billowing black smoke from all over the top of his ship. We were certain the ship was on fire.

The battle was going to continue for another seventy-two hours, and for Komich there were going to be critical moments at another landing zone named Albany, but this was a kind of moment of truth. We were carrying captured NVA troops. We weren't going to leave Harper, his crew, and his passengers there, on the ground, in the middle of the battle. We do not leave each other behind.

I said over the radio, "ORANGE 04, set her down now. You are on fire." Harper's UH-1D went down in no man's land just outside the battle perimeter between the fighting forces, where artillery was impacting around the perimeter. Komich made a voluntary choice to land in the middle of all of that. We began a turnaround to the right, descending, and came in at sixty degrees. We were outside the defensive perimeter between the defenders and the attackers. We set down next to Harper's aircraft, which by now was billowing large black smoke out of the cockpit. We were scared to death landing right next to the aircraft, because if it was on fire it could blow up and kill everybody. Harper's crew of four unloaded with ashen faces, carrying weapons, scrambling to board our helicopter. One of Moore's ground troops, an infantryman with a helmet and no weapon, came out and rounded up the POWs. Komich later said he was very relieved to see that happen because we couldn't take the two NVA with us and we couldn't very well release them, either.

We wanted to get the hell out of there, fast, but a wounded man bounded out of Harper's aircraft and ran in the wrong direction, to the north where the enemy was, his back all red with blood. I said on the intercom, "Go get that man. We don't leave without him." Our crew chief, Richard Smith, leaped out, ran seventy-five yards to grab the wounded man, and dragged him back. For that, I recommended Smith for the Silver Star.

He boarded Harper's crew of four, one infantryman passenger, and three or four wounded. When this was added to the people already on Komich's aircraft, Komich had to take off with fourteen or fifteen total souls on board, almost an impossibility for a Huey helicopter unless it was very low on fuel. Moreover, Komich had to take off straight over enemy positions. From my position in the right seat, it was evident that a lot of North Vietnamese were heading straight in our direction. When all were on board, Komich took off, shuddering. I looked back into the compartment behind us: It looked like the New York subway at rush hour. We were very low on fuel, down to about 150 pounds. The infantrymen were without equipment. But we were flying, just barely.

After coming out of the treetops, Komich pulled it up to 1,500 feet and headed north to Camp Holloway, about twenty minutes away, the only place we knew there was a medical facility for the wounded. I turned and looked out back again. There was blood everywhere. There was blood on the windshield. I lit a cigarette in my cupped hand, after using about three or four matches, turned to my left and gave the cigarette to a wounded man who did not raise his eyes. We had an unwounded soldier on board, whom I call the straphanger, and damned if the straphanger didn't reach out and take the cigarette. I said, "Shit." I then lit another cigarette. I gave it to the straphanger who helped the wounded man smoke. I did that because I'd seen war movies where wounded men were given cigarettes. I lit another cigarette and gave it to Komich.

It's important to remember that all of Komich's actions were voluntary. At XRay and later Albany, he volunteered to evacuate wounded, not only because the infantry was running out of ammunition and if not resupplied would be annihilated but also because medevac unit helicopters refused to land at XRay and later Albany due to the violence there.

**LEE KOMICH** When Dallas Harper's helicopter went down right in the middle of the Ia Drang battle, we had a lot of complicated things to think about. But the truth is, you don't sit back and analyze when they're shooting at you and your buddy is down and everything is moving rapidly. You simply act. We acted and got Dallas and his people out of there.

I remember breathing a sigh of relief as we headed toward Camp Holloway. I had no idea that the Battle of Ia Drang Valley was going to continue for three more days, or that a more difficult experience was waiting for me at a place called Landing Zone Albany.

# Bell UH-1D Iroquois (Huey)

No aircraft is linked in the public mind with Army aviation as much as the UH-1 Huey. The Army alone purchased more than 9,440 UH-1s from 1958 to 1980. The Army's nickname Iroquois, an American Indian tribe, never caught on. Everybody called the helicopter the Huey.

A typical Huey configuration is for ten passengers. In the Ia Drang

Vietnam-era Bell UH-1 Huey helicopter in flight.

*Bell Helicopter*

---

Valley action, a UH-1D model carried two pilots, a crew chief/gunner, and a gunner.

The Army introduced several new helicopters in the 1950s and developed methods to use them. When the Army developed the Huey, one windfall was the invention of the small gas turbine engine.

The first practical such engine, developed by Dr. Anselm Franz, the Lycoming T53, was introduced in 1953. It weighed 3,000 pounds less than previous engines without sacrificing power. It was the perfect match for a new helicopter being developed by Bell.

The new helicopter was originally called the XH-40 and made its first flight on October 22, 1956. Two years later, as the Army introduced a new system for naming its aircraft, this helicopter became the HU-1—the source of the Huey appellation. In 1962, another name change made it the UH-1.

In April 1962, the Howze Board, named for Lt. Gen. Hamilton Howze, was formed to study Army aviation requirements. The board's report, submitted in August 1962, led to the creation of the air assault division. Defense Secretary Robert McNamara authorized testing of the air assault concept and in 1963, the 11th Air Assault Division was formed.

By then, the first Huey helicopters had arrived in Vietnam. The Huey was beginning a production run that would make it the most widely used helicopter in the world.

After the First Cavalry defeated the NVA at Ia Drang, *Time* magazine asserted that the Huey helicopter had "changed warfare forever."

## Bell UH-1D Iroquois (Huey)

**Type:** Four-place military utility/transport, general purpose helicopter

**Powerplant:** One 1,400-shp. (1044-kW) Avco Lycoming T53-L-13 turboshaft engine driving two-bladed 48 ft 0 in (14.63 m) main rotor

**Performance:** Maximum speed 127 mph (204 km/h); hovering ceiling in ground effect 13,600 ft (4145 m); service ceiling 12,600 ft (3840 m); rate of climb at sea level, 2,350 ft (715 m) per min; range with maximum fuel at sea level, 318 miles (511 km)

**Weights:** Empty, 4,717 lb (2140 kg); normal takeoff weight, 9,039 lb (4100 kg); maximum takeoff 9,500 lb (4309 kg)

**Dimensions:** Main rotor diameter 48 ft 0 in (14.63 m); length overall, rotors turning 57 ft 9.5 in (17.62 m); fuselage length, 44 ft 7 in (13.59 m); height, tail rotor turning 14 ft 5.5 in; tail rotor diameter 8 ft 6 in (2.59 m); main rotor disc area 1,809 sq ft (168.06 sq m)

**Armament:** Two door-mounted M60 7.62-mm machine guns

**Payload:** Twelve to sixteen armed troops or four hospital litters

**Crew:** Two pilots plus two

**First flight:** August 16, 1961 (YUH 1D)

# Chapter 7

## Battle of Ia Drang Valley (II)

### What Happened

A small clearing surrounded by enemy-filled Vietnamese jungle meant life or death for American soldiers during the final hours of the four-day Battle of Ia Drang.

On November 17, 1965, the First Cavalry Division's Second Battalion, Seventh Cavalry (2/7th, or "the second of the seventh"), commanded by Lt. Col. Bob McDade, was making its way toward the clearing, known in military jargon as Landing Zone Albany.

The battalion was supposed to be heading away from a battle that many believed had now concluded. But in early afternoon, McDade's cavalrymen came under assault from about 550 North Vietnamese troops. In their history, *We Were Soldiers Once . . . and Young,* authors Lt. Gen. Harold Moore and Joseph L. Galloway wrote: "The most savage one-day battle of the Vietnam War had just begun . . ."

It was at least that bad. One company alone suffered 55 men killed out of 128 who began the battle. There were four companies, in all, caught up in the battle for Albany. Yet this one-day slugfest wasn't even mentioned in the Mel Gibson film based on the book by Moore and Galloway. Near the conclusion of the movie *We Were Soldiers,* Ameri-

**Captain Will Bennett**
**November 17, 1965**
**Bell UH-1D Iroquois (Huey)**
**YELLOW 1**
**C Company, 229th Assault**
    **Helicopter Battalion, First**
    **Cavalry Division**
**Anh-Khe, South Vietnam**

Capt. Will Bennett (seen here as a major), who went into Landing Zone Albany under fire in nocturnal darkness, guided to a landing in tall elephant grass by a soldier wielding a flashlight.

*Will Bennett*

---

cans stack up dead North Vietnamese at Landing Zone Xray following three days of action that ended on November 16, 1965. The celluloid version of the Battle of Ia Drang Valley has ended.

The real battle was not over. Although praised for its respectful treatment of United States soldiers, the film does not portray the final Ia Drang action. "The one-day action at Albany was the bloodiest of the Vietnam war for U.S. troops," said former Specialist Four Robert J. Towles, fifty-eight, of Windham, Ohio. "Of approximately 400 men who went into that action, 155 were killed and 128 wounded."

When he thinks about that battle, Towles remembers what began as a "cleaning-up situation."

"On November 16, we went in to Xray to relieve the 1st Battalion, 7th Cavalry [commanded by Lt. Col. Harold Moore]. The fighting had petered out when we got there. We cleaned up the battlefield, picked up bodies, and policed up equipment. We didn't sustain any direct attacks at Xray, but we were under constant sniper fire. Some men were wounded but none was killed."

Towles was a native of Ohio who'd joined the Army in 1963. He belonged to the antitank platoon of Delta Company, 2nd Battalion, 7th Cavalry. "Yes, antitank. And we arrived in Vietnam to learn that the enemy had no tanks." Towles went into the battle zone carrying rounds for a light armored weapon, plus an M16 infantry rifle.

"On November 17, we walked to Albany," Towles said. "Our platoon sergeant told us this would be combat. We would push the enemy back into an area to be bombed by B-52s. We moved out, led by the 2nd Battalion, 5th Cavalry to which we now became attached. We found some abandoned huts and burned them, which gave away our location.

"We were ordered to halt two miles from the B-52 impact area. We could feel the ground shaking under our feet. We resumed march, entered double and triple canopy, and felt the jungle closing in thick around us. We took a break to eat c-rations. Around noon, we crossed a creek. A couple of deer broke out in front of us, zigzagging. We didn't think much about it, but they were more afraid of what was behind them than of what was in front."

The battle at Albany started at about 1:15 p.m., November 17. The Americans collided with fresh North Vietnamese troops, or NVA, who'd been rushed to the Ia Drang expecting to join combat at Landing Zone Xray. Instead, the NVA ran head-on into Towles and others in McDade's battalion, which was moving north.

Towles became part of a twelve-man line that came under assault from enemy soldiers on the run, firing AK-47 rifles. Towles fired two rounds into an NVA and the man kept coming. Towles shifted to full automatic and emptied the magazine of his M-16. The NVA went down but others swarmed around. "I think we knew by then that we were stalled and using ammunition at a prodigious rate. I think somebody said, 'Isn't this going to be a tough place for the helicopters to help us?'"

In the fighting that followed, Americans all around Towles were hit. Private First Class Marlin Klarenbeek was hit in the leg. Nearby, other soldiers were wounded. Some were killed. Some lay on the ground, writhing.

"Rounds were going off all around us," Towles said. Some of the wounded Americans were now lying on top of each other. Amid confusion, there was an effort to move. Towles broke into a clearing, leading several of his buddies—nearly all wounded.

Towles looked back to see North Vietnamese firing AK-47 rifle rounds at the ground. It appeared they were killing wounded Americans. Towles was ordered to keep moving, Towles entered a clump of trees when two shots went past him, one of them striking Sergeant Jerry Baker in the chest.

Mortar rounds went off intermittently while the point-blank firefight continued. Towles felt himself taking hits, saw blood on one arm, and felt his hand frozen to the pistol grip of his M-16.

As the fighting continued and the men changed position, Towles noticed Private First Class Lester Becker—his best friend—isolated from the others behind a tree where a second man could also find cover. Towles told his sergeant he would help Becker cover the enemy assault from that direction. He ran ten yards to the tree and propped himself behind it.

Instantly, NVA took the tree position under fire and Towles "heard the sickening impact of bullets ripping into tissue" as Becker was struck by AK-47 rounds. Towles and the company commander, Capt. Henry Thorpe, helped move Becker to a safer location while gunfire surged around them. Becker was evacuated but later died.

## Need for Helicopters

On the afternoon of November 17, helicopters began bringing in reinforcement troops and providing support. "We began to think the fighting was now going to wane," Towles said. He was told his unit would be moved out of there. "When a helicopter touched down at LZ Albany, we just walked over and got on."

Towles' war was over. The Battle of Ia Drang Valley, with its bloody climax at KZ Albany, was not.

Capt. (later Col.) Paul Winkel (left) was a UH-1D Huey pilot at Landing Zone XRay. Pvt. E-2 (later Spec-4) William Weber was a UH-1D helicopter crew chief at both XRay and Albany.

*William Weber*

**PAUL WINKEL** As number two in a four-ship flight, Komich voluntarily did something that wasn't planned. He landed at LZ Albany at night using only the flashes of battle, using no landing lights to deliver ammunition while guided by a flashlight held by a brave soldier lying prone in the middle of the battlefield. At the time, night-vision equipment lay in the future. The night landing was all the more remarkable because enemy fire poured into Albany so fast, as one soldier put it, "enemy bullets were knocking bark off trees."

In that action, his flight leader's helicopter was badly damaged. Komich elected to make a second, hazardous night trip to Albany. He was now acting as flight leader, an unprecedented role for a warrant officer. He evacuated three more wounded Americans.

**LEE KOMICH** Albany was the worst thing that ever happened.

For us helicopter crews, it happened at a time when we had been stretched to the limit. Our living conditions were terrible. We had no normal sleep. We flew for as much as twelve to fourteen hours only during daylight. Everybody knew you could only take a Huey into an LZ during daylight. We spent a couple of nights at a Special Forces camp. The food was c-rations but the adrenaline compensated for the lousy taste.

The toughest part was sitting at the ready. Waiting. We hated waiting. Sometimes they told us to start engines and we were all pumped up, ready to go, and then they told us to shut down. At one point I was diverted to make a leaflet drop, accompanied by Dallas Harper.

When we'd begun flying into LZ XRay three days earlier, we didn't yet know Ia Drang was a big battle. I had no point of reference. I thought, "What is a big battle?" When I saw the A-1E blow up just before Harper and I went into Xray and Harper's helicopter went down [previous chapter], I finally must have known this was a big battle.

When we began flying into LZ Albany, there was no doubt. The first lifts into Albany began at 6:25 p.m. on November 17, led by Major Willard M. "Will" Bennett who commanded C Company of the 229th Assault Helicopter Battalion. My buddy Harper flew one of those first lifts into Albany, but I missed that one. It became clear that the battle was going to continue and that we were going to have to go in after dark. We weren't supposed to fly troop support flights after dark—we had no equipment or instruments for night operations—but our cavalrymen were in one hell of a fight at Albany and there wasn't going to be much choice.

**WILL BENNETT** I was given the privilege and honor to take command of Charlie Company, 229th Assault Helicopter Battalion, in March 1964 while stationed at Fort Benning. The outfit was part of the highly trained 11th Air Assault Division, which pioneered helicopter tactics, then acquired a new identity as the First Cavalry Division Airmobile when it went to Vietnam in 1965.

On the late afternoon of November 17, 1965, I led the formation of helicopters that went to Landing Zone Albany in an effort to reinforce McDade's cavalry battalion, which had been moving overland in a column, was ambushed, and was caught up in a sustained battle. You do not want a battle like that to continue late into the day when you're running out of daylight, but McDade had monumental problems in communication and decision making with his troops scattered in a line

Vietnam-era Bell UH-1 Huey helicopter in flight.

*Bell Helicopter*

that may have been a couple of miles long. McDade often seemed to get his ass into a crack at dusk, not the time when you want to be caught up with close-quarters fighting. My helicopters often supported McDade's battalion and it often seemed we were fighting with the sun going down.

One real hero of that fighting was one of my helicopter pilots, 1st Lt. Ken Weitzel. I had assigned Ken as my air observer to McDade's battalion and Ken had humped his way overland from XRay toward Albany with the rest of the battalion. He had a "Prick 25" (PRC-25) radio and was my direct source of communication on what was happening after McDade's troopers got into that fight. Weitzel was in bayonet fights, grenade fights, the whole mess that was getting worse and worse from one end of McDade's column to the other.

Near dusk on the 17th, I led a flight of twelve Hueys into a very "hot" Albany. We had a gaggle of twelve ships, including ships from three companies of the 229th. Among the pilots were Ken Jayne from my company as well as Rob Stinett and Harper. Many of these Huey pilots and crews believed they had seen and survived the worst fighting you could encounter at Landing Zone XRay. When we were going in, we had no idea Albany would be worse.

Our job was to lift a company of assault troops led by Capt. Myron Diduryk. They were the only troops in McDade's battalion who weren't already caught up in the battle at Albany and it was hoped they could offer McDade some relief. One of Diduryk's platoon leaders was 1st Lt. Cyril R. "Rick" Rescorla, an Englishman whose photo has appeared on the covers of several books and who later lost his life trying to save others in the World Trade Center on September 11, 2001.

Going into Albany, there was a great deal of confusion on the radio and it was obvious the fighting was heavy. The smoke of the battlefield was visible from several miles away during the approach.

We were getting low on daylight and fuel was critical. Rounds were going off. Almost all of our ships took hits but we managed to get reinforcements in and to take out many wounded, along with many body bags.

In the book *We Were Soldiers Once . . . and Young*, authors Lt. Gen. Harold Moore and Joseph L. Galloway quoted CWO Rick Lombardo, who flew into Albany with copilot CWO Alex "Pop" Jekel. "On our approach, the sight before me was unbelievable. Grass fires all over the place, tracers crisscrossing the LZ and the smoke. It looked like Dante's *Inferno*.

"Before my skids touched the ground, all the troopers were out," continues the quote of Lombardo from Moore and Galloway. "I glanced down and saw my left skid on a body. Couldn't tell if it was one of ours or one of theirs. Then I realized I no longer had a chin bubble. My feet were on the pedals but there was no Plexiglas beneath them. It wasn't shattered; it just wasn't there! All gauges were in the green so we hauled ass out of there. I told Pop to fly so I could get the dirt out of my eyes. To that point not a word had been spoken over the intercom. Before I could say a word, Pop Jekel keyed the intercom and said, 'I flew thirty-one missions in B-24s in World War II and that's the closest I've ever come to swallowing my balls.' That took the tension out of the crew."

That quote from the book reflects the seriousness of the situation at Albany, which wasn't a very good landing zone by any standard. It was really two clearings rather than one, both very small, separated by an island of trees. It was awash in high grass and, unknown to us there were stumps hidden in that grass—a real enemy to any helicopter pilot. It looked to us pretty much like any other landing zone but it wasn't.

I was flying as YELLOW 1, the flight leader, and was going to land first at Albany. Weitzel or somebody came on the radio and told me to make a go-ahead with the ship behind me because NVA gunfire was too close.

My ship and another one in my company had to make a "go around" at Albany because enemy fire was too close. Otherwise, I would have been first on the ground. YELLOW 1—that's me, the company commander—was always the leader and always went in first, and on this day Rob Stinnett apparently made the first touchdown in Albany, but that was because of my go-around.

## What Happened

McDade's battalion, strung out in column with the front of the column at Landing Zone Albany, continued battling NVA at close quarters after darkness set in and after Diduryk's company joined the fight. In the gathering darkness near Albany, Americans and North Vietnamese were intermingled amid trees, tall grass, anthills, and stumps. When Diduryk's cavalrymen expanded the battalion command post perimeter, they discovered numerous wounded Americans who had been in agony since the beginning of the fight.

After a great deal of radio chatter, it became apparent that some of the wounded would not live until morning, But according to several who fought at Albany, the First Cavalry Division's medical evacuation helicopter crews were not willing to land at the embattled LZ. Their reluctance was understandable. No one had ever evacuated wounded after dark at a tiny, confined landing zone strewn with grass and stumps within eyesight of enemy troops.

By 8:30 p.m., McDade, Diduryk, and others still caught up in the war's worst battle reported that they had to have helicopters. The situation was clear to CWO Hank Ainsworth, overhead in the command OH-13G Sioux helicopter, and Ainsworth passed it along. If anyone was going to make the flight, it would have to be attempted only by volunteers. Most of the 229th Assault Helicopter Battalion's pilots were now at Camp Holloway near Pleiku trying to get something resembling food and sleep after three days of fighting at XRay. When asked if they wanted to go into Albany at night, everyone who was asked volunteered.

**GERALD TOWLER** At around 9:00 p.m., a request came to evacuate more critically wounded. We heard medevac had refused to land. A group of pilots had all just arrived in the barracks from taking showers. Capt. Robert Stinnett walked in the other end of the building at approximately 9:30 p.m. and asked who would volunteer to go with him. Three of us volunteered.

**PAUL WINKEL** As for the helicopter crews who came to help during the night of November 17, 1965, I was a direct eyewitness. I had retired into my sleeping bag in the wood-framed building my platoon mates occupied at Camp Holloway airstrip. I witnessed my platoon leader Stinnett enter the building from the south door.

He met Komich, CWO2 Ken Dicus, and CWO2 Gerald Towler. Stinnett said something to the effect that "the 2/7th Cavalry is surrounded, running out of ammunition, and has wounded that need to be evacuated. Medevac has refused to go. The LZ is hot. I'm going and I need a crew for my aircraft and a second aircraft to go with me. Are there any takers?" Komich said something on the order of, "Hell, I've just had a shower. I'm clean enough to go." Dicus and Towler said something on the order of, "Me, too." Stinnett said something like, "Let's go, then. You guys are so clean that you're probably the only ones the enemy can't smell." This signaled that all four had just volunteered to go into the inferno at Albany.

Other volunteers for the night trip to Albany included CWO2 Robert Kiess, CWO2 Donald Reynolds, and WO1 Robert Mason (who later wrote the book *Chickenhawk*), as well as flight crewmembers Sgt. First Class Keith Maynard, Specialist Five Richard Smith, Specialist Four John Cote, and Privates First Class William Weber and Tommy Dorsey. All were members of the 2nd Platoon, Company B, 229th Assault Helicopter Battalion.

The first sortie was led by Stinnett with Towler as copilot in the lead aircraft and Komich and Dicus in the second aircraft. This pair of Hueys met two more aircraft en route and became a formation of four. These four helicopters picked up several wounded at about 9:30 p.m. at Albany. Towler later reported that the aircraft flown by him and Stinnett

Warrant Officer Robert Mason (center) fought at both of the key Ia Drang landing zones, XRay and Albany, as copilot of a UH-1D Huey. He made the perilous night mission to Albany. Years later, he wrote a best-selling memoir, *Chickenhawk*.

*William Weber*

received at least fourteen hits, one of which went through the windshield. The aircraft was so badly damaged that Stinnett had to ask Komich to "stay with them" as they flew back to Holloway for fear that they might have to make a forced landing in the jungle that night. Stinnett had to ground his aircraft upon return. It was at that point that Komich and Dicus volunteered to lead two other aircraft, Kiess and Mason in one and Harper and Reynolds in the other. The flight picked up more wounded at approximately 11:45 p.m.

**LEE KOMICH** Albany came along at night. Remember I said we don't fly at night? I was in the shower. My platoon leader said he was volunteering and said to everybody in earshot, "We're going." And off we went to Albany. If anybody says XRay was the hottest LZ in Vietnam, that tells me they were never at Albany. I'm not so sure that we were even in the LZ.

Thankfully, we had trained at night in the 11th Air Assault to the point of using the dash lights to guide us. That didn't prepare us for the tracers coming up at us. Albany looked like the Fourth of July. The landing zone itself wasn't clear at all, though we were not about to turn on our landing lights.

Capt. James W. Spires, an officer on McDade's staff, talked us into Albany on the PRC-25 radio. We were trying to keep communication to a minimum and sometimes we would just key our mike to help Spires know we were understanding him.

Spires crawled out in the middle of the LZ when he heard us coming and shined a flashlight to mark the landing spot. He had to be the bravest person on the planet to do that.

When we settled down on that dark black hole of a landing zone, I almost landed on a tree stump that would have ripped out the belly of our Huey. Our crew chief, Richard Smith, saw the stump and yelled at me to pull forward.

We brought in some ammunition but our purpose was to pick up the medevacs. The crew chief from another helicopter got out trying to help and simply disappeared into the dark. At about that time all hell broke loose. We went off. I told Dallas he must have been hit. We picked up the crew chief the next day.

The story of Albany has not been fully told. First Lt. Larry Gwin, a platoon leader in McDade's battalion, wrote a book called *Baptism*. Larry was a huge guy who looked like he belonged on a football field. He apologized to me because he didn't cover the aviation aspect very well. Essentially, they ran into a North Vietnamese reinforcement group that was stretched well out and very upset at the Americans. The NVA attack came so fast, it was a blitz. It really shattered the structure of the American forces and dragged from day into night. I will tell you that some of the bravest Americans that ever lived were in that LZ. Some of our cavalrymen who survived the early hours of that fight got to look at the North Vietnamese executing American soldiers. Then the fight continued into the night and the number of wounded kept increasing. People like Jim Spires, how they held up to all this . . . it's just amazing.

We made two sets of night landings at Albany before midnight on the 17th. But even after midnight, it still wasn't over.

**WILL BENNETT** At about 1:00 a.m. on the 18th, I was told Albany was asking for two ships to bring in resupplies and evacuate critically wounded. Medevacs, again, had tried to help but either couldn't find Albany or found it too hot. I told my operations officer I would fly one ship and asked for a volunteer second crew.

In those days we were not trained to land helicopters in hostile territory in darkness. One American, while under heavy fire, used a flashlight to guide the helicopters amidst all the confusion. Right then, North Vietnamese mortar rounds were coming in on top of us. Although the helicopter pilots did not know the name of the man wielding the flashlight, he was Capt. James W. Spires.

I was concerned we were not going to find the place had it not been for that flashlight. We had a real hard time locating the landing zone because of all the smoke, lights from many flares, and just total confusion in the airspace. Besides worrying about running out of fuel I was concerned about having a flare drop through our rotors. Finally, we saw the tiny flashlight beam and by confirming things on the radio we made the approach and landed.

While we were on the ground, mortar rounds began hitting the landing zone, so we moved about 100 meters. Our brave crew chiefs and gunners dismounted from the helicopters and went out to help carry the wounded to us. These wonderful enlisted crew members returned enemy fire with their M-16 rifles.

In darkness and confusion, despite enemy fire, I refused to lift off until the helicopter was full of wounded and my crew was back on board. Those were very tense moments, knowing rounds were flying past and could hit us any time. The pilot in command of the helicopter can't do anything but sit there, with the night lit up all around him, watching everybody trying to load up the Huey and thinking, *"Come on! Come on!"*

After what had to feel like an eternity, we lifted off. We were engulfed in noise and it looked like the Fourth of July outside. It was a feeling of comfort, although possibly a false one, when we seemed to lift above the reach of North Vietnamese small arms. Because of the confusion of battle, no one is certain exactly how many wounded American soldiers we saved, but the two helicopters contained a couple of dozen.

Getting into the air didn't make us safe. Now we were in a race to get to safety before running out of fuel.

The flight back was a rush against time as the fuel warning lights on both helicopters had been on for a long time and we had critically wounded on board.

The efforts of all men aboard the two UH-1D crews—especially Captain Ken Jayne, pilot of the second UH-1D—saved numerous lives in the battle at Albany, which was one of the bloodiest of the Vietnam war.

I left Vietnam in June 1966 after many more helicopter missions, but Albany was definitely, definitely the worst. I returned for a second combat tour in December 1968. For part of that second tour, I commanded the 227th Assault Helicopter Battalion. That was a great assignment but not as good as being a company commander. They later awarded me a Silver Star for one of my actions, but nothing ever quite compared with Albany.

## Crew Chief at Ia Drang

**PAUL WINKEL** I should interrupt my description of those who volunteered for Albany to explain that crew chiefs did a hell of a lot more than just look outside and spot things for us.

As a pilot, I counted on the crew chief to make certain the engine worked and the airframe and rotors did their thing. I remember once on a combat assault, each time we landed, the crew chief would get off along with the grunts and while the grunts were running for cover the chief would say, "Hold her down until I can get back on board." I turned to look and he was pouring something into a port alongside the engine. I asked, "What in the hell?" He responded that each time we took off and landed that this ship, which had been pulled out of maintenance for the assault, ran completely dry of hydraulic fluid—and had to be refilled after each takeoff. Yes, he had a big five-gallon can of hydraulic fluid on board with him and a little pitcher. What brave souls those crew chiefs! I trusted the crew chief with my life on each flight, each day.

**WILLIAM WEBER** If you've never been a crew chief of a Huey, you have missed one of the thrills in life. In flight, a high console filled with navigational instruments confronts the pilots, limiting their vision. Their view is limited to straight ahead and out the side window. In combat a bulletproof "wing" on the seat, intended to protect the head, limits the pilots' view to the side. To a great extent, they depend on instruments to guide the flight pattern. You would think pilots see out very well but in fact they can't see much from the cockpit.

The crew chief, however, has a grand view. The view is everything from 180 to 360 degrees. With the doors off, as they should be in combat, you sit on the edge of the seat, toes on the edge of the floorboard, wind in your face. When we were flying in the States, there was no machine-gun mount to block your view. You could lean out and look straight down at the earth as it dropped away during takeoff.

In Vietnam, the machine gun mounted on that side blocked some of the panorama. Still, part of your job was to be the pilot's eyes for the left side of his aircraft.

Your eyes kept checking the distance between your chopper and the one flying so closely just behind and to the left of your ship. Close was good. You could read the expressions on the faces of that crew. Too close was bad. If the rotor blades ever touched, even slightly, both helicopters would fall from the sky. I would long for the adrenaline rush that takeoff would yield. My responsibility was not to steer the ship but to guard the ship. I was more that just along for the ride.

One particular takeoff still remains clear. We had been in Vietnam for only a few weeks. There was a group of the 101st trapped in an ambush. A flight of the 229th Assault Helicopter Battalion was called to make an extraction. We had not yet mounted the machine guns, so they lay in our laps. We had harnesses that were six feet long. That would keep us with the ship if we were shot and fell out. Our flak vests were thin, but we wore them. I sat on the one-inch-thick chest protector in case a round came up though the floor.

On our first combat mission, we took off, flew at treetop level, and were on approach when we were called back. They had been reached by a unit on the ground and rescued. That first one stays with me. On our way back, I sang an old hymn, "Coming home, coming home, never more to roam. Open wide thine arms of love, Lord, I'm coming home." Every flight was an adventure, and I made it all the way home.

# Chapter 8

## DUSTOFF Mission in a Hot Zone

### What Happened

Michael J. Novosel could have given Vietnam a pass. Novosel had done his part. No one was asking him to go into harm's way again.

He didn't look like a hero. In fact, he didn't look like much at all. He was "height challenged," the way folks might say it nowadays, a diminutive figure, not the kind of guy who dominates a room or a crowd.

Yet Novosel and his name are now inextricably linked to the helicopter that became the symbol of America's longest war.

Nothing stirs memories of Vietnam like the throbbing of UH-1 Huey rotor blades. A formation of Hueys thrashing its way across a canopy of Vietnamese jungle resonates in the ears like nothing else—in real life, once, mostly only in ghostlike memories today.

When Mike Novosel first saw a Huey, he was already a supremely experienced aviator. Still, other soldiers wondered if he was a bit long in the tooth to be piloting a throbbing, thrashing gadget with a forty-four-foot main rotor that would be called upon to plop itself down in a landing zone, an LZ, with bad guys close enough to pop off at it with

**CWO4 Michael J. Novosel**
**August 25, 1966**
**Bell UH-1D Huey**
**DUSTOFF**
**283rd Medical Detachment (Helicopter**
**Ambulance)**
**Bong Tran, South Vietnam**

Michael J. Novosel went to Vietnam in 1966 after the Air Force couldn't find a use for him. He was already a very experienced Huey pilot, and in Vietnam his skills were tested to the limit. He saved hundreds of wounded. He had no idea that this was only the first of two combat tours in America's longest war.

*U. S. Army*

AK-47s. The Huey eventually became the best-known helicopter in the world, and the age of Mike Novosel eventually became an irrelevancy.

"I wanted to fly it," Novosel said. "It had a reputation for being stable and reliable." He was talking about the Bell UH-1 Iroquois, the Huey, of course, that same stalwart helicopter with a 960-shaft horsepower Lycoming T53-L-5/13 turbine engine and with a well-known reputation for not liking to be riddled with enemy bullets. It was, as Novosel noted, stable and reliable. But Novosel might have been talking about himself.

In a conflict where any soldier over twenty became "the old man" of his outfit, Novosel was forty-two when Vietnam heated up in 1964. He enlisted in the Army Air Forces before Pearl Harbor, struggled to become an aviation cadet (at five feet five, he was officially too short), and became so valuable as a heavy bomber instructor that the brass initially did not want to risk him overseas. Late in the war, he wangled a combat assignment and flew the B-29 Superfortress over Japan. Afterward, he combined careers as an airline pilot and Air Force Reserve officer.

He was also a flight instructor. He worked for a time as a civilian, instructing Army helicopter pilots. He had all the "tickets" (qualifica-

This is a UH-1D Huey medical evacuation helicopter of the kind flown by Mike Novosel at Phu Cat, South Vietnam.

*Norman Taylor*

tions) for a huge variety of airplanes and helicopters, and he knew he was making a contribution—but he wanted to be back in uniform. He was "military to the core," he said. He could instruct in the United States or fly in combat in the war zone, but either way he wanted to be back on active duty.

As a Reserve lieutenant colonel, Novosel sought an instructor slot or a combat assignment to Vietnam. The Air Force, overstaffed, had no slot for him, although it would become desperate for any kind of pilot a year or two later. Novosel found there was only one way he could get back on active duty: He would have to become an Army warrant officer and helicopter pilot.

"But they'll send you to Vietnam," somebody told him.

"So?" He felt he could contribute more teaching others, but he was ready and willing to go into battle.

Novosel joined the Army and began adding to his already impressive total of flying hours in the UH-1 Iroquois, the famous "Huey" helicopter that became so much a symbol of Vietnam for so many. His son Mike, then in high school, watched and said, "I want to do this, too." Mike Jr. made plans to follow in his footsteps.

Novosel was assigned to the 283rd Medical Detachment (Helicopter Ambulance) as a DUSTOFF (medical evacuation) pilot from January 1966 to January 1967. In 1968, he was scheduled to be discharged and to return to a civilian position as pilot with Southern Airways.

As we shall see (Chapter Thirteen), the airline job was not in the

Long before Vietnam, this much younger Mike Novosel is piloting a B-29 Superfortress on a bombing mission to Japan in 1945 as part of the 462nd Bombardment Group (Heavy), the "Hellbirds."

*U. S. Air Force*

cards for Mike Novosel. He didn't need to be here in Vietnam and yet he would be coming back.

**MIKE NOVOSEL**  I was born in 1922 in Pennsylvania. I enlisted in the Army Air Corps in February 1941 and applied for flight training as an aviation cadet. At five feet five, I was officially too short, but we exaggerated my height and the papers went in. Then, it appeared my application had gotten lost. I was a payroll clerk at Sheppard Army Air Field, Texas, and had just passed my nineteenth birthday when we learned that the Japanese had attacked Pearl Harbor.

They accepted me into pilot training then, and I graduated from flight school and was commissioned as a second lieutenant in 1942. Promoted to first lieutenant in 1943, I spent four months on special duty with the Office of Strategic Services and later that year attended B-24 Liberator flight transition training at Smyrna Army Air Field, Tennessee. Promoted to captain in 1944, I became officer in charge of flight test engineering at Laredo Army Air Field, Texas.

At Laredo Army Air Field, I initially trained pilots in the Lockheed AT-18 Hudson, which had a tendency to ground loop and anything but the best training vehicle. Soon, however, they assigned me to train pilots and gunners in the B-24 Liberator. The B-24 was the most numerous aircraft ever manufactured in the United States. The veterans who flew it swear by it. Say a bad word about it around any of them and they'll come down on you like a pile of bricks. But the B-24 was not designed with a guy of my height in mind. I needed a pair of four-inch cushions at my back to comfortably operate the yoke and rudder pedals.

I found the B-24 somewhat difficult to taxi, at least compared to the B-29. I discovered that control forces on the B-24 could be extremely heavy. Someone told me I had the magic touch, and I was also told that I was very good at flying formation, something that wasn't easy in a four-engined bomber. They promoted me to first lieutenant and then to captain while I was instructing. During this period, I found time to try my hand at the controls of a number of other aircraft types, from the P-39 Airacobra to the B-26 Marauder.

I had expected to be in combat. That was what any new pilot expected. But as I kept gaining more experience, they kept saying they needed me too much. I was no longer a new pilot and I began to wonder if I would see action. The chance came when the United States planned the aerial campaign that became the final offensive against Japan. Now the Army Air Forces were shopping for pilots for the new B-29 Superfortress. Suddenly, four-engine experience and formation skills were plusses. By 1944, I met the requirement to become a B-29 aircraft commander, namely a minimum of 500 hours in four-engined bombers. As for my height, no one was using a measuring tape on me any longer. I began B-29 training at Maxwell Army Air Field, Alabama, flying in the left seat, the aircraft commander's seat, from the very first day.

## War Over Japan

By July 1945, I arrived at West Field, Tinian, to join the 769th Bombardment Squadron (Very Heavy), 462nd Bombardment Group, the "Hellbirds." This proud outfit was part of the 58th Bombardment Wing,

---

### Who's Who

Michael J. Novosel, UH-1 Huey helicopter pilot

Michael J. Novosel, Jr., Mike's son and future UH-1 pilot

Tyrone Chamberlain, UH-1 copilot

Specialist Four Herbert Heinold, crew member

Specialist Four Joe Horvath, crew member

1st Lt. (later, Maj.) Thomas Galvin, wounded platoon leader

commanded by Brig. Gen. Roger Ramey, which in turn was part of Twentieth Air Force, led by Maj. Gen. Curtis E. LeMay, an innovative and aggressive bomber general.

By the time I reached the war zone, I was already a very experienced B-29 pilot, now well known among bomber guys as an expert in flying tight formation. I proved that more than once by nudging my B-29 up within a few inches of another B-29 while flying toward the target at 300 miles per hour. I was very late to be getting into the war, though, and flew only a few missions over the Japanese home islands before it was all over. I flew one B-29 named the "Twentieth Century Limited" that has been seen in a lot of war movies.

Fighting in the Pacific ended on August 15, 1945. The period after the Japanese surrender was a time of change and turmoil for those of us who wore wings and stayed in uniform. By 1945, I knew about helicopters but didn't imagine—yet—that I might find myself flying one.

I became part of the Air Force when it became an independent service branch on September 17, 1948. They made me a test pilot at Eglin Air Force Base, Florida. Rank was slow during the lean postwar years, and after a huge amount of experience in peace and war I was still a captain. Tensions were beginning with the Soviet Union but no one really saw what was coming. Because of a reduction in force, they mustered me out on February 11, 1950. Not long afterward, the Korean War began. I was able to remain in the Reserves and was recalled to active duty during the Korea era. When I left active duty again in 1955, I was a senior lieutenant colonel. Today it isn't unusual for a pilot to spend a career flying a single type of aircraft, but in 1955, I had dozens of aircraft types in my logbook.

I became a pilot with Southern Airways (it was later called Republic, and was eventually bought out by Northwest). Part of my work was flying scheduled routes with the most famous airliner of all, the Douglas DC-3, but Southern also had the contract to provide flight instruction to both Air Force and Army pilots. Since I was already an experienced instructor from my World War II days, Southern used me to instruct Air Force student pilots in the Cessna T-37B "Tweet" primary trainer at Bainbridge, Georgia. Continuing as a civilian instructor for Southern, I instructed Army student pilots in the Hiller OH-23D Raven at what was then the Army's helicopter training school at Fort Wolters, Texas. I'm one of the few instructors—conceivably, even, the only one—who has soloed students in propeller-driven airplanes, jet airplanes, and helicopters.

By 1964, when the United States had 15,000 advisers in Southeast Asia (that's how Defense Secretary McNamara spelled the word advisors), I wanted to make a contribution. No one knew then that the number of U.S. troops in Vietnam would go way above half a million. My specialty was instructing younger military pilots. I believed that my knowledge and experience would help younger men who were then part of a major buildup in both the Air Force—which, until then, had been my service—and the Army. At the time, I was thinking of getting back into uniform and instructing in a military environment. I wasn't necessarily thinking about combat, although I was willing.

I had been in the Air Force, and had subsequently instructed Air Force student pilots while a civilian, so I figured the Air Force would find a role for me. I approached them about going back into the service. They said that as a former lieutenant colonel I was too senior for them. A couple of years later, when the big Vietnam buildup was under way, the Air Force probably would have been overjoyed to have me. But in 1964, when I sought a way to use my instructor skills in uniform, the Air Force could find no slot for me.

So I went to the Army, which now had its own aviation arm consisting mostly of helicopters. The Army had been slow introducing helicopters, but had made up for it in the late 1950s and early 1960s. I made an application with the Department of the Army in the Pentagon and almost immediately there was a screw-up with my paperwork. It developed that the only way I could get the necessary pilot's rating, despite my experience, was to go to Fort Wolters as a student. Yes, that's the same Fort Wolters where I spent thousands of hours instructing.

"We need a piece of paper that shows you went there to learn to be a helicopter pilot," somebody said. I had senior ratings in the Air Force and the civilian world but the Army was having none of it. So I went to Fort Wolters. Somebody pointed at a Hiller OH-23D Raven helicopter and said, "You think you can learn to fly this thing?"

"I have 700 hours instructing in it," I said.

My skills were fine but the paperwork wasn't. So I became the quickest student in Fort Wolters history. I arrived there at the end of August 1964. I made one check ride in the OH-23D. When we touched down, the instructor said, "You know more about that aircraft than I do." They completed the necessary paperwork and I officially became an Army aviator.

From the beginning, I had a good feeling about the Bell UH-1 Iroquois, the famous "Huey" helicopter that became so much a symbol of Vietnam for so many. The Huey had earlier been called the HU-1 and the nickname stuck after the letters were flipped. My son Mike followed in my footsteps and for a period of time we had the father-and-son team, both named Mike Novosel, flying Hueys in combat in Vietnam with the same unit. Contrary to myth, there is no military regulation against family members serving in the same outfit.

In the parlance of Vietnam, some Hueys were "slicks," plain transport ships lacking external armament, which shuttled troops from one place to another. Other Hueys were "gunships," armed with guns and rockets to support men and machines arriving at a landing zone. Fewer in number, but never to be forgotten, were the DUSTOFFs—the medical evacuation Hueys that gave many American soldiers their lives. More wounded men survived in Vietnam than in any previous war because of the quick response and flexibility of the Huey. They survived because of the DUSTOFF mission.

They assigned me to the 283rd Medical Detachment (Helicopter Ambulance) as a DUSTOFF pilot from January 1966 to January 1967.

Getting into a hot landing zone and bringing out the wounded required measures that not everybody in the Army liked, especially those who were buying the Hueys. I kept stressing to other pilots the need to get in fast and get out fast. That means you didn't want to gently ease her down on the skids and settle to a nice, comfortable landing. It means you put her down quickly and hard on the ground to save time. You might damage the skids, which can be replaced, or even the helicopter itself, which can also be replaced, but when you're evacuating the wounded you have to move fast.

This is a typical Huey medical evacuation in Vietnam.

*Bell Helicopter*

So I said over and over, "No soft landings, no soft landings." And that was the right advice for August 25, 1966, the battle of Bong Tran, where we were supporting the First Infantry Division, the "Big Red One." In later years, I became acquainted with a platoon leader I rescued that day, Tom Galvin.

**TOM GALVIN** In a fraction of a split second before the grenade blew me up, my only thought was, *"This can't be happening to me! Hey, I used to be the hand grenade officer!"*

I was a lieutenant in B Company, 1/26th, 1st Infantry Division. It was August 25, 1966. We were fighting the battle of Bong Tran, twenty-five miles north of Saigon, against a dedicated foe who had good discipline and brand new weapons and uniforms.

I had been in the Army since 1961. At Fort Benning, Georgia, in 1965, I had been the "hand grenade officer," charged with training other soldiers to use those nasty, thrown projectiles. You do not want to be nearby when one of those handheld bombs detonates. You certainly do not want to be indoors, in a tightly confined space, and have a hand grenade go off within a few feet of your face. I did all of those things.

This hand grenade, however, wasn't the familiar kind I'd known so well at Benning. This was a different model, thrown by a Viet Cong soldier.

While the battle of Bong Tran was unfolding, we cleared an enemy

On August 25, 1966, Tom Galvin was blown up by a Viet Cong hand grenade and medically evacuated by a Huey helicopter piloted by Mike Novosel. When this "in country" photo was taken on September 14, 1969, Galvin had recovered from his wounds and returned to Vietnam as an infantry company commander.

*Tom Galvin*

bunker—or so we thought. The bunkers were square rooms dug so that the interior ceiling was even with the exterior ground surface. The rooms were then covered with two to three feet of dirt.

After firing shots into a bunker several times, I hopped down into the trench that led into the doorway, holding my M-16 rifle at my waist. I was in the center of one of the walls of a square room about fifteen feet on a side, about five-and-a-half feet high. Directly opposite me was a similar entrance to a continuation of the trench on the far side.

Straining my eyes to make out any shapes, I stepped slowly into the room. Looking left and right, I moved one step at a time towards the middle of the room. Gradually, I was gaining a sense of a square empty chamber. Turning my head from side to side, staring into where I thought the corners were, I willed my eyes to see. Everything was still black.

That's when I realized that the bottom of the doorway in front of me was not a horizontal line from side to side. The blackness that formed the bottom of the door was just like the silhouette of a man from shoulder to hip.

My left hand dropped the muzzle of my rifle by about four inches. I fired three rounds. Immediately, both my hands started bringing the rifle's stock up to my shoulder to continue with aimed fire.

As the rifle passed my chest, the silhouette raised a hand. This was a live enemy, lying on his side across the doorway. I'd hit him at least once with my initial burst. I continued firing as the weapon's stock settled firmly against my shoulder. He sent off the grenade then, but I didn't realize it.

Suddenly, everything stopped. I could not see, hear, or feel.

My life didn't exactly pass in front of my eyes, but somewhere inside a brain that wasn't working right, I thought about my wife—I'd been in Vietnam 95 of the 110 days we'd been married—and of my 1964 Volkswagen that was almost paid off. For a few moments, I felt a great sense of tranquil resignation. That's what they say happens when you know you're dying. Then, I had a more ordinary thought: *"That son of a bitch tried to kill me."* My face and head were numb, leading me to fear that the top of my head was blown away.

I placed the tips of my first three fingers of each hand on my eyebrows. In short little pats I tapped them up across my forehead. As I approached the hairline, I expected that each following touch would encounter exposed brain tissue. Getting all the way from my eyebrows to the top of my head without encountering any manmade openings, I said to myself, "I'm getting out of here." I turned and walked back out through the doorway I had entered.

As I stepped out into the light of day, I realized that I could not see through my left eye. My left eye could see only in the lower third of its normal field of vision.

The first thing I saw was my right arm. It was solid red. My pants leg below my hand was spattered blood-red as well. Two steps along the trench was a sapling growing out of the wall at head height. I grabbed the root with my right hand and effortlessly hopped out of the trench. I did not know then that my right forearm was broken.

I came to a soldier who was very pale and speechless. I said, "I'm going to get some first aid." My only conscious thought was that I seriously needed to make my way to my platoon medic. I started walking without plan or direction.

I hadn't gone five yards when I was surrounded by men of my platoon, who made a litter of ponchos and two small trees. In training, they'd told us you could put together a makeshift litter that way, and I hadn't believed it. I was too weak to protest and, in fact, it worked perfectly.

I asked to talk to Platoon Sergeant Kauhane. He materialized instantly. I said, "Call Captain Joulwan and tell him that you are in charge of the platoon. I can't go on. You know what to do and what needs to be done." As I felt myself being lifted, I said to those who could hear me, "If I make it out of here alive, don't send any telegrams."

I was bleeding to death. I was conscious and was in shock. I didn't feel pain. I had been injured in eighteen places—the center of my forehead shattered, a penetrating wound in my left eye, and flesh wounds on my face, shoulders, both hands, both arms, and my left thigh. My right arm was broken and my right eardrum had been blown out. I didn't know all that, of course. Mostly, I knew that a piece of the hand grenade had gone halfway through my right eye, so my field of vision was limited to my lower right quadrant. Even, then I didn't see much because there was blood all over my face. I heard the firefight going on around me. I heard tanks from our cavalry troops knocking down trees to make a landing zone. I heard machine gun fire.

There was fighting and confusion around me. Company commander Capt. George Joulwan (later in life, a four-star general and our supreme commander in Europe) was directing the fight and, at the same time, talking to somebody about getting a helicopter in here. I thought: How can they get a helicopter in here?

Our medic told Capt. Joulwan that I had three chances out of ten to live.

I don't know the details of how they got the helicopter in. At the time, I did not know that the helicopter pilot was Mike Novosel or that he was a wild man. I didn't actually see the helicopter coming, because I couldn't see much, but I heard it. When lift built up under the helicopter, I allowed the whir of the turbine engine to lull me to sleep. If it hadn't been for DUSTOFF—and if it hadn't been for Mike Novosel—I would have bled to death or, if the shock had worn off, I would certainly have died from the pain.

Novosel's UH-1 took me to the 1st Infantry Division's medical company at Phuoc Vinh. I snapped into consciousness just as the UH-1 touched down. I heard medics from the air station talking to Novosel and his crew, exchanging litters and blankets.

Caring hands grabbed my litter, and my bearers took off at a trot for the treatment area. By the sounds of squeaking screen doors and the hollow sounds of footsteps, I knew that I was in a screen-enclosed, canvas-roofed, wood-framed hut with wooded pallet flooring. I felt the litter being placed across two sawhorses.

I sensed people clustered around me. Someone was kneeling on my left, sewing up the back of my ear. A chaplain was holding my right hand. I was glad he was there because I still thought I was going to die, although I had more fight in me now.

Two people standing on either side of me were debating whether to pull out a piece of shrapnel protruding from the corner of my mouth that they were holding with forceps. I got tired of listening to them. "Pull the son of a bitch out," I said. Out it came.

At the same instant they pulled the shrapnel from my mouth, the screen door opened and slammed shut and heavy footsteps came from the door to the head of my litter. A voice asked, "Is this one an amputation?" Sensing indecisiveness, I said, "Get the hell away from me, you son of a bitch."

That night, they got me to the 3rd Field Hospital in Saigon. Doctors splinted my broken arm; cleaned and sutured as best they could the major flesh wounds in my face, hands, arms, and legs; removed the lens from my left eye along with a piece of shrapnel that had stopped just short of the retina; and opened the left half of my forehead to remove the fragments of bone and shrapnel lodged behind the skull and imbedded in the frontal lobe. Weeks later, I was in the Navy hospital in Brooklyn, New York, where I would be a patient for the next seven months.

I could easily have been dead, or blind, or maimed. I would have been without Novosel's UH-1. Instead, thirty months later, I was back in Vietnam, commanding B Company in the same battalion, same regiment, same division, same part of the country. I may be the only combat officer who did two tours in the same outfit. I didn't have to go back and fight again—now that I know Mike Novosel, I know he didn't, either—so why did I return to Vietnam? Well, God could have made me tall or given me a good singing voice. He didn't. He made me good at soldiering.

American troops and Huey helicopters in Vietnam.

*Bell Helicopter*

---

**MIKE NOVOSEL** Many years later, when I heard from Tom Galvin, I had a very gratified feeling. Of course, while the war was going on I didn't know Tom. I'd never heard his name.

At the end of my first tour in Vietnam, I didn't know what I would be doing next. The same aviation bug that took a chunk out of me also bit my son, Mike Novosel, Jr. He, too, wanted to fly Army helicopters. I didn't know it yet when my first tour was wrapping up, but the younger Mike was taking the steps that would put him into a Huey cockpit.

There was something else I didn't know yet, too.

I didn't know I'd be returning to Vietnam.

**MIKE NOVOSEL, JR.** I started out as an Army brat around my Dad. I don't remember when I first wanted to fly helicopters but there's no doubt that I had a strong fatherly influence working on me.

We moved down to Savannah, Georgia, and lived at Hunter Army Airfield. They had just opened it up in 1967. It was during my senior year in high school. I got a job working at the officers club annex, out by the flight line. Everybody I hung around with were young Army

aviators, many just back from Vietnam. I was around those guy
the time.

On the day before my nineteenth birthday, I traveled to Fort Jack
son, South Carolina, and on my birthday—November 19, 1968—I took
the test to become a warrant officer. I did real well on the test because I
understood a lot about helicopters and flying. As a young dependent, I
had often gone down to the Link Building. I knew the instructors there
who were NCOs; they allowed me to sit in the Link and "fly" it from the
time I was nine or ten years old.

I knew exactly where I was going. You go to flight school. You go
to Vietnam. Everybody told me I didn't have to go because my Dad was
there. I could have been exempted because of that, but I wanted to go.

# Chapter 9

## Blades of Wood
## Flown by Men of Steel

### What Happened

At the height of a furious battle in Vietnam on April 11, 1966, an Air Force pararescue jumper, a PJ, descended from a helicopter in the sky and gave his life to save others. His helicopter pilot was Capt. Harold "Hal" Salem.

The PJ was Airman First Class William H. "Pits" Pitsenbarger. The helicopter was the HH-43F Huskie helicopter. The unit was the 38th Aerospace Rescue and Recovery Squadron. Pits was a three-striper, equivalent in rank to today's senior airmen.

On April 11, 1966, Salem's helicopter was called in to evacuate American casualties from dense jungle at Cam My, thirty-five miles east of Saigon. The Army's Charlie Company, 16th Infantry Regiment, 1st Infantry Division—the "Big Red One"—was caught up in point-blank firefight with Viet Cong troops. From overhead, Pitsenbarger volunteered to ride a rescue hoist 200 feet down through triple-canopy jungle. On the ground, he organized rescue efforts.

Though he could have ridden home in his helicopter, the pararescueman took up arms with the besieged infantry. In the vicious fighting

**Captain Hal Salem
April 11, 1966
Kaman HH-43F Huskie
PEDRO 73
Detachment 6, 38th Aerospace
   Rescue and Recovery
   Squadron
Bien Hoa, South Vietnam**

Just before heading off to Vietnam to become pilot on a Medal of Honor mission, Capt. Harold "Hal" Salem poses with an HH-43B Huskie helicopter almost identical to the HH-43F he flew in Southeast Asia.

*U. S. Air Force*

that followed, the Viet Cong breached Charlie Company's perimeter and fatally wounded Pitsenbarger.

One of Charlie Company's embattled soldiers, Sgt. Charles F. "Fred" Navarro, described how Pitsenbarger repeatedly exposed himself to enemy fire to care for the wounded. "He risked enemy gunfire to gather and distribute vital ammunition to the American defenders," Navarro said. "As he crept from one isolated position to another across the broken perimeter, Pitsenbarger fired his M-16 rifle, gathered ammunition, and tended to wounded men."

Salem said: "What Pits did was far and above. Here was an Air Force guy, helping Army soldiers he didn't know." Salem pointed out that Pitsenbarger piled a body on top of Navarro to prevent the sergeant from being killed by flying bullets.

Col. Arthur W. Beall, commander of air rescue forces in Southeast Asia, recommended Pitsenbarger for the Medal of Honor. The recommendation went to Pacific Air Forces in Hawaii. But officers there returned it to the United States command in Saigon, which was run by the Army. There, the number two officer in Vietnam, Army Lt. Gen. John A. Heintges, signed a recommendation that Pitsenbarger be awarded the Air Force Cross instead.

Bill Pitsenbarger was the pararescue jumper on Salem's crew who lost his life fighting with the infantry and was later awarded the Medal of Honor.

*Harold D. Salem*

The Air Force Cross is a serious recognition. But for decades, those who fought with Pitsenbarger wondered why the pararescueman did not receive the higher award.

Pits' posthumous Air Force Cross award was given in a small ceremony. Air Force chief of staff Gen. John P. McConnell presented it to the family at the Pentagon on September 22, 1966. Salem saw an article in *Airman* magazine and said, "What the hell happened to the Medal of Honor?"

Was the Army in Saigon miffed because the Air Force initially sent the recommendation forward through its own channels? Years later, it is impossible to determine why Heintges downgraded the award on behalf of his boss, Gen. William C. Westmoreland.

In the 1990s, a handful of Americans sought to rectify the injustice. Among them were pilot Salem, Secretary of the Air Force F. Whitten Peters, Joe Linebarger, an official with the Air Force, and *Air Force Times* columnist Robert F. Dorr. It took thirty-five years, but largely as a result of work by Peters and Linebarger, the result was an extraordinary Medal of Honor ceremony at Wright-Patterson Air Force Base, Ohio, on December 8, 2000.

Usually, the President presents the Medal of Honor at the White House. But Pitsenbarger's posthumous award was made inside a giant hangar that serves as part of the Air Force Museum. The ceremony brought together the largest group of pararescue jumpers—PJs—ever to convene in one place, an estimated 400. Peters presented the Medal to Pitsenbarger's father, Frank Pitsenbarger, who was frail and ill. Having lived to see his son receive the nation's highest award, Pitsenbarger died months later.

Once he reached the ground, Pitsenbarger fought like a soldier. But his job was aboard a helicopter. And it was a helicopter—Salem's helicopter—that carried him into his final battle. Years later, after there was no going back to change any part of what happened, Salem described flying a box-shaped, twin-rotored machine into harm's way at a moment in history.

**HAL SALEM** I was born in 1932 in Douglas, Arizona. I went to Arizona State College in Tempe where I met my wife Edna. In 2004, we celebrated our fiftieth wedding anniversary. We're the parents of four girls and a boy. She, and they, waited while I was in Vietnam.

Going to college, I had four jobs going so we could put food on the table. I graduated in 1955 and got a Reserve Officer Training Corps commission. I went into the Air Force in April 1956 as a second lieutenant and signed up for a commitment of four years to become a pilot. If I had failed in pilot training my obligation would drop to three years.

I was in Flying Class 57-O. We began flight training at Bartow, Florida. Ours was the first class to begin with the Beech T-34A Mentor primary trainer, which was entering service then, and to progress to the North American T-28A.

I did well as a student pilot and made good grades. My instructors in primary flight training were civilians, but we had military check pilots. I'll never forget John Duris, an instructor of mine who was really,

really good and made you feel that this was an important and worthwhile experience.

After a flight one day, John said, "I'm going to give you something I've never given anyone else." He pulled off his shoe, lifted up a pad, and removed a shiny penny he had kept under the sole of his foot for years. He said, "I've kept this here for good luck as long as I've been flying. Now I'm going to give this to you." Maybe he said that to every student pilot, but I believe he was being truthful. He saw potential in me and wanted to recognize it.

Everyone understood that the hottest pilots became fighter pilots. Duris said, "You're going to be a fighter pilot." I said, "No, I want to be a helicopter pilot."

Nobody believed me.

My Dad didn't believe me. He said, "Why do you want to fly them?" I said, "Dad, I don't know but I want to fly them." I went next to Laughlin Air Force Base in Del Rio, Texas, where I started to do fighter pilot stuff by flying the T-33 Shooting Star jet trainer in the final segment of advanced flight training.

There's not a lot to do in Del Rio. One of the guys joked that the town was so small, the local Baskin-Robbins only had one flavor. We ran into an ex-captain who'd bought an ex-hotel on a little lake twenty miles from the base. He rented suites to Harry Rudder and me. They were still saying the best pilots flew fighters, and that I was one of the best pilots. "I want to fly helicopters," I said to anyone who would listen.

My T-33 experience at Laughlin was interrupted very suddenly. I was up doing the silver-winged, jet-jock thing one afternoon after two weeks at the base when we got a call: "Return to base immediately," we were told. "Report to the base theater for a briefing." We assembled as ordered. The base commander got up in front of us and said, "We've just gotten word that we're going to close down all flying training here. This base is going to be turned over to a top-secret project. Gentlemen, you have two hours to make a decision as to where you want to go." It was late 1956, and none of us had any idea what was going on. Many years later, I learned Laughlin became the first base for the U-2 spy plane, which had a critical role in the 1962 Cuban Missile Crisis. At the time, I knew only that my T-33 flying at Laughlin was over.

I had become commander of the student pilots and I didn't know what to advise them. In the case of me and my family, we ended up going to Goodfellow Air Force Base near San Angelo, Texas, with our daughter who was just two weeks old, just before Christmas. Our fighter pilot class was wiped out and now we were going to be multi-engine pilots so we got into the TB-25 Mitchell, the twin-engined medium bomber of World War II that was now being used as a multi-engine trainer. Harry Rudder and I were together again flying B-25s. I graduated in June 1957 and got my pilot's wings.

The way they worked it there, your next assignment was decided by your standing in class. Again, it was time for a meeting at the base theater. They posted available assignments up on the screen for everyone to see. As they called your name in order of your class standing, you got up and said what you wanted. They were offering pilot slots in the KC-97 air-refueling tanker, among others. I got up and said, "I want helicopters."

Someone said, "That Salem sure is one stubborn son-of-a-bitch about wanting to fly helicopters."

## Into Helicopters

We went to Randolph Air Force Base in San Antonio, Texas, for helicopter school for three months. We flew H-13, the bubble-topped Bell helicopter from the movie and TV series "M*A*S*H."

On my very first flight, we ran into a problem and had to autorotate—using the lift from the rotors, with no power, to make an impromptu landing. The instructor had failed to fill us up and we'd run out of fuel. After we touched the ground safely, he said, "I want you to know that was the real thing, fella."

One problem with the H-13 was that people got too comfortable with it, and it killed a lot of pilots later on. The accident rate in the H-13 after training was fairly high. Without much regret, we soon advanced to the bigger H-19.

There's a lot of classroom work that goes with flight training. One of our instructors, Mr. Morris, had all kinds of helicopter pictures hanging on his classroom wall. I looked at one that I didn't recognize and said, "What's that?" He said: "That's an H-5." He said: "You'll never see one of those again. You're not ever going to see an H-5 because they're all gone from inventory." So I went off to my first operational assignment at Lake Charles, Louisiana, in late 1957 and found myself flying H-5s for the Strategic Air Command. Later, I flew the H-21 and the H-19 in SAC.

I was introduced to the Kaman HH-43B/F Huskie in the early 1960s and soon after that I was in Vietnam. I spent most of my combat tour with Detachment Six of the 38th Air Rescue and Recovery Squadron and flew 358 combat missions between September 5, 1965, and August 31, 1966. We flew with the same crew as much as possible, and I had a regularly assigned crew of Potter, Pitsenbarger, and Hammond.

For a period of a few weeks, I was uprooted to the helicopter detachment in Korat, Thailand, where things were not going well. I was ordered to fix it. I made changes and got things working better.

While in Korat, I had a visit from Gen. Howell Estes, commander of the Military Air Transport Service (this was about the time it was renamed Military Airlift Command on January 1, 1966). His job made him the boss of the Air Force's rescue assets, including our squadron and my detachment. He came to tour Southeast Asia because rescue was under him. He had a hell of a big job.

I said, "General, I'm having a serious problem. We send our rotor blades back to the depot for repair and maintenance. They come back to you with the records changed but no actual work performed." Estes's ears perked up. A colonel in his entourage said, "Sir, we have this resolved." Only a lowly captain, I said, "I beg to differ, General, but that's wrong." As a result of Estes's visit and my talk with him, we got our blade problem resolved.

Estes took me out on the ramp where we could talk alone. He asked some hard questions. I said, "General, I talk with guys flying in the north. They don't have dedicated air support." He changed his schedule to go to Nakhon Phanom, Thailand, to visit rescue people up there who were having problems. "Naked Fanny," we called Nakhon Phanom in

This is Hal Salem (second from right) in South Vietnam with his HH-43F Pedro crew. Left to right: Airman First Class Gerald C. Hammond, helicopter mechanic on Salem's helicopter, Airman First Class (later Staff Sgt.) William H. "Pits" Pitsenbarger, pararescue jumper (PJ), Capt. (later Lt. Col.) Harold D. "Hal" Salem, pilot, Capt. Dale L. Potter, copilot.

*Harold D. Salem*

those days. The Fortieth Aerospace Rescue and Recovery Squadron with a pair of HH-43B/Fs and HH-53B/C Super Jolly Greens were the guys closest to North Vietnam and went all the way into the north.

Estes' visit apparently prompted the decision to use the A-1 Skyraider to escort helicopters in a support job that became known as the "Sandy" mission. I don't know if I had anything to do with it, but by putting a bug in a four-star general's ear I may have caused Sandy to come into existence. Anyway, I cleaned up things in Korat and went back to Bien Hoa.

## Pitsenbarger Medal of Honor

Years later, I put together my recollection of how Pitsenbarger descended to the jungle floor to assist in the evacuation and treating the wounded and survivors of Charlie Company of the "Big Red One," the 1st Infantry Division. The facts were verified by other eyewitness survivors Army 1st Lts. Martin L. Kroah and John A. Libs, and Army Sgt. Charles F. "Fred" Navarro.

"Let's go!" somebody said. It was 3:07 p.m., April 11, 1966, at Bien Hoa.

We'd just received word that Charlie Company had suffered many casualties during an encounter with the Viet Cong. They were surrounded. Help from friendly ground forces was hours away. The jungle was very dense and the only way to evacuate the wounded was to hoist them out.

Hal Salem's HH-43F Huskie helicopter at Bien Hoa, South Vietnam, in July 1968.

*Harold D. Salem*

We knew that area well. Our crew had spent a large part of the previous night trying to get in and extract the wounded but we were held on orbit close by. Charlie Company had been engaged in fierce combat with 500 Viet Cong soldiers. We watched as air strike after air strike pounded the area.

Within minutes after receiving the call, two HH-43F Rescue Helicopters, Pedro 97 and Pedro 73—that's us—lifted off the pad at Bien Hoa. While en route, our crew discussed what lay ahead. It was going to be a tough one. Pitsenbarger said he didn't feel good about this one. We all agreed. None of us did.

My crew consisted of Pitsenbarger; A1C Gerald Hammond, helicopter mechanic and primary hoist operator; myself as rescue crew commander; and Major Maurice Kessler as copilot. Kessler had elected to fill in for Captain Dale Potter who was in Saigon. Our regularly assigned crew had flown many rescue missions together. We had come to respect and trust each other. We could anticipate each other's actions.

Both helicopters arrived on scene at 3:45 p.m. and made contact with Sidewinder 23, an Air Force forward air controller in a Cessna O-2A Skymaster spotter aircraft. He belonged to the 19th Tactical Air Support Squadron which consistently supported the "Big Red One."

He cleared us to begin the rescue effort and advised that Charlie Company had been severely hit. Thirty-three survivors were left out of a company of 180 men and most of the survivors were wounded. Pedro 97 was primary bird for the day and positioned himself to move in for the first pickup. The jungle below was very dense with a triple layer of canopies; the upper canopy was close to 150 feet tall, with the second layer at 100 feet and the lower at approximately 50 feet. There was a small hole in the lower canopy that would be just large enough to "snake" a Stokes litter through. To make the recoveries, it was going to be necessary to hover in a conclave area with 100-foot trees below and 150-foot trees towering on all sides. The hover reference point was a large tree within three to five feet from the rotor tips.

Pedro 97 moved into the hole and completed a Stokes litter pickup. They pulled out to transfer the patient from the Stokes litter to a folding canvas litter in the cabin. There was only room in the chopper for two litter patients.

I brought us into the hole for a pickup. Hammond snaked our Stokes litter down through the trees and into the hands of survivors below. The infantrymen were having a tough time figuring out how to get the next patient into the Stokes. Once they figured out how to rig the sling assembly, they placed a wounded soldier, stretcher, and all in the Stokes litter. They reattached the sling and gave us the thumbs up for hoisting. We did not realize that they had not strapped the wounded patient in. The stretcher had been made from a poncho and two long tree limbs. These limbs extended about two feet past both ends of the litter.

This complicated the pickup because the stretcher poles extending out of the litter caused the litter to continually get hung up in the trees below. When the Stokes litter was finally hoisted up near the cabin door, Pits and Hammond had to swing it out far enough and away from the chopper before they could pull the patient in feet first.

It was a struggle. They finally got him partway into the helicopter, with part of the Stokes litter, wounded patient, and stretcher poles still extending outside the door. The hoist cable remained attached to the litter. We had no choice but to pull out of the hole and head for Binh Ba, site of the Army field hospital, with only the one wounded soldier aboard. There was no room or way to pick up another person.

It had been an exhausting pickup. It consumed forty-five minutes, twice as much time as normal. While in a hover you're a sitting duck for enemy ground fire, so we were trying to keep our hover time as short as possible. The more time you take on a pickup, you reduce your window of opportunity to complete more pickups. We didn't want that.

En route to Binh Ba, we agreed there had to be a better way to hoist those people out of there. We couldn't afford to waste more time. It was very hostile and we had to make every minute count if we were going to get the rest of the wounded out of that hellhole. We had no direct communication with the people below, except though hand signals. We couldn't advise them on how to speed up the process. We hoped some of the wounded could be sent up on the forest penetrator, which was faster but couldn't be used to hoist the critically wounded.

Pitsenbarger offered his solution.

"Captain, on our next trip in why don't you put me down on the ground? I can help out. I can show those guys how to rig the Stokes litter and load it right. It's a wonder we didn't drop and lose the last guy out of the Stokes. A couple of times when the Stokes popped loose, after it had been snagged in the trees, it started to spin and wobble. I thought we might lose him for sure. Captain, if you will just put me on the ground I can get everything organized and it will speed up the pickups. In between pickups I can help some of the wounded and determine who needs to come out first. Maybe we can send some of them up on the forest penetrator. It will be much faster and you can put more people in the bird. I know it will make a difference!"

I said, "Pits, I don't want to take the chance of losing you! You are really needed here. It's hotter than hell down there! Are you really sure you want to go down?"

Pits said, "Yes sir! Captain, I can make a difference!" Hammond agreed. He said, "Those poor guys on the ground are going through

This is a HH-43F Huskie similar to Salem's.

*Harold D. Salem*

hell. Most have never even seen our rescue gear and don't know our procedures. Pits could help, even though I really don't want to see Pits go down there!"

I said, "I'll think it over." I pondered it and decided to give it a try. Over the intercom, I said, "Pits, Hammond, we will be ready to go back into the hole in about five minutes. Pits, I'll go along with you on a couple of conditions: As soon as you have things under control down there, I want you back up here. And if Hammond gives you the signal to come up, you come up! Okay?" Pits said, "Yes sir. That's great. I know it will make a difference." I gave him an opportunity to have second thoughts. He said he had none. "I'm taking my M-16," he said. "Ready when you are!"

I discussed the situation with Pedro 97. He agreed. He also had a pararescueman aboard and could insert him if needed.

We wished Pits good luck over the hot mike. I maneuvered the helicopter into the pickup hole. Hammond strapped Pits onto the forest penetrator. Just before Hammond disconnected Pits' mike cord I wished him luck again. I quickly took a glance at Pits over my right shoulder and caught his eye. I nodded and he responded by nodding. Hammond began to lower Pits to the ground and to the waiting soldiers below. Pits had a big grin on his face and held onto his medical kit in his left hand and his M-16 rifle in his right. His arms were wrapped around the forest penetrator. I said a silent prayer for him. I'm sure American infantrymen were surprised to look up and see a U.S. Air Force PJ being lowered down into their hellhole.

On the ground, Pits motioned for Hammond to send down the Stokes litter. Pits quickly showed soldiers what to do and helped load the next patient into the litter. Hammond hoisted the patient without a hitch.

I pulled out of the hole. Pedro 97 moved in for another pickup. We proceeded to Binh Ba, where our patient was transferred to the field hospital. We refueled quickly and headed back.

With Pits now on the ground attending the wounded and getting things organized, Pedro 97 was able to make a patient pickup using the Stokes litter and two patients using the penetrator, which was much easier and faster than before. Pits really made a difference! I thought, *If we can just keep this pace up, we may get everyone out to safety.*

Reentering the pickup point, Sidewinder 23 told us that the VC had launched a mortar and small arms attack on Charlie Company. We held in orbit close by, soon joined by Pedro 97.

Sidewinder 23 finally said that the firefight had petered out and cleared us to go back in. Pedro 97 went first. Pedro 97 completed two Stokes litter pickups in a very short period of time. Thanks to Pits, everything was organized! Pits was medically treating the wounded and determining which wounded should be sent up first.

When Pedro 97 pulled out of the hole, we went in for another pickup. Hammond spotted Pits signaling for a Stokes litter. Hammond hooked up the litter and began lowering it to Pits. We heard the firefight increasing down below, but Pits was ignoring it and kept motioning for us to continue lowering the litter.

When the litter was just a few feet above Pits, all hell broke loose. We were getting hit hard by enemy ground fire. The helicopter lurched from the rounds hitting the bird—it suddenly yawed severely to the left. At the same time, we experienced a severe loss in rotor rpm, causing the bird to begin a slow descent. I was able to control the yaw with full right rudder and realized I had no control over the engine—we apparently had taken hits in the throttle quadrant and in the flight controls. The right rotor blades also went severely out of track as we must have taken hits in one or both of the blades. The tracking motor would not bring the blade back into track. The out-of-track blade produced a heavy beat in the helicopter.

My immediate concern was to keep the chopper flying and not hit trees that were just feet away from the tips of our rotor blades. Hammond kept the litter going down while signaling for Pits to grab hold so we could pull him out. I was finally able to keep the helicopter fairly steady now using full right rudder, but did not have any control of the fuel throttle. Finally, the rotor rpm began to increase slowly and stopped our descent. Again, my concern was to find some way to get Pits on board.

He must have known that we were taking heavy ground fire! Hammond was now frantically motioning to Pits, but Pits continued to give Hammond the wave-off and appeared to be hollering for us to "Get the hell out of there!" This was his second wave-off. Pits was making a conscious choice to stay on the ground with Charlie Company!

Not knowing how much longer our HH-43F was going to hold together, we had to get out of there and put this bird and crew on the ground as soon as possible. As I began to maneuver up and out the pickup hole, the Stokes litter on the end of the cable became snagged and hung-up in the trees sixty feet below. We were now "tethered" to the trees!

Hammond said it was really hung up. He couldn't get it loose. He wanted me to cut the cable. I flipped the hoist-cable emergency arming switch and pressed the hoist-cable cutter button on the cyclic stick grip. The cartridge fired and successfully cut the hoist cable. The cable fell away and we again began a gradual pull out of the pickup hole. We headed for a small clearing I had spotted earlier. It was about two klicks away. We realized that if I set her down in the clearing, we might be up to our armpits in VC.

I figured that we would just have to take our chances on the bird holding together a bit longer. Upon reaching the first clearing, I spotted another small clearing about a klick farther away and we headed up for it. As we got closer, we could see Binh Ba several klicks away and decided to take a gamble the bird would stay together and get us there. We didn't know how badly the flight controls or rotor blades had been hit, so I felt it best to not make abrupt flight control movements and to be gentle on the controls. I made a slow, shallow approach to a running landing. The bird held together and we arrived in one piece.

Because the fuel control had been hit by enemy fire I could not shut the engine down. Hammond lowered the inner cabin doors. He took a hammer from his tool kit and smashed the fuel control levers to the "off" position. The engine finally quit running and I was able to pull on the rotor brake, stopping the rotors. Our chopper was now totally out of commission. Bullet holes were found on other parts of the chopper. One bullet had cut more than halfway through one of the wooden blades, on the right side. This caused the severe-out-of-track condition. If the blade had failed where the bullet struck, the helicopter would have crashed.

As for Pits, we felt Pedro 97 would get him out. But Sidewinder 23 told Pedro 97 that there were seven more known causalities and Pits was still on the ground. Before Pedro 97 could maneuver into the pickup point, Sidewinder 23 advised that no more pickups could be attempted because the area was again under very heavy enemy contact. This time the enemy was also too close to the survivors for close air support to be called in. Artillery was directed in and the pickup point soon became fully encircled by artillery fire. Shortly after dark Sidewinder 23 advised Pedro 97 that no more extractions could be attempted and advised the Pedros to return to home base.

The next morning, we learned that Pits did not survive. He had paid the ultimate price! He had been killed at approximately 7:30 p.m. on April 11, after helping numerous wounded, returning fire, and saving Navarro by shielding him with another soldier's body.

## Continuing the War

For me, of course, the war went on. After reading about the problems the Cavalry had at Landing Zone Albany (Chapter Seven), I have to make the point that nobody said we couldn't fly our HH-43F at night. When you go out in the middle of the night to try to locate these guys in the jungle down below, that's hard. You've got to be careful on the pickup because you can only leave your lights on for so long without being spotted.

There was one mission that was kind of spooky. We got a call. We had some elite forces out—an Army officer, a green beret type, another

American, and a couple of foreign troops who fought on our side. We got this call that one of the foreign troops had turned against our guys and killed one of the officers. The others grabbed him and had him all bound up. They wanted us to extract our guys and the turncoat from a rubber plantation where they would shine four flashlights for us. I went in at 5,000 feet so that I could see down below and spot these four lights. I did a corkscrew landing to get down quickly. It was really tight. I came in. It was a real hot area. There were a lot of Viet Cong around. They carried the bound turncoat up to us and plopped him into our helicopter and we got the hell out. I never learned any more about it.

On June 6, 1966, we were making a pickup. (We had lost Pits on April 11.) Staff Sgt. (later CMSgt.) Rick Connan, a helicopter mechanic and my hoist operator, was squatted in the cabin right behind me, facing outward, looking down to make his pickup. We also had a PJ on board whose name escapes me. Remember, you can't stand up in that H-43; you've got to squat. Another limitation is, it's hard to jockey the Stokes litter around to move it into the aircraft.

A bullet went up behind Connan and hit the oil cooler. Bullets hit the iron plate under my seat and clanged around. If it hadn't been for that plate, I would have been dead. I kicked the rpm up because I knew if I were going to freeze I'd want as much lift as I could. They'd torn up my helicopter real bad and I had to put it down quick. When we slammed into the ground, Dale Potter and I bounded out and made sure all our guys had guns. The enemy was right around us.

The Army had a bunch of gunships hosing down the area. Our PJ was Sanger. I don't recall the rest of his name. When an Army helo arrived to carry us out of there, they didn't have room for all of us. Sanger said, "You go ahead, Captain. I'll take the next one." I grabbed Sanger by the collar and shook him. "Don't give me this hero shit," I said. "I've lost one PJ. I'm not going to lose another." They lifted my crew out in an Army helo. Another helo came to get me. It didn't have the power to get off, bounced, hit the ground. On the fourth bounce he got enough altitude, put his nose down, and barely got the rotors to clear the trees and get us out of there. We eventually hitched another helicopter to take us back to Bien Hoa.

All that, and in my glass case at home I have a Distinguished Flying Cross.

# Kaman HH-43B/F Huskie Helicopter

In 1956, the United States Air Force held a competition to determine the most suitable helicopter for a newly defined Local Crash Rescue Mission (LCRM). The helicopter would scramble to the site of a local air base crash, dousing it with firefighting chemicals, and rescuing survivors. The Bloomfield, Connecticut, company founded by Charles H. Kaman entered the LCRM competition with an Air Force version of a boxy-looking helicopter it was building for the Navy. The U.S. Air Force's popular name for the aircraft was Huskie. In Vietnam, where it was used on combat rescue missions, it was called the Pedro. The nickname was drawn from their radio callsign.

The helicopter used Kaman's unique, meshing rotor design, which

## Kaman HH-43F Huskie (Pedro)

**Type:** Four-place rescue and utility helicopter

**Power:** One Lycoming T53-L-1B or T53-L-11A gas turbine engine; derated to 825 shaft horsepower (615 kW), driving two intermeshing 47-ft (14.32-m) two-bladed wooden main rotors

**Performance:** Maximum speed 110 mph (177.02 km/h); cruising speed, 107 mph (173.44 km/h); range, 277 miles (445.77 km) on internal fuel; endurance, 4 hours; ceiling 25,000 ft (7620 m)

**Weights:** Empty, 4,620 lb (2095 kg); useful load, 4,350 lb (1973 kg); gross weight, 9,150 lb (4150 kg)

**Dimensions:** Main rotor diameter, 51 ft 6 in (15.69); fuselage length, 25 ft (7.62 m); height 17 ft (5.18 m)

**Armament:** Up to four .30-cal or 7.62-mm machine guns

**Crew:** Four (two pilots, pararescue jumper, flight mechanic)

**First flight:** December 13, 1958 (H-43A)

made a tail rotor unnecessary. To some, this made the helicopter look as if it were trying to slice itself to pieces.

Kaman built 262 H-43A, B, and F models (redesignated HH-43A, B, and F in 1962).

In Vietnam, the H-43 drew a job it was never meant for—combat rescue. At Bien Hoa airbase near Saigon, a sign mocked the aging design of the Huskie's rotors: BLADES OF WOOD FLOWN BY MEN OF STEEL.

One of the final chapters of the H-43 story was a tragic one. On July 19, 1969, a B-52D Stratofortress bomber crashed on takeoff at U-Tapao, Thailand, after confusion between the aircraft commander's airspeed indication and the copilot's. As the crew escaped the burning bomber, the tail gunner became separated. An HH-43B/F crew rushing to the scene assumed he was still on board and attempted a rescue, although the gunner was, in fact, already safe. On a pass over the blazing wreck to drop fire retardant, the Huskie was caught in the final explosion and both men aboard the helicopter were killed.

The Huskie, alias Pedro, was still in service when the January 27, 1973, cease-fire ended American combat in Vietnam.

# Chapter 10

## Night Mission into North Vietnam

## What Happened

The mission was simple: Take off from the deck of a destroyer and fly in daylight to rescue the pilot of any battle-damaged aircraft that came out of North Vietnam and ditched in the Gulf of Tonkin. But Clyde Lassen's helicopter crew left the relative safety of the Gulf, crossed the coast, and flew twenty-five miles inland in sheer darkness; it was an unprecedented move for the lightweight Seasprite helicopter. As copilot LeRoy Cook put it, "Nobody had ever done a night inland rescue. It just wasn't done."

Lassen, Cook, and crew were launched when a surface-to-air missile blasted an F-4 Phantom, callsign ROOTBEER 214, out of the night sky near Vinh. Pilot Holtzclaw and back-seater Burns parachuted into the darkness. The Phantom and its crew belonged to squadron VF-33, called the "Tarsiers," from the carrier USS *America* (CVA 66).

Offshore aboard the destroyer *Preble*, at the controls of what was supposed to be a "fly over the water and pick people out of the ocean" helicopter, pilot Lassen and copilot Cook launched into the moonless black night. Before it was over, Lassen's crew was caught up in a point-blank battle, Cook was firing an M-16 from his copilot's seat at

**Lieutenant, Junior Grade
 Clyde E. Lassen
June 18, 1968
Kaman UH-2A Seasprite (Bureau no. 149764)
CLEMENTINE TWO
Helicopter Composite
 Squadron Seven (HC-7)**

Lt. (later Comdr.) Clyde Lassen in the cockpit of the UH-2A Seasprite he flew on his Medal of Honor rescue mission in Vietnam. The copilot on the flight was Lt. (j.g.) LeRoy Cook, at right holding an M16 rifle.

*U. S. Navy*

North Vietnamese troops swarming around the UH-2A, and crew members Bruce Dallas and Don West were fighting for their lives with M-60 machine guns. Lassen is credited with a never-equaled feat of airmanship.

**LEROY COOK** Our squadron sent out independent detachments to operate from ships like the guided missile destroyer USS *Preble* (DDG 46). First, we identified the group that was going out. We took about seven enlisted men and two officers. The enlisted men represented all the mechanical trades. We had mechanics, we had hydraulic men, we had metalsmiths, and we had electronics technicians. Out of those six or seven, there were at least three sailors who were collateral air crewmen. They flew with us. We flew with two at a time so there was one on the ship and two on the aircraft with the pilot and copilot.

At the squadron in Japan, preparing to embark on a ship, we formed up about six to eight weeks before embarking. We would have an aircraft in the squadron that we would fly, and we would learn to operate as a group. We had full responsibility for that aircraft. We flew it. We maintained it.

When it became time to deploy, we left that aircraft in Japan. We went to an Air Force base. All of our sea boxes, all of the parts that we were going to need to maintain a helicopter, and all of our personal effects were flown down to Clark Field in the Philippines. We took all of the equipment over to Subic Bay. We had an airfield there at Subic. At that point, we got the helicopter that had just returned from deployment with another detachment. We got the crew to sign it over to us. They went back to Japan and we assumed responsibility for this aircraft. We would spend about four weeks in the Philippines pulling maintenance on that aircraft that they could not do while they were on a ship.

When the time came, we were linked up with a ship that pulled into Subic Bay—in this case, the *Preble*. We loaded all the people on. When the ship cleared the harbor, we flew on board. We lived with that destroyer.

The way we know a mission is coming is, somebody gets shot down. That's the whole reason for us being out there. We had two similar detachments out in the Tonkin Gulf at any one time, one up north and one down south.

The carrier would send us electronic traffic saying, "Here's the missions that are being flown tomorrow. We need an aircraft launched at such-and-such time, to go up and pre-position and fly twelve to fifteen miles off the beach and wait there. If anything happens, our jet pilots will try to get back out over the water and you will then go and pick them up."

This was during the day. We were restricted to flying day visual flight rules [VFR] only because the ship had very little in the way of navigational equipment for us. We could do some night VFR if the moon was out but it was never intended that we would operate at night.

Just before that June 18, 1968, mission, we were in bed asleep. It was after midnight. While we were on the line, we had degrees of alert status. The highest alert status was a fifteen-minute alert, where you had to be in the aircraft and off the deck in fifteen minutes. Then you'd go down to a thirty-minute alert, and then you'd go down to an hour. We had been on fifteen-minute alert for two days.

The commodore for the squadron of destroyers, callsign HARBOR-MASTER, had decided that the higher alert status should be shifted to the other helicopter up north, and that we should stand down from alert status. We had just been north, where the helicopter on station used the callsign CLEMENTINE ONE. Just two days before we had come south. They said, "Okay, you guys stand down a little bit now and we'll take the helicopter that's up there now, the new CLEMENTINE ONE, and put them on high status ready alert." Our callsign was now CLEMEN-TINE TWO, and we were at the lowest level of alert status.

It depended on where the jets were going to strike. Sometimes we'd fly off the beach and watch them come in and bomb something that was just a few miles inland. That night, we were down there and they said, "You're off alert status." But they flew that one sortie that night. The F-4 pilots got hit by a surface-to-air missile [SAM] and went down, and we got the search-and-rescue [SAR] alert from HARBORMASTER and they said, "Get the helicopter in the air." The F-4 Phantom was using the callsign ROOTBEER 214. They were flying with an A-6 Intruder and his callsign was BUCKEYE 504.

They went down just a little before midnight. When we got the call, they'd been on the ground about half an hour. The ship got its orders from the chain of command. The ship went to something like general quarters except the Klaxon was saying, "SAR alert! SAR alert! SAR alert!" and the bell was going bong, bong, bong. The ship's company had specific activities that they needed to do to get us off the deck. We got out of bed a few minutes after midnight and we were airborne by about twenty minutes after. So even though we were off ready alert, we still got the aircraft into the air in about fifteen or twenty minutes of being notified.

My pilot Clyde Lassen went into the combat information center, the

CIC, to get a five-minute briefing from the watchstander on what we were doing. I got the aircraft started and got everything ready up to the point of being ready to release the rotor brake. We had put the aircraft to bed with the switches in all the right places so that all we had to do was plug in power, turn on the switch, and start the engine. It would come up.

When Clyde came in and strapped in with all of his survival gear on—we had all of this stuff stored in the aircraft, so we could put it on right there and jump in—he released the rotor brake, which started the generators going. We got safety power going and the aircraft became self-sufficient electrically, and we disconnected the power cord. There were several people on the deck guiding this process. One of the detachment crew people stood out in front of the aircraft and signaled when we were clear to go. The process was very rudimentary because it was what we would call today a "beta-test project." Remember, we would land on ships that they would not allow anybody to land on today. That included the *Preble*.

The H-2 was an all-weather aircraft with running lights and instrument panel lights.

I don't recall the ship's standoff distance, but I'd say we were seventy-five to eighty miles from the downed F-4 crew. They were about twenty-five miles inland. The ship had to stay out at least twenty miles, I think. Once airborne, we used to hold at about fifteen miles offshore.

## Launching from Ship

One of our crew members held up two sticks with the red and green flags. When we were ready to take off, he held up the green. While we were sitting on the deck, we had a tiedown chain from the each wheel, left and right, to a tiedown pad in the deck. We had wooden chocks in it. We had a sailor standing by each of those wheels. The pilot said he was ready to go and gave the thumbs-up. The crewman standing out in front of us outside of the rotor arc held up the green flag and signaled the chock and chain watchers to release us from being tied down to the ship. He then signaled us to fly away. The process was similar to the way airplanes are launched from a carrier, but without a catapult.

Clyde was flying. How did we find our way to the survivors? An aircraft controller guided us. When the F-4 was shot down, he had a wingman with him. The wingmen reported that a SAM had shot down the F-4. The controller on the shop at sea fixed the location by tracking the wingman on radar. The wingman said, "Okay, I'm going to fly over and when I say 'Mark!' you put a grease pencil on your radar screen and you'll know where the survivors are." When we launched after them, the radar crew on the USS *Jouett* (DLG 29), where HARBORMASTER resided, knew their position. The *Jouett* took the original Mayday call and HARBORMASTER had the final say whether we went in. That was Capt. Emerson. I don't think I ever knew his first name. HARBORMASTER was the commander of the squadron of destroyers and Capt. Robert S. Hayes was the commanding officer of the *Jouett*.

So they're all in CIC by this time. They get notified that they've got an aircraft down. HARBORMASTER is the one who has to make the decision to launch. He's the one who sends the message up to the *Preble* and says, "Okay, get the helicopter airborne."

Once we're airborne and we tell HARBORMASTER that we're airborne . . . and by the way, we talked about the H-2 being underpowered? During the day, we sometimes had to leave one crewman on the deck and go up and dump some fuel. We never did fly with a full load of fuel because it was just too hot and humid out in the Gulf and the extra armor plating on the H-2 made it heavier, so we always had limited fuel capacity. Sometimes we'd lift up in a hover over the ship and we didn't have enough power to hold that hover and we'd set it back down. Although the freeboard was only about twelve feet above the water, we would actually dive down to about six feet above the water and build up air speed and then we would start climbing and get hot.

During this night launch, fortunately we didn't have to leave a crewman out but we still took off at twelve feet above the water and dove down to about five feet over black water without any moonlight to get airborne.

Once we were airborne, the aircraft controller on the *Jouett* said, "Okay, here's where I want you to go." All the ships had an electronic arm out there called TACAN—tactical air control and navigation, I think is what it stood for—and that TACAN capability gave us azimuth readings and distance measuring equipment, or DME, readings. So they said, "Okay, we want you to goon Guard at a 260 radial and hold at ten knots and fly a racetrack pattern around that fictitious point in the sky." The ship is moving and that point is moving, too. We're maintaining ourselves on that radial off of that ship. They put us there until HARBORMASTER decided what he was going to do.

Nobody had ever done a night inland rescue. It just wasn't done. One of the most difficult decisions in combat search and rescue is the "go" or "no go" decision. That was HARBORMASTER's decision.

HARBORMASTER had to have three pieces of information before he would come up with that one.

First, he had to know that the survivor was, in fact, a survivor and not a dead person. The way they got positive identification was that prior to every deployment every pilot filled out a piece of a paper saying, "Here's my favorite dessert, here's my wife's maiden name, here's my grandmother's maiden name," things that only that pilot would know. Now, whenever the pilot got shot down, the on-scene commander—who was almost always the pilot's wingman—would say, "I have voice communication with ROOTBEER 214."

There were two F-4s providing cover for the A-6. They were on a night mission to look for trucks on the highway. We pilots had survival gear that we wore over our vests. In that was medicines, candy bars, and water, but we also had a crystal radio called a PRC-63, or "Prick 63," a handheld ultra-high frequency [UHF] that had three frequencies on it, including Guard [the international distress frequency]. It would send out an emergency signal that sounded like *Peow! Peow! Peow!*—meaning, "I'm in trouble." Or you could go to voice and talk to somebody. So the on-scene commander was talking to Holtzclaw and Burns, who were the pilot and the radar intercept officer [RIO] of the downed F-4.

Burns was the senior person and the mission commander. They had their PRC-63 working on the ground and the aircraft above was talking to them. So HARBORMASTER indicated to the aircraft overhead to break out the personal identification information and verify that it really was Holtzclaw and Burns. They did.

So now HARBORMASTER would have been thinking, "We have

two of the elements we need to order the helicopter in. We know that the survivors are alive and we have positive identification. The third thing we need to know is that they are successfully evading and that this is not a trap." At that time of night—by this point, it was quarter of one or later—HARBORMASTER's decision would have been, "You know what? If we wait until morning, there's no chance we're going to get them out of this area." It was north and west of Vinh Son, one of the most heavily defended areas of North Vietnam. They had triple-A [antiaircraft artillery] everywhere. The whole coast for miles up and down had nothing but red circles on our map. So HARBORMASTER just made the decision: "We'll have to go in tonight. Otherwise we're not going to get them out."

Clyde told the crew we were going in. My copilot's job is to monitor the temperatures and equipment and do some of the radio work. The pilot—Clyde Lassen—did some of the radio work, but he did the flying.

We had two crewmen in the back, Bruce Dallas and Don West. They were rescue swimmers. If we needed to pick anyone up over water, they would do it. They each had an M-60 machine gun that was mounted in the aircraft and pointed out the side doors, left and right. The copilot had an M-16 rifle available to him.

We went in at about 5,000 feet. We were more concerned about being shot down by small-arms fire than by heavy stuff. We had never faced heavy stuff, really. Our major fear was, you go down below 2,000 feet and you're in range of somebody shooting you down with an AK-47 or whatever weapon of choice they happen to have at that time.

We went feet dry [over land]. We went in just a little north of Vinh Son. There's a little valley down there—to call it a valley is a bit of a stretch since heights were only about a thousand feet—so we began flying up this valley. We were doing about 110 knots, maybe 120 knots. By this time, we had overhead rescap [rescue combat air patrol] from A-4 Skyhawks. Their callsign was CHAMPION. They were off the carrier *America*.

We had no defensive electronic equipment on the H-2 that would have detected a radar-guided missile. We were a shipboard, "fly over the water and pick people out of the ocean" rescue vehicle.

The on-scene commander changed about three times that night because of fuel status and the need to get back to the carrier. Holtzclaw and Burns had joined up on the ground and stayed together.

As we were flying up the valley at 5,000 feet, somebody on the ground shot something very big at us because it made a huge *whoosh!* as it went past my side of the aircraft and it left a big trail of sparks. Without threat analysis capability in the aircraft, we could only guess what it was but it must have been a SAM [a Soviet-built SA-2 "Guideline" surface to air missile]. Am I certain it was a SAM? Not really. It was big enough that with the doors closed and over the noise of the aircraft and the transmission it still made this big loud *whoosh!*

We went in. We had difficulty finding the survivors. We could see the wreckage burning to our left at about ten o'clock, maybe ten or twelve miles in the distance. We had Rescap above helping to direct us to the site because they had a visual on the site where the survivors were. They were doing great circles above us trying to stay somewhere around us while we approached at our relatively low speed.

The survivors were on the ground talking on their radio. We had the ability to dial into that frequency. We had a needle pointing to where they were. That needle was on our noise wavering back and forth, plus or minus five degrees. We knew they were up there someplace, but we didn't know exactly where.

Rescap overhead was telling us where they were. Now we were having voice communications with the pilots on the ground. They told us they were on the side of a hill. They called it *karst*. That was the first time I ever heard that term and I had no idea what it was. Clyde hadn't either. I looked at him and said, "What's karst?" He said, "Hell, I don't know."

They were in the jungle. They had 200-foot trees for canopy. The canopy kept their flares from penetrating. You know those pencil flares? A pencil flare is half an inch or three-eights of an inch in diameter. It's a hollow tube about five inches long that has a plunger on it. It's spring-activated. You slide this knob back. You reach that little button. The firing pin hits it. And the thing becomes like a Roman candle.

But the jungle canopy was so dense that their flares would not penetrate it. The survivors had strobe lights. You couldn't see those down through the canopy unless you were right on top of them in a clearing. The on-scene commander had flown over and said he saw the strobe. So he was directing us to it. Then somebody gave us directions, telling us when we should start looking.

They also carried five-shot .38s. They also had pistol flares. These were magnesium flares similar in appearance to tracer rounds, another tool for us to locate them. Those went up through the jungle canopy so we could pinpoint where they were. But it also gave away their position to the North Vietnamese. Now it was more hazardous for them, too, because all of the attention wasn't focused on our helicopter any longer.

We wanted to get from 5,000 feet down to ground level as quickly as possible. We did that in a very steep, spiraling descent. At night, on instruments, that was very tricky for Clyde to do.

He did it. We flew around the area until a survivor said, "Oh, you've just passed us." When we passed them that ADF (automatic direction finding) needle, it swung to a point behind us, pointing at their radio transmission.

We could figure out pretty closely now where they were. We did finally get overhead of them and see them. But then Clyde noticed that this jungle, this karst, sloped down to some rice paddies, down to a little delta area. There were three or four hamlets that we could see—just little black dots where the hooches were. By this time, Rescap had gone to parachute flares that illuminated the ground so that we could get visual references. I think they were called Mark 24s. They were phosphorus lights that burned bright on their way down. At any given moment we had two or three parachute flares up there. They descended slowly, burning for a time and then burning out.

## First Attempt

Clyde came in. He landed at what was essentially the edge of a rice paddy. There was some mud there, so he could not set down the weight of the aircraft down on the tires. He basically held a hover with the wheels in the mud. So there was no relaxing for him. He was flying constantly, all the time.

We said, "Okay, guys, we're here. Come down the hill." And they said, "I'm sorry. We can't." The jungle was so dense at that point that after they got together on the ground—and after stumbling their way into one of the hooches and backing off—they found their way up to the jungle. They said they had to go together like football players on a blocking dummy just to get through the undergrowth in the jungle. So they said, "No, we're up here only about a hundred yards away but we can't come down right now. You have to come and get us."

## Second Attempt

Clyde said, "Okay." We took off. We went around. We got sight of them again. Clyde tried to come in on a hover and the H-2—because it was limited in its power—could not hold the hover above the trees. Clyde said, "I'm going to have to dump some fuel in order to get lighter so I can come back and do the hover."

## Third Attempt

We did. We dumped some fuel. That was my job. Then we came back around and went into a hover.

Now, we were just barely holding the hover. The gauges that were giving us the rotor rpm and the engine speed at the same time—you want to keep those two needles matched up at 100 percent on the gauge—they were barely doing what we wanted.

By this time, Bruce Dallas, the crew operator on the right-hand side of the aircraft, and Don West, the crewman on my side—they're talking on the ICS, the intercom communications system—are peering out and reporting North Vietnamese. Dallas has the door open—he and Clyde share the same great, big door—and he's right behind the pilot. He could reach up and touch the pilot on the shoulder. He's operating the hoist. It's going down. But we only have 200 feet of cable on that hoist. Now the horse collar on the end of the cable is dangling within a matter of a good three feet above Zeke Burns and John Holtzclaw. They can't reach it because of the jungle.

To hold this hover, we needed references. We did not have any of the electronic equipment that was later installed in that aircraft. Everything was manual. We needed to see the trees and to have references so we knew if we were moving at all. Just when we needed references most, all the parachute flares went out and the world got very black.

That's when we hit a tree.

The nose pitched down and we almost crashed, but Clyde righted it, and got back up in the air and got out of there.

## Fourth Attempt

We went up. We decided to settle down and get our nerves back and our adrenaline under control. We told them, "Guys, that's not going to work. We can't pick you out of there with the hoist. You're going to have to come into the clearing." They would have to get down to where we could land and pick them up.

Sometime during these events, we had another missile fired at us. Dallas and Don West saw that one.

Because of all the noise in the helicopter and because of the flares and the lights in the sky, we'd had people running out shooting at us since we got there. We could see their muzzle flashes coming up at us. They were just shooting at sound. They didn't see a target.

In these hamlets I mentioned, people came out of the hooches like spokes of a wheel. They knew something was going on and they were all converging on a central point, where we were at the center of everything. As we were flying around in the sky, we saw all sorts of muzzle flashes. The number continued to increase. We saw more and more of them. They concentrated as they drew closer.

Fortunately for us, they had to run across their rice-paddy dikes. They couldn't come in a straight line. They would come from ninety degrees, like tacking in a sailboat, trying to get to us. The paddies had several feet of mud and water, knee deep, which was kind of an obstacle to them in trying to get to us quickly. That slowed down their progress but the paddies also impeded us in what we could do and where we could set the helicopter. We couldn't really land it anyplace.

We flew around. We told Claw and Zeke that they had to come out of the jungle and they kept saying, "No, come get us."

During this time, as they were going into the jungle, Zeke lost his

PRC radio that was sending out this *"Peow! Peow! Peow!"* sound. That was overriding some of the voice communications between us and them. You could pick up only about every other word. So communication was pretty well hindered. To make ourselves understood about what we wanted took awhile. So we repeated, "You guys have to come down the hill because we can't get you out up there. We can't hover over the trees." By this time they had been on the ground for an hour and a half or two hours and were still saying, "No, no, come get us, come get us."

They could now hear people running on the trails in the jungle. Some were running very close to Claw and Zeke, within feet. Every now and then, they shut up and went silent and a little later they'd say, "Well, we had company so we couldn't talk right then."

So we're telling them, "You've got to get down here. You've got to get down here through all that dense undergrowth. And you have to come out into the open because we can't come to you."

Our two guys in the back were manning their machine guns, not constantly but sporadically. One of the things we had going for us was that nobody could see us. We had no running lights turned on. Everything was black. We were a dark gray aircraft without any white markings—we had only black markings for that very reason—against a black sky. They didn't know how fast we were moving. They would shoot at our sound when we weren't there any longer.

We landed back on the side of the hill again. We sat. We waited. And we waited. And, again, we could see [North Vietnamese] coming into the light from the parachute flares. We started to see figures. So again we said to Zeke, "Come on down." And he said, "We're not there yet. We can't make it yet. It's going to take us a little while longer." So we took off and flew around a little.

Zeke said, "Okay, we're ready for you to come back." We flew back. We landed. Now, this was the third time we'd landed in that same part of the rice paddy sloping down from the jungle to our left. So we were really on the edge of the rice paddy. We were maybe seventy-five yards from the jungle but it was still moist and muddy. So we sat there and we waited, and we waited, and we waited.

A Kaman UH-2A Seasprite helicopter like the one flown by Lassen, Cook, Dallas, and West on their dramatic night rescue mission deep inside North Vietnam in 1968.

*U. S. Navy/PH2 Jeffrey K. Halsey*

It seemed like we waited a very long time but it might have been thirty seconds or so. Then Zeke said, "No, we still can't get out into the clearing."

So we had to take off and come back a fourth time. By this time we were running out of fuel. We had dumped some of it to hover, which took away our reserve. We were now at a point where Clyde, watching the fuel gauge, said, "Well, we'll keep going until we have just enough fuel to reach the Gulf and go feet wet. Then we'll put this helicopter in the water and call for rescue ourselves. But we're going to do everything we can to get these guys out of here tonight."

So we made our final approach. We were at about 150 feet, coming in. Of course, everything on our aircraft was dark. The parachute flares burned out again. And again the world went black. We were right down low and close to the ground, which made it a not-very-good time for everything to go black.

On the collective that the pilot had in his left hand, there was a box with a number of switches. One of those switches turned on the lights. We had four different lights—two in the nose that pointed ahead at angles-off, slightly to the left and right of the centerline, another that would swing down and point forward—or with a little button on that collective box, you could move it left or right, or up or down, like a spotlight. And the fourth one was the hover light that shone right straight down to the ground from the belly of the aircraft.

Clyde turned on all of those.

Now the North Vietnamese had no doubt where we were. We saw their faces as they ran at us, shooting at us. They were literally maybe a hundred feet away, fifty feet away, something like that. We had them coming at us from the front and the side. The crewmen were telling us that they were coming at us from behind, too. The only direction where we weren't taking fire from was on the left, where the jungle was.

So we're sitting there in the middle of this big *thing* of light that goes out about twenty feet on either side of the helicopter. It encircled us. We were lighted up like a Caribbean cruise ship.

We could see the North Vietnamese. But we couldn't see beyond the edges of the jungle.

Don West was on my side of the helicopter. He had his M-60 machine gun pointed out toward the jungle. I had my M-16 pointed out toward the jungle. I said to Don, "If you see faces coming out of that jungle and you see muzzle flashes, you start firing."

Two faces in black pajamas—or so it seemed from our perspective—came bursting out of the jungle, running at us. Don and I were waiting to fire.

Fortunately, it was Zeke and Claw.

During the ejection process, Zeke had been out of position so he'd suffered a broken ankle, a broken shinbone, something like that. Still, he outran Claw to the helicopter.

Dallas got out of the helicopter on the right side. The damn fool. There were people on the right side shooting at us. He was in the light, looking to see where the survivors were going to come from. And Clyde looked down and said, "What in the heck are you doing down there? Get back in the damn aircraft!" He got back in the helicopter and began shooting at North Vietnamese. This was the point at which Zeke Burns came running straight at the aircraft. But Zeke and Claw did not want to run into our circle of bright light and become targets themselves, so they skirted around the nose and came in from the right-hand side.

We started taking fire from the jungle where they had just emerged. That's how close the North Vietnamese were, the ones who were chasing them. So if we didn't get them this time, they probably would be captured.

Dallas is a big guy. He's six-one, something like that. Don West is a big guy, built like a linebacker. When Zeke came around the side, Bruce grabbed him by the scruff of his flight suit and, one-handed, threw him into the back of the aircraft. Zeke later said, "I landed on my back upside-down, wondering how I got there."

About that time, Holtzclaw came around and got the same treatment. Holtzclaw's survival radio was still putting out this *Peow! Peow! Peow!*—drowning out our ability to communicate on the headsets.

So we had some confusion. "Are the survivors both on board?" "Are they not?" "Are we ready to go?" "Can we get the hell out of here?" West, Dallas, and I were all operating weapons, firing back at people who were shooting at us. Finally, it became clear that, yeah, everybody was on board and we could get out of that spot.

## Out of North Vietnam

When the confusion was cleared up and we said, "Okay, let's get the hell out of here," I put down the M-16 because my job as copilot now was changed back to helping the pilot inside the aircraft. I think I just threw it up on the dashboard.

We got airborne. We got out of there. Bruce and Don continued to fire their M-60s out the doors as we went along. As I said, the North Vietnamese were close enough that you could see the features of their faces—in the glow of our lights, not of the parachute flares.

So we did that. Now, Holtzclaw's radio in the back was still overriding all communications between us and HARBORMASTER, whom we now were trying to contact and get a steer toward because now we were down to approximately twenty minutes of fuel and twenty-five minutes of flight time.

We were trying to find the shortest route out of there. In the process, we flew north and we actually flew a little farther into North Vietnam before we got turned around and pointed toward the *Jouett*. Clyde comes on the ICS and says, "Turn off that damn radio!" He says, "I don't care if you have to strip naked to find it. Throw that radio out the door." So they finally found the radio in Holtzclaw's pocket and were able to turn it off so we could get in communication with HARBOR-MASTER and get steered toward them.

Capt. Hayes, the CO of the *Jouett*, was listening for our fuel state. We said, "We're going to get feet wet, but we may not get all the way to you." Hayes made the decision to steam his ship into shallow water to close the distance on us. Otherwise, we wouldn't have made his ship.

On the way out, we were taking some additional Triple-A. Then there was something else. I don't know what it was. But one thing you learn quickly as a pilot is that anything that's on the horizon is something that's at your altitude. I saw what I can best describe only as a handful of flaming arrows coming straight at us on the horizon. I scared the hell out of Clyde. I yelled, "Get down!" I grabbed the collective and put us into a dive. But they exploded a mile or two away, harmlessly.

As we were climbing out, another problem arose. The H-2 had an air-speed restriction with the doors open. You could not exceed a hundred knots. You wanted to have the doors shut by about eighty-five to ninety knots. We were able to pick up speed pretty quickly now—we had probably 400 pounds of fuel in the front tank and that was all—so we were climbing pretty quickly. Clyde told Bruce Dallas to shut the door. It was a common door with the pilot and crewman on that side. Bruce reached out and tried to push the door forward and the door departed the aircraft. It separated and fluttered to the ground and became a souvenir for some Vietnamese. It had been damaged when we hit the tree. When Bruce touched it, it just fell out of the tracks.

The other damage that we suffered when we hit the tree was we banged the tail rotor and the horizontal stabilizer. That made the aircraft go through these little shudders all the time that we were flying after that. The horizontal stabilizer is just like a little wing that helps give some lift to the tail.

We got feet wet. The *Jouett* closed. They turned on a bunch of their lights, which made them a target for shore batteries—if the North Vietnamese shore gunners had been awake, but fortunately they weren't. As

Lassen's helicopter crew went into North Vietnam to rescue the crew of F-4J Phantom II bureau no. 155546 of squadron VF-33, called the "Tarsiers," from the carrier USS *America* (CVA 66). This aircraft, bureau no. 155568, is a sister ship from the same squadron but is seen after the squadron transferred to another carrier.

*U. S. Navy*

---

the *Jouett* got closer we told him, "Okay, we need you to turn in to the wind. We need to make an immediate landing. This will be a straight-in approach."

After that, it was kind of an anticlimax. Clyde came in. He made our landing. He got it on the deck. He shut it down. We had less than five minutes of fuel left. If Capt. Hayes hadn't gotten the *Jouett* crew to close in on us, we'd have landed in the water.

While we were taking fire, each time the muzzle flashes got bigger we were certain we were taking hits. We thought we were getting the hell shot out of us. Clyde said, "We're pretty shot up."

In fact, nobody touched us. Our helicopter did not have a single bullet hole.

One postscript about our helicopter, bureau number 149764. It was transiting from one of the destroyers to another ship. They got a bad steer. They ran out of fuel. They had to set that helicopter down in the Gulf of Tonkin and Bruce Dallas got to swim away from it.

As for Clyde Lassen, who won our highest award for valor, he was a modest, mild-mannered person. He knew exactly what he wanted. He started out in the Navy as an enlisted person. He got picked to go to OCS and to flight training. When I learned that I was going to be his copilot, I was very pleased. He was a very sharp individual. When he left the Navy, he did the stock market and real estate and became very successful. He died of cancer at age fifty-two.

## What Happened

The success of the ROOTBEER 214 rescue was due in part to the work of Radioman 1st Class Allen R. Melton, who was the voice of HARBORMASTER aboard the *Jouett*.

The ROOTBEER 214 mission resulted in an award of the Medal of Honor to Lassen, the Navy Cross to Cook, and the Silver Star to Dallas and West. On January 16, 1969, President Lyndon B. Johnson presented the nation's highest award "for conspicuous gallantry and intrepidity at risk of life, above and beyond the call of duty" in a ceremony in the Blue Room of the White House. On April 21, 2001, the Navy commissioned the guided missile destroyer USS *Lassen* (DDG 82) in honor of the UH-2A Seasprite pilot. On April 1, 1994, Clyde Lassen died after a brief but courageous battle with cancer.

## UH-2A Seasprite Helicopter

The Kaman H-2 Seasprite series of helicopters was a response to a 1952 United States Navy design competition for a high-performance, all-weather utility helicopter. The Seasprite was the brainchild of the same company that built the Air Force's H-43 Huskie (Chapter Nine), the Bloomfield, Connecticut, company founded by aviation pioneer Charles H. Kaman. The series began with four prototype and twelve production models known as HU2K-1s.

The HU2K-1 nomenclature was changed to UH-2A on October 1,

1962. By then, the low-slung little Seasprite helicopters were beginning to appear on Navy warships. The initial batch of 88 UH-2A models, all equipped for all-weather operation, was followed by 102 UH-2Bs, which lacked all-weather instruments and were intended for daytime flying. In the Vietnam conflict, the Navy operated UH-2As, UH-2Bs, and HH-2C models that had a chin-mounted mini-gun turret. Crews complained that the gun never worked properly and, because of weight and balance issues, it was almost never used. In post-Vietnam years, the Navy added a new chore to this helicopter's work schedule, using the Seasprite in bigger, more robust versions with twin engines for antisubmarine patrol duty.

## Kaman UH-2A Seasprite (HU2K-1)

Type: Four-place search-and-rescue helicopter

Power: One 1,250-hp (932-kW) General Electric T58-GE-8B turboshaft engine driving 44-ft (13.41-m) four-bladed main rotors

Performance: Maximum speed 165 mph (265 km/h) at sea level; cruising speed, 152 mph (245 km/h); maximum rate of climb at sea level, 1,740 ft (530 m) per min; service ceiling 17,400 ft (5385 m); range with maximum fuel 422 miles (679 km)

Weights: Empty 7,050 lb (3193 kg); normal takeoff weight 12,800 lb (5805 kg); normal fuel capacity 276 UG gallons (1045 litres)

Dimensions: Main rotor diameter: 44 ft (13.41 m); length, rotors turning, 52 ft 7 in (16.03 m); fuselage length 36 ft 7 in (11.15 m); height, rotors turning, 15 ft 6 in (4.72 m); stabilizer span, 9 ft 8 in (2.94 m); height, 13 ft 6 in (4.11 m); tail rotor diameter 8 ft 0 in (2.44 m); main rotor disc area 1,529.59 sq ft (141.25 sq m)

Armament: Two crew-served .50-cal. (12.7-mm) machine guns, plus personal arms

Payload: Up to 1,800 lb (944 kg) of personnel or equipment

Crew: Two pilots plus two

First flight: July 2, 1959 (HU2K-1)

# Chapter 11

# Killing Field at Khe Sanh

## What Happened

Marines who fought at Khe Sanh, South Vietnam, in 1968 say that without Maj. David Althoff they might not have survived the seventy-day siege of the combat base.

Althoff, now a seventy-two-year-old retired lieutenant colonel in Tempe, Arizona, flew 1,080 combat missions and logged 1,000 combat air hours in Vietnam. He piloted the CH-46A Sea Knight helicopter, the Vietnam-era version of the CH-46E flown by Marines today. Boeing manufactured the Sea Knight in Philadelphia, Pennsylvania.

Althoff and crews from Marine Medium Helicopter Squadron 262—nicknamed "Tiger Airlines"—performed what a Boeing observer called "audacious flying" to supply the mountain outposts that were the eyes and ears of embattled Khe Sanh. The flying was done at low altitude where, as Althoff said, "there was a lot of metal flying around." The thin skin of a CH-46A can be punctured with a handheld pencil: Flying metal from North Vietnamese guns can slice through a CH-46A like a knife through butter.

Althoff was shot down on four occasions when he had to land immediately "and many other times when I could just barely make it back

The CH-46A Sea Knight helicopter had twin, tandem rotors, one behind the other. It was the workhorse of the Marines in Vietnam. Here, a CH-46A is being refueled at Dong Ha, South Vietnam, in 1966.

*U. S. Marine Corps*

to a base." Getting hit was the rule, not the exception. "You could sometimes count a hundred or a hundred and twenty bullet holes in the chopper."

Althoff remembered that, "The CH-46 had superb visibility forward, but there's no visibility aft. You need to rely on the crew chief for that."

Every pilot relies on the troops in the back to scan the area around the helicopter—doubly so in an aircraft like the CH-46 with two main rotors. Althoff goes further than most, however, in emphasizing that the crew deserves credit for any pilot's achievements. He repeatedly credited his crews not only with successful missions with him at the helm, but with his survival. Together, Sea Knight crews repeatedly shared the experience of being hit, something that doesn't come naturally to everyone trained in aviation. "You're going into a hot zone," Althoff remembered. "They're firing at you from 360 degrees. You start to take hits. You know you're taking hits. The crew chief is telling you, 'Okay, we're leaking here. The gas line's hit there.' If they're shooting into the cockpit, the gas lines are under the gauges so they're leaking all over your feet. You can hear the bullets cracking into the fuselage."

Second Lt. Michael Mullen, another pilot in HMH-262, said in 1968 that Althoff was "the squadron's idol. He would never ask one of his junior pilots to fly a mission he had never flown. When we went on a hairy mission, we went with the knowledge that it could be completed because [Althoff] had already done it several times before."

Corporal Travis Flowers, also a member of Althoff's helicopter squadron, said, "When we inserted a reconnaissance team into a hostile area, Major Althoff would tell the guys to keep their heads and arms inside the chopper because we were going in low and fast and he didn't want any of them getting something knocked off by a tree. He really meant it. You had to look *up* to see the trees."

**DAVE ALTHOFF** I was assigned to Marine squadron HMM-262, the "Flying Tigers," a part of Marine Air Group 36 operating from Quang Tri, Marble Mountain, and other locations in South Vietnam. The long, twin rotor Sea Knight was our standard transport helicopter for getting from Point A to Point B, and for taking assault troops into a landing zone. It was equivalent in some ways to the Army's "slick'" Huey troop transport, but a lot bigger. We had two Sea Knight models in "Tiger Airlines"—the CH-46A and, soon after I arrived, the updated CH-46D. They both used a pair of General Electric T58 turboshaft engines with about 1,850 shaft horsepower.

The mission for the CH-46A Sea Knight pilot was to haul Marines to a landing zone. Or, sometimes, the job would be to carry in supplies or ammunition. Then we would carry out whatever needed to be extracted. Sometimes, that meant acting as a medevac bird for the wounded. Unlike the Army, we did not have dedicated DUSTOFF birds. For us, medevac was always an integral part of our duties.

The Sea Knight had two rotors, one behind the other. When you're sitting up front, that's a lot of helicopter behind you, believe me. In fact, from the tip of the front rotor to the tip of the back is almost ninety feet [Author's note: eighty-three feet, four inches]. So when you're sitting in the cockpit, you've got seventy or seventy-five feet of rotor behind you. When you're going into zones with trees and stuff, that makes it pretty difficult to maneuver.

**Major David L. Althoff**
**1967–1968**
**CH-46A Sea Knight**
**Marine Medium Helicopter**
   **Squadron 262 (HMH-262),**
   **"Flying Tigers"**
**CHATTERBOX 64**
**Khe Sanh, South Vietnam**

*U. S. Marine Corps*

You're on headset with other crew members. They have to help you get in and out. The guys in back are your "spotters" when it comes to every danger to the helicopter, whether it's tree branches or Viet Cong machine guns.

The bird had those big fuel sponsons on stub wings on each side of the fuselage. The fuel tanks inside the sponsons were self-sealing. And they had some ingredient added to them so they didn't catch fire. I've taken tracer rounds and had all kinds of holes on those sponsons, but they never caught fire. At one time, I had a Viet Cong B-40 rocket with its red-hot rocket motor burning go right into that stub wing and not catch it on fire.

## The Crew

Without the crew members in the back, you'd be dead in a hurry trying to take a loaded CH-46A into a small landing zone. The crew members have to talk you down practically foot-by-foot when you're getting in to where it's really close. You have to really know and understand each

This is a formation of Marine Corps CH-46A Sea Knight helicopters like the aircraft flown by Althoff.

*U. S. Marine Corps*

other, so you can communicate quickly without any misunderstanding. Often, you're trying to bring that bird and its cargo of Marines to the ground while the foliage is pressing in from all sides and the enemy is shooting at you.

The crew consists of a pilot in the right seat, the copilot in the left seat, and the crew chief who roams back and forth, to and from the cockpit. He keeps you informed on how many hits you're taking and what kind of damage it's doing. He talks you into the zone. When you're going into a tight zone, he's looking out the back. He's telling you, "Forward . . . forward . . . forward . . ." or "right . . ." or "left . . ."—guiding you into the zone. We're communicating on the ICS [intercom system] during that whole time. The whole crew is on headphones throughout the mission.

In addition to pilot, copilot, and crew chief, on the right window you've got a gunner with a .50-caliber machine gun. On the left side, you've also got a gunner with a .50-caliber machine gun. Marines are familiar with the weapons. They fire rifles and machine guns in training and they have to remain current with them. They know about weapons because they're Marines. So there's no special armament training for the enlisted flight crew members, but before they serve on the crew, we take them for several familiarization hops. We take them out into free-fire areas where they can get some practice shooting at things while we're traveling at 150 miles per hour. That's when they learn about leading the target and about how the bullet trajectories work. That'll show them how the tracers work and how to bring the guns to bear on certain targets. Also, even the best-trained Marine needs the experience of shooting from air to ground from a moving platform. Some simply don't get the knack for it.

The crew chief's job is to watch the systems, guide you into the zones, and supervise the loading of people and cargo. At times, he'll be outside the aircraft, attached by a cable to his headphone, helping Marines load or unload. If you have the right coordination between pilot and crew chief, the pilot is going to know exactly where that crew chief is, every second of the mission, especially during those critical moments when you're on the ground in a landing zone with hostile troops nearby. I'll have to say it again, I can't say it too often: The crew chief is vital to this mission. A pilot with a good crew chief is a happy pilot.

You've got to realize the importance of the crew working together. The crew chief, gunners, copilot, and pilot were just absolutely one team that couldn't be beat. I flew 1,080 combat missions. At one time or another, I probably flew with everybody in the squadron. I never encountered a Marine who was deficient. I never flew with a Marine who couldn't take it. I never flew with a Marine who wasn't great in the most stressful situations, even under direct fire.

Some of these guys were eighteen or nineteen years old. They wouldn't hesitate when they had to go out into the elephant grass, maybe sixty or seventy yards from the chopper, under fire, and recover Marines. They would never, never hesitate. Those enlisted Marines saved my ass. Some of them were hydraulics men, metalsmiths, and so on, who had full-time jobs apart from their flying duty. They would fly all day—some days we flew fifteen hours—and afterward they would spend the night repairing holes and working on that aircraft. Many, many nights, they slept in the chopper. At times, they survived on rations. They would work on repairs until they reached exhaustion. They would sleep for a couple of hours, then wake up and do more work on repairs. The next day, they'd go out and fly a mission. Then they would repeat the same cycle. They never hesitated. They never complained.

Squadron HMM-262 started out at Que Ha, moved to Marble

Mountain, and then became part of the Special Landing Force, which was aboard one of the carriers offshore, the assault ship USS *Tripoli* (LPH 10). There was a period when we had some aft pylon failures on the CH-46A—we were in the news for weeks, and you would never have known from the stories that these choppers would serve the Marine Corps for decades to come—and so the whole squadron went back to Okinawa for refitting and rework. It was widely publicized as a major mechanical failure of our helicopter, but it took only a relatively modest program to make the fixes. After about a month of rework on Okinawa, we put eight of our CH-46A Sea Knights back on the *Tripoli* and back into Vietnam. We operated off the carrier from October until December 1967.

## CH-46A Sea Knight Mission

I have been asked to describe how we flew a typical mission. With over a thousand of them, it's not easy to find one that's typical. We did many kinds of things, but most of our flying consisted of resupply and troop movements. We did this in all kinds of weather and terrain.

When an operation is being planned, the air group operations officer will brief the squadron commanders as to exactly what the deal is. That sets the wheels in motion. The squadron commander, together with his operations officer, goes back to the squadron area, gathers the pilots together, and lays out the flight schedule. He tells us what time we'll take off. He gives us an opportunity to discuss any issues we need to talk about, including weather, terrain, formation flying issues, the likelihood of enemy fire, and so on.

The squadron commander then briefs all of the crew members, as well as the standby crews. Those assigned to the mission typically will use our squadron's static callsign CHATTERBOX, followed by a two-digit number for each aircraft. Those on standby typically use the radio callsign SPARROWHAWK, again with a two-digit numeral assigned to each helicopter, and are supposed to be on alert and ready, if needed. We pay a lot of attention to callsigns and communications procedure because when we get into the hot zone we don't want any misunderstandings.

Marines climbing aboard a Sea Knight helicopter like the one flown by Althoff.

*U. S. Marine Corps*

He says, "Okay, now, here's the deal. We're going to take a battalion from Point A to Point B and insert them in there." He wants us to know everything we can about what's going to happen. The briefing covers the enemy's situation. It covers how many helicopters will fly the lift. You're told where you'll have to go for emergency maintenance if you're shot down, who's going to pick you up, and what frequencies you're going to operate on. You're told what the landing zone is like and what the weather is like. Part of the key to getting ready to fly into a hostile area is to have the best information you can get, have it briefed properly to everybody who needs to know about it, and have everybody in the squadron ready for whatever is going to happen. It's not unusual to go over some of these points two or three times to make certain everybody is prepared.

Depending on the size of the lift and the urgency, you might have the whole squadron in on it. Sometimes we would launch all twenty-four birds in the squadron. It depended on how big the zone was, how much you could get in at one time, and other factors. Normally, it would be at least four, usually eight, helicopters. When Khe Sanh was under siege, we often operated in much smaller numbers, sometimes even a two-ship formation or a single ship operating alone when the weather was really severe. And of course we always had birds on standby for emergency medevacs.

You lift off in formation and cruise at medium altitude toward the place where you're going to insert troops or supplies. The pilot flies the

Marines in South Vietnam climbing aboard a Sea Knight helicopter like the one flown by Althoff.

*U. S. Marine Corps*

aircraft when you're going into a hot zone. The copilot is on the controls with you so that if you take a round from a hit he immediately takes over. He has certain added duties like lowering the ramp and, if it's night, working the lights. The copilot will switch radio frequencies as needed but the pilot is normally the one who communicates on the radio. You're constantly on the headphones with each other, using standard aviation terminology in very short and simple exchanges. For example, if one of you takes the controls over from the other, you both acknowledge this verbally: "You have the aircraft," and, "I have the aircraft." Going into a hot zone requires the best in teamwork and coordination, but it also requires a pilot who is unmistakably in charge.

## Siege at Khe Sanh

Khe Sanh was down in a U-shaped bowl with a mountain around it, with peaks of 2,000 to 3,000 feet. That's the only place you can have a base when you have mountains like that. The peaks offer an outlook on all the valleys, roads, and trails leading from Laos into that part of Vietnam. We had companies on the hills all around trying to block the NVA from moving down out of the north. The NVA came down anyway. There were so many of them. We killed a shit pot full of them with air and artillery.

The siege of Khe Sanh is sometimes seen as a long-distance duel by artillery but there were many, many nights when the North Vietnamese were charging the wire. Marines at Khe Sanh saw them coming, even saw their faces, many nights.

The action at Khe Sanh began on January 20, 1968, and we lost our first plane out there on that day. From then on it just turned into pure hell. At first, C-123s and C-130s were bringing all supplies for both the base and friendly troops in the hills, going right into the runway at Khe Sanh. We would wait on the runway to pick up the stuff that was for the Marines in the hills and take it to them by helicopter.

Then, the fixed-wings started taking unacceptable losses and stopped landing. They just made parachute and low skid drops. We would still go into Khe Sanh, pick up those supplies, and carry them to the troops in the hills.

We had close air support and helicopter gunships by the hundreds, dropping bombs and shooting rockets in the hills around Khe Sanh but also down in the valley, right up to the base, sometimes within a very short distance of our own Marines. There were hundreds and hundreds of artillery shell holes.

We always referred to a formation flight of helicopters as a "gaggle," like a gaggle of geese. When you have as many aircraft in the sky as we had on our Khe Sanh resupply runs, it's a supergaggle.

To bring something into Khe Sanh, I would take off from Quang Tri, head for a forward location, and pick up supplies, ammunition, and water. We medevacked some troops. We brought replacement troops in. We didn't have a squadron that was dedicated to medevac. We would be assigned medevac. We would be out doing resupply and somebody would come up on the wire and say, "God, I've got five guys shot here. I've got to get them out of here." So, we would go in there and bring them out. SPARROWHAWK was the callsign for standby emergency medevac.

The weather was extremely bad during January and February at the height of the siege. Going in and out of there was really treacherous. They had GCA there [ground-control approach, meaning a capability to guide an aircraft to a landing using radar], but the NVA were smart enough to know how that worked and they had the glide slope zeroed in. So when they directed me to make a GCA landing, I purposely stayed a couple of hundred feet above the glide slope. They thought they were pretty smart because they could predict our moves, but we

A Marine CH-46A Sea Knight helicopter.

*U. S. Marine Corps*

could predict theirs, too. We would be in the soup with solid, wet gray in front of us, and still they would be shooting at us. I would see the rounds going past below and in front of us. I've also gone in there at night. There were no lights on the airfield at Khe Sanh. You had to use the radar altimeter to guide you down, and that method was notoriously unreliable. That was really scary.

Toward the end of February, it was even getting too tough for helicopters to work out of Khe Sanh. So we had to start staging supplies at Dong Ha, out on the coast. They didn't take much "incoming" there and we could refuel. But Dong Ha was twenty miles from Khe Sanh, so considering fuel requirements we had to fly more sorties and use more helicopters.

Khe Sanh started out as a commitment for my squadron, HMM-262. But by the time we stopped staging supplies at the Khe Sanh airstrip, we'd lost more than half of our aircraft to enemy fire. So in order to come up with twelve Sea Knights, we were reinforced by HMM-364.

Each night we'd pick the hill we were going to the next morning and brief the fixed-wing people. We planned all the takeoff times so that when the fixed-wings arrived from Chu Lai, the Huey slicks would be there to control them. Meanwhile, we'd have launched our twelve Sea Knights from Quang Tri, gone into Dong Ha, picked up our external loads, and be heading for the objective.

We'd arrive over Khe Sanh within two minutes of the time the fixed-wings had finished their prep of the hillside, and they'd save enough ordnance to make a last pass or two as we were going in. We usually did this three times a day—about nine o'clock in the morning, one in the afternoon, and five in the evening.

No pilot is ever going to tell you his aircraft is perfect. No Marine is ever going to tell you the CH-46A is perfect. But when you remember that our helicopter was designed before Vietnam, and that no one could have predicted how it would be used, you have to give credit to the engineers who came up with that sturdy, tandem, twin-rotor design. Of course, there were also problems, too. In fact, some of the problems attributed to the CH46A received quite a lot of press attention.

The aircraft has two hydraulic systems but the backup system is located very close to the primary system. Here's what that can mean: I was shot down one time by a single round. It could have been an AK-47 round. It was just one bullet. It went through both the primary and secondary hydraulic systems. They could have been designed so that couldn't happen. And the CH-46A could have been designed so the control function wasn't right behind the pilot's head. Later, when I went back to Boeing and spent a week talking with their engineers, I went through this. They incorporated some of my suggestions.

Another feature that could have been designed differently: Along the very top of the back part of the helicopter [author's note: the spine of the fuselage], the main control cables and the hydraulic lines running through there are vulnerable to fire. You could sometimes count a hundred or a hundred and twenty bullet holes in the chopper. The pattern of the holes showed that they were firing at the systems they knew were vulnerable. They studied the design of our helicopters, looked for weak points, and made sure their troops knew about the weaknesses.

In some ways, you might think our tactics were designed to help out the North Vietnamese. They weren't, of course, but when you're using helicopters to support ground troops in combat, there are only so many ways you can do it. If you're using a landing zone surrounded by bad guys, there are only so many choices. If you're able to take off, then, of course you take off. But then you're more vulnerable than ever because you're flying over enemy troops at ten, fifteen, or twenty feet. They can look right at you and shoot. With automatic weapons, they can string their bullets all along your fuselage.

I'm going to describe what happens when you take off and they bag you.

The moment of takeoff is critical, especially in a place like Khe Sanh. You're taking off. The gas gauge is going crazy. The fuel pressure is dropping. You've just gotten off the ground and you can hear the hits, like rain pattering against metal, and the helicopter is hesitating. You know you can't fly without fuel pressure, so you've got to auger it right into the ground, right where you're at. That was a decision I had to make at moments when I knew we could easily be surrounded and overwhelmed. You pick the least bushy area and smack it right down to the ground. If the chopper were damaged, sometimes you'd have to climb out the side window. That was a very tight squeeze.

Once you're on the ground, everybody piles out and forms a perimeter around the aircraft. The pilot and copilot would normally be out near the front. A lot of folks carried M-14 or M-16 rifles on the helicopter. I preferred to carry two pistols. You would follow a straight line corresponding to the nose of the aircraft and meet in front while the rest of the crew formed around the aircraft. You formed that perimeter and tried to fend off the enemy. They were always very alert to what we were going to do when they hit us, and they tried to overrun us more than once. I've been close enough to see them coming at us and to see their muzzle flashes moving as they came.

We try never to have a helicopter crew operating alone. You would have others with you. Normally you have other birds on station, Hueys or Cobras, so they strafe the area around you. Still, I've been on the ground for as long as twenty minutes with very aggressive enemy troops coming at us right around the helicopter.

When they can, they'll land some Marines around you as a security force. They'll also bring in another pilot and copilot to take a look at the aircraft, see what kind of damage it has, and see whether it can be flown out—or if it has to be airlifted out. Sometimes they can replace a fuel line or a hydraulic line. In that case, you can shake it out of there and fly it to a secure location. Otherwise, they'll have to call the Jolly Greens or the CH-53s and have it airlifted out. At times, a crew in my squadron simply had to abandon a helicopter that couldn't be repaired or recovered. When that happens, you just blow it up. You just start firing at it until it catches fire and it goes up.

**M. J. STEINBERG** Joining HMM-262 in July 1967, Major Althoff was assigned as operations officer. During the two months following, the squadron participated in several battalion-sized operations. All of these were marked by a thoroughness of planning and execution that resulted in extremely successful operations. Working tirelessly, Major Althoff ensured that the necessary and essential coordination was achieved among all participating and ground units prior to each assault.

## What Happened

Althoff earned the first of three Silver Star awards on February 1, 1968, as flight leader of a section of two CH-46s assigned to extract an eight-man reconnaissance team surrounded and pinned down by 100 North Vietnamese soldiers five miles west of Dong Ha. A Marine Corps press release later described the action:

> In spite of the fact that he was forced to rely solely on his instruments because of fog, rain, and darkness, Major Althoff landed through intense enemy fire near the beleaguered Marines. As the team moved to board his helicopter, he directed the delivery of suppressive fire from all of his helicopter's weapons. Although his aircraft had received damage from hostile fire, he was able to lift out of the hazardous zone, only to receive an increasingly heavy volume of enemy fire that

seriously damaged several internal systems of the helicopter. Despite the severe damage, he skillfully flew the aircraft to Dong Ha and a safe landing.

Marines talk about Dave Althoff with a special kind of awe. "He would just keep flying back into the furnace," said one. Althoff's fearlessness was kept in balance by his care and concern for his crews, and for all the Marines who flew aboard his CH-46A. "He's an old reliable," said Major Bob Neff, a fellow pilot. "It's a comforting feeling just to hear his voice on the radio."

Althoff holds numerous other military awards and was given the Alfred A. Cunningham Award in 1968, making him the "Marine Aviator of the Year." In 1991, he was inducted into the Arizona Aviation Hall of Fame. Althoff and his wife Phyllis have five grown children.

# Boeing Vertol CH-46A Sea Knight

In 1961, the Boeing Company's Vertol (formerly Vertol Aircraft and later, simply, Boeing) won a 1960 competition to build a new assault helicopter for the Marine Corps. When the Pentagon system for naming aircraft was overhauled on October 1, 1962, the new aircraft was known initially as the HRB-1 and was renamed the CH-46A. The CH-46A made its first flight sixteen days later.

The Sea Knight was the latest in a long line of twin-tandem helicopters designed in the 1950s by Frank Piasecki and dubbed "flying bananas" by the press. Boeing designed the CH-46A with folding rotors for stowage aboard aircraft carriers.

Boeing began to deliver Sea Knights to Marine squadrons in 1964. The Navy also used the helicopter for delivery of supplies to ships at sea.

The CH-46A arrived in Vietnam in March 1966, and began to replace the Sikorsky UH-34D (Chapter 5). Improved CH-46D models followed soon after. Sea Knights served with squadrons HMM-164, -165, -262, -265, and -364. They were often in the thick of battle. Boeing manufactured 624 of the helicopters and the North Vietnamese shot down 106 of them. The CH-46E—unlike, for example, the CH-53E (Chapter Nineteen)—has been through several modernization programs to introduce new equipment and "zero out" the airframes for longer life. For more than fifteen years, the Marine Corps has intended to replace its current Sea Knight fleet with the MV-22B Osprey tilt-rotor aircraft, and plans were still proceeding when this volume went to press.

## Boeing-Vertol CH-46A (HRB-1) Sea Knight

Type: Four-place, twin-tandem transport assault helicopter

Powerplant: Two 1,250-shp (1010-kW) General Electric T58-GF-8B turboshaft engines driving separate tandem sets of three-bladed 50-ft (15.24-m) main rotors

Performance: Maximum permissible speed, 168 mph (270 km/h); maximum cruising speed, 159 mph (253 km/h); maximum rate of climb at sea level, 1,375 ft (419 m); hovering ceiling in ground effect, 5,250 ft (1600 m); hovering ceiling out of ground effect, 7,400 (2255 m), service ceiling, 17,000 ft (5180 m); range with maximum fuel, 682 miles (1097 km); typical range, 230 miles (370 km)

Weights: Empty, equipped, 12,406 lb (5627 kg); maximum takeoff weight, 21,400 lb (9707 kg)

Dimensions: Main rotor diameter (both), 50 ft (15.24 m); distance between rotor centers, 33 ft 4 in (25.40 m); length overall, rotors turning, 83 ft 4 in (25.40 m); fuselage length, 44 ft 10 in (13.66 m); height to top of rear rotor hub, 16 ft 8.5 in (5.09 m); rotor disc area, each, 1,963.5 sq ft (182.41 sq m)

Armament: Typically, two 7.62-mm or .50-cal (12.7-mm) door-mounted machine guns

Payload: Seventeen to 25 fully armed combat troops, or 15 litter patients and two attendants; or 4,000 lb (1814 kg) of cargo

Crew: Two pilots, plus two

First flight: October 16, 1962 (CH-46A)

# Chapter 12

## Blown Up by a Booby Trap

### What Happened

The life of a Vietnam helicopter pilot included frequent point-blank skirmishes. It also meant challenges in the cockpit, flying in a country where weather and terrain could be as unfriendly as the Viet Cong.

For retired Lt. Col. Robert Kelley, sixty-five, of Vienna, Virginia, the experience included returning for a second tour as a combat aviator after being wounded so severely that, "doctors said I would never fly again."

By the time an enemy booby trap destroyed his helicopter at the battle of Soui Doi, Kelley was an Army captain and a mature soldier and pilot.

Born in 1939, Kelley grew up in Erie, Pennsylvania, and took reserve officer training at Gannon College, where he was graduated in 1961.

Kelley went to flight training in 1964 and to Vietnam in 1966 as a pilot in the 118th Assault Helicopter Company, the "Thunderbirds," at Bien Hoa.

The unit was equipped with UH-1C gunship and UH-1D transport versions of the Huey helicopter.

**Captain Robert Kelley
March 19, 1967
UH-1D Huey
65-9909
118th Helicopter Assault Company, "Thunderbirds"
Bien Hoa, South Vietnam**

A somewhat damaged portrait of Bob Kelley and UH-1C Huey helicopter at Phu Loi, South Vietnam.

*Bob Kelley*

"We flew combat assault missions where we hauled troops into a landing zone. Of course we were taking them there because the enemy was there."

Kelley was under fire repeatedly. Enemy rounds hit his helicopter a number of times.

Going into a landing zone near Soui Doi on March 19, 1967, Kelley was at the controls of a Huey when the helicopter in front of his was blown to bits by what he described as "a 500-pound bomb rigged as a booby trap."

An Army report calls the device a "non-Artillery launched or static weapon containing explosive charges (mine)."

The explosion sent his wiring harness and fragments of the cockpit ripping into Kelley's legs and groin. "We made a controlled crash with the hydraulics shot out."

Kelley remembers a crew chief ramming a morphine shot into his leg. "Others ran over to us and pulled me out of the helicopter."

For days and weeks to come, Kelley's life was something of a "controlled crash" as he went to hospitals in the field at Vung Tau, South Vietnam, and in Japan.

At one point it wasn't clear he would walk again, but Kelley returned to duty in August 1967 walking with a cane and crutches. After an assignment at Rucker, he returned to flight status in March 1968.

Today, Kelley wonders if doctors approved his return to flight prematurely: He still has little feeling in the lower part of his left leg.

Kelley returned to Vietnam. After a period as a logistician, in January 1971 he took command of the 128th Assault Helicopter Company at Phu Loi, equipped with UH-1C gunships and UH-1H transports.

Kelley said that memorable missions included trips by helicopter to insert Special Forces "A teams" behind enemy lines. On both Vietnam tours, he flew numerous "Firefly" missions in which helicopters prowled the perimeter of a firebase or base camp at night and engaged enemy infiltrators.

Kelley later worked in space and computers, acquired a graduate degree, and went to artillery school. He served on the Hawaii-based staff of the United States commander in the Pacific during the 1975 evacuation of Vietnam. Kelley retired from the Army in 1983 and now works for a government agency. He and his wife Pam have three sons.

**BOB KELLEY** I went through Reserve Officer Training Corps at Gannon College, Erie, Pennsylvania. I joined the Army in 1961, initially as a Private E-1, and went into artillery. They sent me to Alaska. It was cold as the dickens up there. We had 75-mm pack howitzers there, left over from World War II. They told us we were the first line of defense against the Russians.

In June 1964, I went to fixed-wing aviator training in the L-19 Bird Dog at Fort Rucker, Alabama. I was second in my class. I would have been first, but I failed my last check ride in the last fifteen minutes. The inspector, a guy with a clipboard, was taking notes. I leaned over to look at his clipboard to see how he was grading me, and that cost me my first-place slot.

Everybody in my flying class went to Vietnam. I got orders to Vietnam in late 1966. First, I went back to Fort Rucker to train in the UH-1

Huey helicopter. For guys who were already fixed-wing aviators, they used the OH-13 Sioux and they had an abbreviated eight-week course.

I arrived in Vietnam for the first of my two tours in December 1966 and was assigned to the 118th Assault Helicopter Company, the "Thunderbirds," at Bien Hoa. We had the UH-1C Huey gunship and the UH-1D lift helicopter, meaning the "slick," or transport, used to haul troops. The Huey was maturing as a combat system and while it still needed more power and a few minor improvements, it was very highly regarded.

On arrival a pilot went through four to six weeks of flying which included an evaluation of your flying skills, a test of your knowledge of emergency procedure tests, and an in-country introduction to the locale and geography.

## First Tour in Vietnam

As helicopter pilots newly arrived in country, they worked us hard and required us to learn fast. Standardization instructor pilots (SIPs) with lots of in-country experience gave us a series of tests in the Huey—autorotation, emergency procedures, and so on—as well as tours of the area so we'd know where the important safe-harbor bases were.

We began flying combat assault missions. We took troops in. The public thinks of the two guys in the front of a Huey as the "pilot" and "copilot," so I'll use those terms, but we actually called ourselves the "aircraft commander" and the "pilot." Contrary to practice elsewhere in the helicopter world, in Vietnam the aircraft commander of a Huey flew in the left seat.

The object was to get everyone qualified to carry out any mission. You were a copilot until an aircraft commander who flew with you determined that you were capable of handling the mission. Eventually, you became one of the more experienced guys, and then you were training the new guys.

Every day we were flying, we needed to get out to the flight line by six in the morning. They tried to give us one day off a week. Sometimes you didn't get that day. We were flying six to eight hours a day. You'd fly. You'd go wait somewhere, some secure area. You'd wait. You'd go again. We wouldn't get back home until six or eight o'clock at night, every night.

So we had twelve- to fourteen-hour days. Then you had to look at the helicopter, inspect it, report the main problems, look for bullet holes, and that kind of stuff. So it was always difficult to know what happened on a particular day. It was constant: "Go . . . get your mission. . . ." For the combat assault missions in 1966 and 1967, you were always flying South Vietnamese or American troops into combat. And you were taking them there because the enemy was reported to be there. So when you went in, you expected to be shot at. If the enemy was really strong there, they'd fire at you and if not they'd lay low. In 1967, they were building up big-time for the Tet Offensive, which came in 1968.

I can't say enough about the helicopter crew chiefs and maintenance men who worked with us. Our maintenance crews worked 24/7. The night crews would repair bullet holes. We always had civilian sheet-metal personnel assigned to every unit and they had a role in patching up our ships. Vietnam put a lot more wear and tear on the helicopter than anyone had in mind when they designed the Huey for medevac and general transport duty. We were constantly demanding more from the aircraft than it had been built for.

## Getting Shot Down

My moment of truth came about five months after I arrived in Vietnam. We were given a mission in the Tay Ninh Province area of III Corps in Vietnam with twenty helicopters. It was March 19, 1967.

This was on Palm Sunday, 1967. On Thursday of that week, I was notified that I was being transferred from the lift ships (the "Slicks," or transports) to the gun ships ("Guns"), based on my ability and skill. I flew Friday. Saturday, I was told, "You have Sunday off to write your efficiency reports for the men under you. Report to Guns on Monday morning."

Well, on Saturday night my platoon had a going-away party for me, a get-together at the bar. We had a grand time. At about one o'clock, I said, "Well, guys, I've got to go to bed." I left the party with a clear head. Sure, they'd told me the following day would be a nonflying day for me, but you could never tell. The one thing that was certain in Vietnam was uncertainty.

Well, at four-thirty that morning somebody's shaking me in the bed. I was instantly awake and alert. Somebody asked, "Would you please fly for Capt. Moore 'cause he is inebriated and can't?" I said, "Okay." I got up and went out with the unit.

The mission required my ship to lead the flight in. The company commander was flying with us. We had a discussion. I told him that we were really not flying a good mission that day. They had not done an adequate job in advance of suppress fire in the area. It just wasn't the right time go fly into that particular landing zone with a formation of slick Hueys. We had been there recently, and that had caused the enemy to become very well acquainted with us.

"We'll be okay," somebody said. "We were okay there before."

My point of view on that was that if you went back to a landing zone that you'd been in within ninety days, it was generally going to be booby-trapped. That was a ploy the enemy used to great advantage. But the company commander had a point of view, also. There were a lot of Americans on the ground out there. It was our job to go in when they needed additional troops and supplies. Yes, they said they were in intermittent contact with the enemy, but our guys would do their best to suppress fire and we would go in.

Our company commander flew the lead ship. We were in a line-up formation that covered a lot of sky and undoubtedly made us readily visible. I drew the task of flying the trail ship, which was the twentieth Huey in the formation.

As we approached, there was a lot of chatter in the earphones. We started taking heavy fire. There was stuff criss-crossing in front of us and people were shouting warnings. It was the usual confusion you encountered when a battle was under way.

The helicopter in front of me was a "loaner," not one of our regularly assigned Hueys. Standard operating procedures (SOPs) were for every helicopter unit on a mission to have a standby helicopter (loaner) designated as a backup in case of the inability of one of the original helicopters were unable to make the original assignment. On this day, the mission required twenty helicopters and only nineteen were flyable—so another unit furnished the loaner helicopter. My recollection was that the original helicopter failed a preflight inspection and was grounded until repaired. There's no significance to the fact that we had a loaner helicopter except that they weren't able to complete the mission.

The loaner helicopter was descending toward what the pilot must have thought was a perfect, nose-high landing with its rotors thrashing when it landed right on a 500-pound bomb that had been rigged as a booby trap. It was not a helicopter after that. It was a ball of fire. Right in my face.

My helicopter (the records show it was UH-1D serial number 65-09909, purchased by the Army in May 1966, with 566 hours on the airframe) flew into the middle of the fire.

## The Battle of Soui Doi

This was a very big battle. This was called the Battle of Soui Doi. We had an artillery firebase in there, with some infantry. On the ground at that time in 1967, the commander was Lt. Col. John W. Vessey, Jr., executive officer of the 25th Infantry Division. He must have been a senior lieutenant colonel because he moved up quite fast after that. Vessey had won a battlefield commission at Anzio and had fought in Korea. He later became chairman of the Joint Chiefs of Staff from 1982 to 1985. One of the veterans of that battle told me later that Vessey, a veteran of Anzio and of Korea, was the "fightinest" officer he'd ever seen.

The big deal was, our artillery was shooting flechette rounds. This was the first time they turned the tubes down and shot right at the enemy. By the end of the day, this point-blank artillery tactic drove the North Vietnamese off. They counted 675 bodies, dead North Vietnamese. This was a huge battle and it was the first time they ever turned the artillery pieces horizontal and shot directly at them. They were charging them that fast. Those flechette rounds really shredded those people.

There may have been other booby traps at that landing zone. As I had pointed out, the enemy had had plenty of time to seed the place with explosives. I have no doubt, and an official report later confirmed, that the 500-pounder was command detonated, meaning that somebody watched our Hueys approach. The official report said my helicopter was at an altitude of five feet when it happened. They determined the size of the explosive later by studying the crater.

Out of the twenty ships we took in, eighteen managed to get out in one way or another but twelve of them were severely damaged and five of the twelve crashed. My helicopter was one of those. Unlike the one in front of us, we weren't immediately blown out of the sky but the damage to our Huey was mortal—and the damage to me was nearly so.

We had a controlled crash. We had to go in because some of our shipmates saw that we were in trouble and flew behind us and tried to snatch us out of harm's way. The problem was, all the hydraulics were shot out and all of the controls were locked, because shrapnel from that 500-pound bomb had got into the transmission and others things. So, we were trying to slow to a level which would give us a gradual descent but we couldn't control it and we were headed into a big mountain.

We got just so far. Our people who were flying safety for us, going along with us, radioed, "Everything is starting to fly off of your helicopter. It's coming apart." The guy who I was flying with, Major Bill Benton, really saved the day. I was in the left seat as the aircraft commander and Bill was in the right seat as the pilot. He was from New Orleans and I'd call him an old grayhair who really knew how to manipulate the controls.

I had flown the helicopter into the landing zone but I couldn't fly it out because it was locked up. The perception I had was, the helicopter was going out on an angle. In my own mind I was kicking the pedals. I had the sensation of kicking the pedals. But the helicopter would not turn. So I looked down there to see why it wouldn't turn.

The pedals were there. But the whole inside of the front of the fuselage, inside the cockpit, was red with my blood. I couldn't see any feet on the pedals. My legs weren't there. I didn't know where they were. The nerves were damaged in my legs and I couldn't move them and, of course, I wasn't doing anything to the pedals. I didn't know what was going on with my legs.

Bell UH-1C Iroquois (Huey) like Bob Kelley's aircraft, in Vietnam.

*Norman Taylor*

As we were going in, Benton turned the throttle off totally about twenty feet in the air and we pancaked in. I was vaguely aware that we had gone in and that another helicopter was touching down beside us to try to help out. Mainly, I realized the aircraft crew chief was getting out the morphine and giving me a shot.

The other helicopter crewmembers ran over to our helicopter and pulled me out while others secured radios and stuff like that. They hauled me to a MASH hospital in the city of Tay Ninh. The military had one there. It was just like the TV show, a MASH hospital. My memories of getting there are a little muddled, but I distinctly remember my arrival.

## Wounded Helo Pilot

I was the very first patient in that day. They were given a big alert that a horrendous battle was on and they needed to be prepared for it. So when I got in there, another circumstance of fate took place.

I had been blown up by a very big booby trap but suddenly I found my life influenced by a newspaper article about a very small booby trap of a very different kind. The *Stars & Stripes* newspaper, three days prior to my action, showed doctors trying to extract a grenade from the inside of a Vietnamese person, up in the northern part of South Vietnam. They had bunkers around the person and were working on the extraction. When I was brought into the hospital into triage, they looked at me and thought about that newspaper story.

What had happened was, the entire wiring harness from the aircraft and shrapnel came in and got my legs and my groin. So I was bleeding and I had all of these wires hanging out of me. So the doctor took one look and said, "Oh, my God. He may have a grenade inside him. Put him aside for now."

They had their minds made up. They were not going to be blown up by me.

So they put me inside for a while. I can't tell you for how long. This happened at about ten in the morning. I was taken to another room, given another shot of morphine, and wrapped up to stem the bleeding and left there. It had to be a long time because they were bringing other people in there and leaving them there. I came in and out of consciousness and didn't know what was happening.

So here I am in, apparently now in some building next to the hospital, but not getting treated because they think I'm going to blow them up. Finally, as it was starting to get dark, they came looking for me. They were looking throughout this area because, little did I know, they had put me in their mortuary! All the people they brought in there were not seeing the light of day.

I guess they got over their fear that I was some kind of a limping bomb. They took me out of the mortuary and brought me back into the hospital. They worked on me. They decided they couldn't do anything for me. There was a six-inch-in-diameter hole in my thigh that they didn't have the capability of closing. So that was the end of my stay at the MASH, and from there, they took me to a hospital in Vung Tau.

This was a surgical hospital. I had a doctor who was about a week from leaving. He looked me over and said, "It's tough enough to graft here because of the climate, so I'm going to just try to close it—squeeze it closed, sew it up. After four days, we'll take one stitch out at a time and let it open back up and reheal, because that's the best way to do it."

That part was okay, but the problem was, my perennial and sciatic nerves were damaged. Both of them were damaged. I had no feeling from this part of my leg all the way down. It was totally numb. When your foot's asleep, you favor it because it doesn't support itself and that's what I wanted to do. I had no feeling there and it was like my foot was asleep.

They worked on me at Vung Tau. I was there about two-and-a-half weeks. One of my good friends from flight school, Michael Millett, came to see me. He was in the unit across the street. He saw me and wrote a letter to my wife Pam.

At Vung Tau, they needed to clear beds because the battle at Hamburger Hill was going on and they were taking 500 wounded casualties a day. The hospitals needed to treat these people. So I was shipped to Japan, to the old Ishini Barracks. I couldn't tell you what city that was in.

## Trying to Recover

I was there. But even in Japan, they didn't have what was needed. They said, with this type of nerve damage, they couldn't do anything for me. They needed the beds, too, because of the influx from Vietnam. So they moved me to Walter Reed Army Hospital in Washington, D.C., in early May. My wounds were considered minimal compared to others. Some were double amputees, quadriplegics. One was Max Cleland, later a senator from Georgia who had multiple wounds.

I was movable. If I held on to something, I could hobble. I trained myself to walk on a numb foot. I learned how to do that. But the problem was, I had no control of my ankles or toes or anything on my left leg.

So I would get treatment twice a day. I had occupational therapy. I pedaled a bike to try to make feeling in the foot come back.

In August 1967, they said, "We can do no more for you. You're walking with a cane now. So we're going to get you back on limited duty." They indicated that if I wanted to apply for medical retirement, I could. When I was there about a month, they had said they didn't think I would walk again because I didn't have control.

I did not elect to do that. I went back to Fort Rucker. They offered me any assignment in the world. I had a friend in the assignments office. He was very frank. He said, "I'll send you anywhere you want, but here's the bottom line. Whether you go to Europe or you go anywhere else, within nine months you'll be back in Vietnam."

I wanted an assignment in Germany. He explained the options to me. "I can send you to Germany, but all I can guarantee you is nine months there. After that, we're sending you back to Vietnam." A normal tour in Germany is three years. I said, "Where can I go for the longest?" I was thinking I needed more time to recover from being wounded.

I said, "Well, wait a minute. I can't walk. I'm using crutches and a cane." He said, "We have desk jobs for pilots, too. We need people to run the operations. We are short." I said, "Where can I go so I can stay the longest?" He said, "Fort Rucker."

I went to my old office. They were glad to see me. They grabbed me up in a minute. They gave me a two-year assignment. This was middle to late 1967. I was promoted to major in August 1968.

At Rucker, I was an instructor in meteorology and rotary wing aerodynamics. They taught me how to do that in about six weeks. I stayed there until 1969. They wanted to send me back to Vietnam then because my two years were up, but they realized I had not been to an advanced course. So I went to Fort Sill, Oklahoma, for a year and then went back to Vietnam after that—after attending advanced artillery school at Sill.

## Second Vietnam Tour

I went back for a second tour. They assigned me as a logistician with the 12th Aviation Group for five months beginning in August 1970. After that, they selected me to command the 128th Assault Helicopter Company, the "Tomahawks." That unit was assigned at Phu Loi, Vietnam, which was twenty-five miles northwest of Saigon. I took command in January 1971. We had both slicks and gunships. We had UH-1C gunship models, just as on my first tour, but the UH-1D transport Huey from my first tour had been replaced by the UH-1H, which was a lot more powerful. We didn't have Cobra gunships at that time. The United States was in a drawdown mode and there were only so many available. The Cobras were being given to the First Cavalry Division. They were at Anh Khe and Khe Sanh. They were the ones who fought the real heavy-duty battles.

Huey helicopter pilot Bob Kelley at the Vietnam Veterans Memorial, better known simply as the Wall, in Washington, D.C.

*Sean Kelley*

The UH-1C gunship was modeled after the old B-model Huey, which was a smaller model. The Charlie model gunship had a bigger engine and a bigger blade structure than the B. This gave it a little more lift and a little more speed. The reason they wanted Cobras was, the Charlie model Huey could not keep up with the UH-1H helicopters. So they had to go ahead and join in near the LZ. Or, they generally had two gunships closer to the landing zone and two coming along with the transports. The UH-1C couldn't carry a lot of weight. Eventually they went to a UH-1M model, but I did not see any of those. In the UH-1C, you had two pilots and two gunners, one on each side. That was the crew on the slick models as well. One person was always a gunner, someone who was really good with the weaponry. The other guy was the crew chief, who was the master of that helicopter. He would take along all the maintenance and report forms and work on it in the field.

Your armament on these aircraft: You always had the 7.62-mm machine gun on the door on either side. And you had either a 40-mm grenade launcher on the front or rocket pods on the side. The rocket pods held 2.75-inch rockets. You couldn't carry both the grenade launcher and the rockets. The pilot operated the rockets and the grenade launcher. In the summer months, you couldn't carry a full load of rockets unless you reduced your fuel load, because the UH-1C didn't perform as well in heat and humidity. They had been working for years to improve the hot-weather performance in the Huey, which was why they had the UH-1H model, though it was never used as a gunship. The earlier Huey was supposed to be able to carry ten people but in the heat and humidity, you were down to maybe seven Vietnamese and they were very light people.

One of the typical missions flown by Tomahawks helicopter crews was known by the term "Firefly." The Firefly mission was a night mission that was assigned to the helicopter units in Vietnam. These missions would have a helicopter with a very large, bright light on it and two gunships, and they would fly the perimeter and maybe outwards a mile or two of the fire bases or base camps or airfields to determine if there was any enemy activity out there go out and turn on the lights. These were flown every night. You probably had throughout Vietnam several dozen of them flying every night. I flew them once a week.

I left in August 1971 to go home. I returned to the United States from my second tour in Vietnam and went to the University of Southern California to finish a master's degree. After that, I went to Fort Sill and was assigned to the post computer center until August 1973. I went to command and general staff college at Fort Leavenworth, Kansas. Then, I went to our Pacific Command staff, known as CINCPAC, in Hawaii. I was a plans officer for Thailand and the Philippines. After three years there, I went to Fort Belvoir, Virginia, for further work with computer systems development.

I retired from the Army in 1983. Today, I work for a company called SAIC and I'm on a detail to the Central Intelligence Agency.

# Bell UH-1C Iroquois (Huey)

Bob Kelley flew both the UH-1C gunship and the UH-1D transport helicopter. The technical description applies to the UH-1C model. The "C model" as described here is significantly smaller than the UH-1D. After arriving in Vietnam, some UH-1B/C Hueys received newer engines, but most were delivered with the underpowered T53-L-11.

# Bell UH-1C Iroquois (Huey Gunship)

**Type:** Four-place military utility/transport, general purpose helicopter

**Powerplant:** One 1,100-shp (905-kW) Avco Lycoming T53-L-11 turboshaft engine driving two-bladed 44-ft 0 in (13.41-m) main rotor

**Performance:** Maximum speed 127 mph (204 km/h); cruising speed, 124 mph (200 km/h); hovering ceiling in ground effect 16,800 ft (5120 m); service ceiling 16,700 ft (5090 m); rate of climb at sea level, 2,350 ft (715 m) per min; range with maximum fuel at sea level, 318 miles (511 km)

**Weights:** Empty, 4,519 lb (2050 kg); normal takeoff weight, 8,500 lb (3856 kg); maximum takeoff weight, 9,500 lb (4309 kg); normal fuel capacity 330 U.S. gallons (1250 liters)

**Dimensions:** Main rotor diameter 44 ft 0 in (13.41 m); length overall, rotors turning 53 ft (16.15 m); fuselage length, 42 ft 7 in (12.98 m); height, tail rotor turning 12 ft 8.5 in (3.87 m); tail rotor diameter 8 ft 6 in (2.59 m); main rotor disc area 1,520 sq ft (141.02 sq m)

**Armament:** M-5 armament subsystem, consisting of a nose-mounted M-75 automatic grenade launcher with 315 rounds and/or two to four packages of 2.75-in. (70-mm) folding fin aircraft rockets; two door-mounted M-60 7.62-mm machine guns

**Payload:** Twelve to sixteen armed troops or four hospital litters

**Crew:** Two pilots plus two

**First flight:** August 16, 1961 (YUH-1D)

# Chapter 13

## DUSTOFF Mission in a Hot Zone (II)

### What Happened

Mike Novosel, Jr., is in many ways a look-alike for his dad but with differences under the skin. Both are among the most accomplished helicopter pilots in the world. Both have logged tens of thousands of flight hours. Both are credited with thousands of combat rescues. But while Mike's dad served two tours of duty in Vietnam and was given the nation's highest award for valor, Mike fought a similar war during his one tour, under similar circumstances—and, like so many from that era, with little recognition.

**MIKE NOVOSEL, Jr.** It was important to me to be very good at the controls of the Huey. I had the best inspiration a young pilot could have—my dad—and I had the ability to fly the aircraft with considerable skill. I flew 1,550 missions. That's a thousand hours of combat. I evacuated 2,500 people. I got shot down several times. I almost got blown up three or four times. And I didn't even get a green weenie, which is what they call the Army Commendation Medal. I didn't get diddly jack shit.

When I went into the Army in 1968, I was following in the footsteps

**CWO4 Michael J. Novosel**
**October 2, 1969**
**Bell UH-1H Huey**
**DUSTOFF 88**
**82nd Medical Detachment (Helicopter Ambulance)**
**Binh Thuy, South Vietnam**

Mike Novosel wearing the Medal of Honor presented to him by President Richard M. Nixon for an action during Novosel's second combat tour in Vietnam.

*U. S. Army*

of my father. He was still on active duty then, a career soldier and pilot who had already completed a Vietnam tour and was going back for another. He knew I had been fascinated with flying since I was a little kid, and he didn't object.

Yes, I know the military is a tradition in a lot of families. What is different about our father-son relationship is that we two Novosels—both named Michael, both called Mike—were in combat in the same outfit at the same time.

There are many examples in history of fathers and sons who fought. Theodore Roosevelt was awarded the Medal of Honor for his charge up San Juan Hill in 1898. His son Ted Roosevelt received the same award for action on the Normandy beachhead in 1944. But Dad and I don't know of another example where a father and son were in combat together. The Army tells us it cannot find an example.

America didn't require us to do this. In fact, ever since the loss of the Sullivans—the five brothers who died aboard the same warship in the Pacific in World War II—there has been this myth that there's a rule against close relatives serving together, or even serving at the same time. The movie *Saving Private Ryan* was loosely based on a situation involving brothers being exposed to enemy action at the same time. Tra-

Michael J. Novosel, Jr. (left), and his father, Medal of Honor recipient Michael J. Novosel, served together in the 82nd Medical Detachment in Vietnam beginning in January 1970.

*U. S. Army*

ditionally, the military discourages exposing members of the same family, but there is absolutely no regulation against it.

So we ended up together, not at the behest of the Army or the nation but on our own initiative, as a father and son team in the 82nd Medical Detachment in South Vietnam in 1970. We wanted to serve, and fate handed us an opportunity to serve together.

I started out as an Army brat around my dad. We lived at Hunter Army Airfield, Georgia, after we moved to Savannah during my senior year in high school. They had opened the airfield in 1967. I got a job working at the officers' club annex out by the flight line. Everybody I hung around with was a young Army aviator, many just back from Vietnam. I was around those guys all the time.

On the day before my nineteenth birthday in November 1968, I traveled to Fort Jackson, South Carolina. On my birthday, I took the examination to become a warrant officer candidate. I did real well because I understood a lot about helicopters and flying.

I went to Fort Walters, Texas, a familiar place to my family, and then to Hunter Army Airfield—even more familiar—for advanced flight training, although most people went to Fort Rucker. I trained in the two-seat TH-55A "Mattel Messerschmitt" at Walters and in the UH-1A, B, D, and H versions of the Huey at Hunter. I became a warrant officer and an Army aviator on December 15, 1969.

I knew exactly where I was going. You go to flight school. You go to Vietnam.

Following in his father's footsteps, Michael J. Novosel, Jr., is seen in Army basic training in 1968 and in helicopter training at Fort Wolters, Texas, in 1969.

*Courtesy Mike Novosel, Jr.*

In late 1969, I completed pilot training. My father was beginning a second combat tour in Vietnam.

**MICHAEL NOVOSEL** Just before Mike signed up for the warrant officer program, I was completing my plans to get out. In 1968, I was scheduled to be discharged and to return to a civilian job as pilot with Southern Airways. That might have given me an opportunity to do more instructing, which has always been my main interest—mentoring others in helicopter flying.

Unfortunately, the physical examination prior to leaving the service discovered that I had glaucoma. That meant I would never be able to fly for the airlines again. However, the Army was at the point of its greatest need for helicopter pilots in its entire history. I was able to obtain a waiver to continue flying with the Army. I was now one of the oldest helicopter pilots on duty. I was also one of the most experienced. I could make the Huey do things that weren't in the pilot's manual.

So the Army and I sorted out our relationship with each other. And as if it were the most natural thing in the world, I returned for a second tour of combat duty in Vietnam.

The job was familiar. The mission was the same. But by then we had another generation of soldiers in Vietnam, so in some ways it was like starting all over again. I was made the head of medical evacuation operations for the detachment, and quickly made it clear to the new guys that I had done this before.

Other soldiers found me somewhat unconventional in my approach to Huey flying. Having begun in fixed-wing aircraft, where the pilot in command flies in the left seat, I usually flew left seat as a Huey commander. This was not unusual in the Army in Vietnam—in the Ia Drang battles (Chapters Six and Eight), the aircraft commander sat on the left—but soldiers also found that I had my own opinion of the rulebook. Bred to rely on checklists, manuals, and procedures, I became well known in the outfit for believing

## Who's Who

Michael J. Novosel, UH-1 Huey helicopter pilot

Michael J. Novosel, Jr., Mike's son and fellow UH-1 pilot

Tyrone Chamberlain, UH-1 copilot

Specialist Four Herbert Heinold, crew member

Specialist Four Joe Horvath, crew member

that it was more important to think than to read, and for routinely flying by the seat of my pants, relying on feel, touch, sound, and instinct. With my instructing experience, I knew more about the rulebook than almost everybody else and I knew which parts of it to reject. I believed the Army's helicopter-training syllabus devoted too much attention to procedures to follow in the event of a systems failure, and not enough to instinctual flying based on the assumption that equipment would work the way it was supposed to. I had supreme confidence that the American taxpayer had given me a helicopter, an engine, and a system that would work when it needed to. The Huey, the T-53 engine, and the organization behind us proved me right on that, every time.

On October 2, 1969—already in combat for nearly eight hours that day—I was directed to make a pickup along the Cambodian border, near a geographic landmark called the Parrot's Beak.

By most standards, it was a job somebody else should have done. My crew—consisting of copilot Tyrone Chamberlain, crew chief Herbert Heinold, and medic Joe Horvath—had been flying missions all day. A unit of South Vietnamese troops was surrounded and outgunned in a field of high elephant grass. They were being chewed up. They were on the verge of being overwhelmed. Communications were poor. An attempt to support them by F-100 Super Sabre fighter-bombers apparently had not been much help. There was an O-1 Bird Dog forward air controller (FAC), callsign SWAMP FOX 15, circling over the scene at

just a little over treetop level, taking fire and trying to find a way to help the friendly troops. The F-100 and O-1 pilots were doing their best to lay ordnance down to help the South Vietnamese, who were on the verge of being overrun, but those guys had a rulebook attitude toward procedures and they were obviously having communications problems. The battle had been under way for several hours before anyone even called my detachment for help, and then the communications were a little garbled.

This was one situation where the good guys were in a real fix. He had a little difficulty connecting with me on the radio, but when he came on he said essentially that the situation was hopeless.

In my biography, *Dustoff: The Memoir of an Army Aviator,* published by Presidio Press in 1999, I described the conversations we had. Here's how I described it:

> We had worked hard during the last three missions, which were viciously contested by the Viet Cong. We were returning from our latest extraction and all was quiet. We thought we might have a respite from additional missions. But when we were within a few minutes of Binh Thuy, the RTO called, "DUSTOFF 88, I have a mission for you. Are you ready to copy? Over?"
>
> "Aw, shit, what have you got for us now?" I copied the transmission and checked the time. It was just after 1600. After decoding the mes-

sage, I plotted the coordinates of the pickup site. "Damn, that's a good forty minutes flying time from our position," I exclaimed. "Chamberlain, how long have we been flying today?"

He checked the aircraft logbook. "According to our entries, we've logged seven hours up to now."

"Well, we've got what looks like another long mission before we're through for the day. We're headed next to the Parrot's Beak. It'll take us a minimum of half an hour just to get there."

One point I may not have made well enough in the book is this: Although I was in charge, there was no hesitation on the part of my crew members. When we progressed toward the battle scene, they overheard radio traffic between me, using the callsign DUSTOFF 88, and the forward air controller, SWAMP FOX 15, as well as a ground controller known as CONCERT BRAVO. They knew we were going into a scene of noise and confusion, where communications were flawed, visibility was poor, and the Viet Cong might soon be mixed in among the South Vietnamese we wanted to help.

## Taking Fire in the Hot Zone

I made a high-angle insertion into the "hot" landing zone. Automatic weapons fire swirled around our Huey. In the middle of this firestorm, CONCERT BRAVO was telling me about a lone friendly soldier who had gotten separated from the main force and was hidden in the elephant grass. I made three attempts to locate and rescue the man, taking hits each time. Finally, Heinold and Horvath spotted this man. I watched our air speed dropping as I tried to maneuver and get closer to the friendly soldier while making us hard to hit. My copilot, Chamberlain, said we were taking fire from all directions and we could feel rounds striking our Huey. There was some confusion at the worst possible moment as the friendly soldier tried to decide between hiding safely beneath the high grass and appearing in the open to be rescued by us. It didn't help that our rotor wash was beating down on the grass, making it harder to keep him in sight. Also, visibility was declining because daylight was waning. The Viet Cong had us in their crosshairs now and

A Vietnam DUSTOFF, or medical evacuation, mission.

*U. S. Army*

were pouring it into us. I managed to get us as close to the friendly soldier as we dared and, after further confusion, Heinold and Horvath hauled him aboard. But then more South Vietnamese troops materialized amid the swaying grass.

This was the start of a series of protracted "in and out" visits to the hot landing zone as we sought wounded South Vietnamese troops who seemed to be scattered all over the difficult terrain. I had to pause several times to climb above the reach of Viet Cong weapons fire because it was simply too intense to stay there. Still, to get those guys out we had to expose ourselves, so we kept returning, descending again, and plucking friendly troops to safety. As daylight began to wane and enemy fire grew more furious, I filled up our Huey with ten South Vietnamese soldiers who had no other way out of their trap.

We lifted out of there without mortal damage to our Huey. I pointed our Huey toward a Special Forces camp at Moc Hoa, the nearest friendly place where we could get these wounded men some help—one of them was gut shot, another was trembling violently, and there was a lot of blood on the floor—to say nothing of our own need for fuel. Now we were seriously running out of daylight, we had half a dozen potential write-ups on our Huey, and we were low on gas. My copilot Chamberlain was handling himself well but was still a rulebook kind of guy in an environment where many of the rules no longer applied. Of course, the Viet Cong were still on the verge of overrunning the South Vietnamese and it didn't matter to the VC that night was coming.

When we were overhead at Moc Hoa, I eased her down. We came to a halt on the skids, rotors turning, and I ordered Horvath to find us some fuel while Heinold unloaded the wounded. We needed half a tank if we were going to do the unthinkable—head straight back toward that battle.

Someone probably suggested that it was time for us to stand down but there wasn't any real discussion. When Horvath gave me the sign that he had finished refueling, we all knew what would happen next. Chamberlain pointed out that it was now mid-evening and we had eaten nothing since before sunrise, but he was only making conversation. Exhausted but operating on adrenaline, I looked at my crew and they looked at me. Nobody needed to say anything. I took off and pointed our Huey back toward the scene of the battle.

Now we had enough fuel but almost no daylight, and no one seemed to have set up any fire support for the embattled South Vietnamese troops. CONCERT BRAVO and SWAMP FOX 15 both sounded forlorn when they told me that there was no supporting artillery or mortar fire for the friendlies, no sign of the Air Force—nothing. I asked the men on the ground to fire an occasional M-79 grenade to keep the Viet Cong distracted.

We went in again, came under fire again, and picked up more friendly troops. Then, suddenly, relief appeared. SWAMP FOX 15 told me that a pair of F-100 Super Sabres was coming in to make life interesting for the VC. Then—in a reversal that had me fuming—we were told they couldn't attack until we got out of the way. This had me really pissed. It was the rulebooks again. Somewhere it was written that friendly aircraft had to be a certain distance away, and the F-100 pilots had no flexibility.

Was I the only pilot in Vietnam who knew that sometimes you could use maturity and knowledge to break the rules? I followed instructions and backed off as the F-100s, working with a minimal knowledge of the enemy's location, splattered napalm across the area. This opened the way for me to take us back in, and to pick up some wounded soldiers who were eager to get out of there. Once again, Viet Cong gunfire thunked into our Huey. The F-100 air strike apparently hadn't touched the enemy.

## Cobras to the Rescue

I took us out of range of enemy gunfire, waited for what seemed the right moment, and took us back in. Heinold and Horvath picked up several wounded men and hauled them aboard. They were badly wounded. One man's intestines were coming out. Another had lost a hand. Another had been shot through the mouth.

Now a pair Army AH-1G Cobra gunships showed up. One of them separated from the other, rolled in, and began searching after the Viet Cong with its guns winking. Where had they been until now? I'm not sure but now it seemed everybody in the world was calling DUSTOFF 88 on the radio. We had now picked up nine more friendlies. But now a tenth survivor stood up in plain view.

When you're in the middle of a hectic situation, you maintain awareness of many things at once. First, there was the simple fact that this was anything but a rulebook extraction: We had inadequate communication, little guidance, and no fallback plan if anything went wrong. Second, there was now a friendly soldier who'd just emerged from the high grass and was standing in the open and waving an item of clothing at us. He could be an enemy decoy, maybe, but we were sure he was not, and our job was to rescue people, rulebook or no rulebook. Third, there was the simple fact that the Viet Cong were in small units, scattered around the friendlies, perhaps even mingled among them. I was processing all this information, knowing our helicopter was damaged but not knowing how badly. I was determined to finish this day alive, somehow. But I was also going to do the job we'd come here to do.

On the intercom, I told my crew that I was going to back our Huey into the spot where the guy was waving at us. By approaching him backwards, I would be placing our tail, tail boom, and lower fuselage between the Viet Cong guns and my crew members and passengers. A backward-moving hover in a helicopter is easy to perform if you're in a big, open space but it becomes difficult down low. The pilot has little visibility to the side and rear. I briefed Horvath and Heinold that they would have to grab the guy we wanted to rescue quickly. I told Chamberlain that we would both grip the controls while we were backing in. If one of us were hit or killed, the other would control the Huey.

There was a patter of rounds hitting us again, and as we went into this maneuver, I had the Huey somewhat tail-up. An observer would have thought it was gliding backwards and might have wondered how that was possible but, aerodynamically, it was a simple move. Never mind that Chamberlain was saying we were taking fire from around the clock. Never mind that the rudder pedals jerked when bullets hit us.

Even while flying steel whipped past the Huey—there was "no way the helicopter could survive a torrent of gunfire like that," one of our wounded said later—the wounded man on the ground initially balked at being rescued. Maybe the sight of a UH-1H backing up in his direction confused the hell out of him. I wondered if the man thought it would be safer to cower in the tall elephant grass because he abruptly stopped waving his shirt at us. I thought, "He's probably scared to death being underneath a huge machine that's beating the air and thrashing the grass all around him." Heinold or Horvath said something over the intercom about how they understood that they would have only seconds to grab the guy. I have always been impressed with how my crew maintained its calm and did almost everything exactly right.

Another factor, as I contemplated our getaway: We were very close to the Cambodian border—forbidden territory. If we succeeded in getting out of here, we were going to have to watch our navigation.

Just when the intercom boomed with the magic words I wanted to hear—Horvath, hauling our wounded man aboard—a Viet Cong soldier stood erect about thirty feet in front of our helicopter. He just popped right up out of the grass. At that instant, Horvath lost his grip on the wounded man, but the man became entangled with our skid, and Horvath was able to grab him again and haul him in.

We had armor around our side and back at the pilots' stations in the Huey, but we were protected from the front only by flak vests. That Viet Cong remained in the standing position and emptied the full clip of his AK-47 automatic rifle straight at me. There was no way he could miss at this range and he didn't. At least three AK-47 rounds glanced off my flak jacket and clattered to the floorboards. In its backward, tail-high attitude, the helicopter went out of control momentarily. Unaware how seriously I was hit, I beckoned to Chamberlain to get us the hell out of there. Only much later would I learn that my bullet wounds were superficial, although one round had done significant harm to my legs.

Still taking fire from all directions, we got the hell out of there. As darkness descended, Chamberlain mistakenly took us over Cambodia where the North Vietnamese controlled the terrain, and rounds came shooting up at us. We got out of there, too.

I recommended the members of my crew for the Silver Star. I had no idea there was also a recommendation in the works that involved me. I completed my second tour in Vietnam—a part of it spent serving jointly with my son, Mike Jr.—and went on to complete my Army career. One of my last assignments was flying fixed-wing airplanes for the Army's Golden Knights parachute team. They were some of the finest soldiers I've ever known. It was an honor to help the Army tell its story through them. It was also a hell of a lot of fun.

In his account (below), my son Mike describes how I was invited to the White House in June 1971 with my wife Ethel and other family members.

As a master Army aviator and an Air Force command pilot, I have been told that I'm the only holder of the top pilot ratings of both service branches. When I retired in 1985—still flying, with a waiver for my glaucoma—they told me I was the last active duty aviator on flight status who had flown combat missions in World War II. I had been on military flight status for forty-two years, logging 12,400 hours of flight time, including 2,038 flight hours in combat. In two Vietnam tours, I was credited with rescuing 5,589 wounded soldiers. Today, I live in Enterprise, Alabama, which is not far from the home of Army aviation at Fort Rucker.

**MIKE NOVOSEL, JR.** While I was in flight school, my dad had begun his second tour in Vietnam and had flown that famous mission on October 2, 1969. Mom visited me in training and sent photos of me to Dad and everybody else she could think of. He told his fellow soldiers about my progress. He was very proud.

I got to Vietnam on January 6, 1970. I flew DUSTOFF the whole time. I volunteered for DUSTOFF. In Saigon, we had a conversation

Following in his father's footsteps, Michael J. Novosel, Jr. is seen in Army basic training in 1968 and in helicopter training at Fort Wolters, Texas, in 1969.

*Courtesy Mike Novosel, Jr.*

about where I would be assigned and I asked to go to my Dad's DUSTOFF outfit, the 82nd Medical Detachment. They called my Dad and asked him what he thought about that.

We had a deal between the two of us: He didn't treat me any different than anyone else. We flew together in Vietnam. He gave me my in-country check ride. We were in a detachment with twelve pilots. We were supposed to have fourteen. My dad assigned me to Rexford Smith, who was one of the finest aircraft commanders I ever saw—apart from my Dad, of course. We were flying the UH-1H, which was the Army's ultimate single-engine Huey. Unlike the other service branches, the Army never purchased a twin-engine version.

Dad welcomed me into the unit but made no offer to let me share his hooch, the only one at Binh Thuy with air conditioning. He treated me like he treated every other pilot in the outfit. "I wasn't overly concerned about the risk Mike was taking," he said later, and I wasn't too worried about him, either, although he was now twice the age of your typical Army pilot.

Throughout my tour of duty in the combat zone, I trusted the techniques my father taught would keep me alive, like flipping the tail of the aircraft into the direction of fire so bullets would have to travel through the body of the aircraft before entering the crew compartment.

When we actually flew together, I didn't doubt for a second that the outcome would be good. I also had a lot of faith in Smith and the other aircraft commanders he put me with because they had all "been there and done that."

In March 1970, my UH-1H was hit by gunfire and we had to put it down. Dad heard the "Mayday" call from fifteen minutes away. With assurance from my aircraft commander that our crew had survived the crash and found shelter, Dad completed his own mission and then flew to our aid.

As I told the Army's magazine, *Soldiers,* when they asked me for an interview many years later, I returned the favor seven days later when my Dad was shot down. *Soldiers* told its readers that I was just nineteen at the time. Actually, I was a lot more mature than that. I was twenty. And saving each other was no big deal. Saving lives was what we did.

Awards? Like I said, who had time to write the awards? All you had time to do was sleep. I got thirty-seven Air Medals but those are just for flying hours. I understand a crew chief named Bill Weber (Chapter Seven) told you, "Once a month, they gave me an air medal and a malaria pill." That's about the way it worked.

The aviators and crew members of the 82nd Medical Detachment thought about what we did a lot—saving lives is a unique opportunity and an honor—but we didn't think much about recognition. The truth is, we were too damned fatigued most of the time. I remember Dad had to give up sleep in order to write up his crew members for recognition. They got what they deserved. Dad did not know, until a few days before it happened, that he was going to receive the greatest recognition of all.

On June 15, 1971, Dad was invited along with members of our family to the White House, where President Richard M. Nixon awarded him the Medal of Honor for that October 2, 1969, mission. The official citation said he'd flown his Huey into a hail of enemy fire to save twenty-nine soldiers. The actual number may have been higher, and there's no question some of those men would have died if that UH-1H hadn't shown up.

We were deeply touched by the ceremony. I was impressed that President Nixon knew that I, too, had flown in Vietnam. The president asked about me, and that was when I was able to shake his hand. Later, First Lady Pat Nixon was our host for refreshments. There were also five other Americans who received the Medal of Honor that day.

By the day of the ceremony, I, too, had completed my combat tour of duty in Vietnam. It never occurred to me to get out. I loved flying

Army helicopters. I continued my career in the Army and became an instructor pilot in the UH-1H Huey. I stayed with the Huey all the way to my retirement. The Army never purchased a twin-engine version, but I wouldn't buy one of those model 412 helicopters because they have a low-inertia rotor system. That means, when you lose power, the rotor rpm are more difficult to maintain.

In civilian life, I have checked out in several helicopter models and flown them commercially. Currently, I fly the Bell 407, which is like a stretched OH-58 with a larger engine than the OH-58D. You can fill it up with people and fill it up with gas and go.

Until early 2004, when not flying, I was running the Flight Line Cafe just outside Eglin Air Force Base near my home in Fort Walton Beach, Florida. The walls of the restaurant pay tribute to Dad and to aviation history with models, photographs, and artifacts. My wife Margaret and I enjoyed having this small business, but with me still flying helicopters, it turned out to be a little too much for us to handle. I wanted to continue flying, so we sold the business.

Our combat days are over, but Dad and I reminisce about a past that makes us comrades as well as kin. We live only a few miles from each other and spend a lot of time together talking, of course, about the present and the future but also remembering the past. When two guys from Vietnam get together, they call it a reunion. But Dad and I have that every day. My father is an old friend from the war and an old combat buddy. How many fathers and sons share that?

# Chapter 14

# Cobra in the Crosshairs

## What Happened

A new kind of helicopter with a new mission joined the United States Army in Vietnam on September 4, 1967.

On that day, Maj. Gen. (later Lt. Gen.) George P. Seneff, Jr., and Chief Warrant Officer J. D. Thomson flew into an impromptu battle near Can Tho, South Vietnam, and logged the first combat for the Bell AH-1G Cobra (also called the HueyCobra), the Army's first helicopter to be designed from the start as an air-to-ground gunship.

In that action, Seneff shot up a Viet Cong sampan.

In Vietnam, the Cobra received high marks for escorting troop-carrying helicopters and for carrying out close-fire support missions.

Soldiers warmed to the AH-1G. "It didn't happen to me immediately," said former Chief Warrant Officer Three Kenneth Whitley, fifty-eight, of Cleveland, Ohio—who grew up in rural Texas. "The first time I walked out on the flight line and climbed into one, I thought it was more like a jet fighter than the helicopters I'd flown in flight training. I thought, 'Oh, my God, this country boy is in over his head.'"

Asked if there was anything wrong with the high-speed Cobra, Whitley remembered that it was difficult to control in a high-speed at-

CWO4 Ken Whitley
Bell AH-1G Cobra (HueyCobra)
67-15458
TIGER 34
October 14, 1969
D Company, "Smiling Tigers,"
   229th Helicopter Assault
   Battalion, First Cavalry
   Division
Dau Tieng, South Vietnam

Warrant Officer Kenneth Whitley of D Co., 229th Aviation Battalion, 1st Cavalry Division poses in Vietnam in 1969 with his two-man AH-1G Cobra gunship helicopter. In the Cobra, the pilot in command sits in the rear seat. The unit's "Smiling Tigers" insignia is located just forward of Whitley's right foot.

*Kenneth Whitley*

---

tack. "The Cobra needed air brakes," Whitley said. "When you got into a dive, it started gaining speed so rapidly that you wanted more time to properly aim and shoot."

On many missions, the Cobra worked as part of a two-ship team along with a scout helicopter, the Hughes OH-6A Cayuse, also called the Loach (from the Army's term LOH, for "light observation helicopter"). The two very different helicopter types—Cobra and Loach—"made a perfect team," said retired CWO4 Rod Barber, sixty-two, of Seattle, Washington, who flew both. "You could see real well out of the Loach but you didn't have the weaponry. The Cobra has all the guns and rockets."

In later years, pilots came to refer to the Cobra as the "Snake." The Loach, in shorthand, is often simply the "Scout." To Ken Whitley, the Cobra was the machine that almost killed him. The Loach was the machine that saved his life.

**KEN WHITLEY** An enlisted man came into my sleeping area and shook me as though he was attempting to awaken the dead. Moving quietly,

The Army's AH-1G Cobra, also called the HueyCobra, had a slender frontal cross-section, just 38 inches, but it was a kind of flying tank. This Cobra, at Phu Cat, South Vietnam, on April 20, 1971, is carrying canisters of 2.75-inch rockets under its stub wings and has a gun and grenade launcher installed in its chin turret.

*Norman Taylor*

as if he were the shadow of the night scurrying about, he arrived moments prior to the sun rising over Dau Tieng's horizon. Dau Tieng was our Cavalry base at the end of a range of hills called the Razorbacks near the Michelin Rubber Plantation.

The walls of my room had been constructed from discarded rocket boxes. We emptied more rocket boxes than our fair share. We were on the northwest directional corridor from Saigon toward Cambodia. None of us could rest easily. The enemy might come to remove us from our roost at any time. It was our task to prevent the North Vietnamese from walking openly into Saigon.

Nailing our rocket-box boards into walls and rooms was our usual pastime around Dau Tieng camp. We had plenty of wood left over after emptying these boxes. We had our own blowtorch, together with assorted gas bottles that we used to burn the walls on their rough surfaces. Each room builder had to burn the wood differently so it wouldn't blend into uniformity. The crewmembers worked hard until they were pleased with their personal sense of charm and decoration inside their own private space. The walls were there to give us a touch of privacy and gave us a sense of stability and ownership over our ever-changing theater of war.

Sunrise in Vietnam gave me the feeling I was nearer to my family and ranch back in Brazos, Texas. It's a poor little town, with about forty people, about fifty miles west of Fort Worth off Interstate twenty near the banks of the Brazos River and the Palo Pinto Creek. It has no post office so its mail goes through the Santo post office. Brazos used to be named Angora after a Spanish goat breed because goats were big business there but the population changed its name to Brazos—after the river.

I pretended that they, back home, could look at their sunset, while I looked at my sunrise, which together could let our eyes from both worlds actually observe the same sun simultaneously. It helped remind me that once upon a time I was born far away and in a distant land, but it seemed such a long time ago. The rest of each day and night, I forgot about my family and thought of two things—staying alive and killing our very capable enemy.

This particular enlisted man sent to awaken me usually lugged along a heavy flashlight that beamed brightly into my sleep-filled mind and eyes. Speaking softly, so as not to awaken the others nearby, he whispered in my ear, "Sir, it's time to get up, you have a flight mission waiting for you at dawn."

I rolled my feet around and out of bed, placing them firmly on the floor. It was a dirty concrete floor and I could feel the grit there under my toes. We in the 1st Cavalry Division had no Vietnamese hooch maids like other American units in South Vietnam. Our division commander, figuring properly for once, had decided all Vietnamese were spies. None could be trusted within our living area unless they were under armed guard. That way they couldn't tell the enemy later where their rockets had hit or how to walk them accurately into our important buildings. The enemy was left guessing whenever they fired any kind of explosive device into our living and working base area.

The enlisted man's voice transformed my sleeping twenty-three-year-old form into a Vietnam gunship helicopter pilot.

## Ready to Fly

Dressing quickly, I put on my odd-colored green, itchy, but much-needed, fire-resistant flight suit. Every day, the suit made me too hot and sweaty under the Vietnamese sun. I would have preferred wearing jungle fatigues because they were so much cooler, but my third platoon leader had caught me wearing them and had gone to my company commander complaining, "One of the men in the third platoon is not following orders, sir. It's that pilot, Whitley. He's flying without proper fire protection."

I pulled on black leather boots and secured them tightly to my feet. Once dressed, I went to our mortar-scarred, hole-infested mess hall to grab a few powdered eggs. Those tasteless eggs matched my miserable life in this hellhole. A slice of fried Spam and a cup of bitter-tasting, carbon-black coffee made up my breakfast tasting event.

An FNG was a "fucking new guy" in 'Nam slang, because all the new guys were dumb in warfare fighting ability. An FNG would be my copilot during today, but he seemed all right. First Lt. Robert Cashon, my copilot, was a map-reading instructor who'd just arrived. Cashon was considered by all here a long timer, which meant he had a full year left to fight, while I was a short timer, with just six more weeks left on my tour.

Cashon was new to the Cobra. Unless one had the proper outlook, meaning a strong attitude toward success, a Cobra was not an easy nut to crack.

There were many differences between UH-1 Huey helicopters and AH-1G Cobra helicopters. The Cobra was tall, skinny, and fast, while the Huey was ponderously slow in comparison and much wider. The Cobra gunship had tandem seating—two seats, one behind the other—while the Huey, by its very name (after baby Huey in the old comic books), had super baby strength, which meant it could carry a much larger load than previous helicopters. The two pilots sat side by side in the Huey and could actually look across at one another, shoulder to shoulder, seeing each other completely. Inside the Cobra, the front seat pilot had a tiny rearview mirror that was used to glance back and see the rear pilot's face and helmet and vice versa.

The crew on the Huey added up to four people, two pilots and a crew chief on one side door as a door gunner and a weapons specialist on the other rear side as the door gunner. The Cobra carried two pilots aboard with no room for anyone else. If we were to try and rescue anyone using the Cobra they had to ride facing backward on the rocket pods that were hanging from the little wings on each side of the ship. In an emergency, passengers could be on the outside of the aircraft, facing aft, but only two men could ride in this manner, one on each stubby side wing.

Cashon's previous experience flying the Huey in 'Nam certainly wouldn't dishonor him in my eyes. At least he'd been in combat. Copilots that hadn't been under enemy fire were harder to keep calm. Their nerves kept getting in the way when the bullets flew too close. Before learning anything else, they had to learn to remain together under extreme circumstances. Only after being baptized by bullets could they learn the Cobra's attacking abilities. A pilot who became overpowered by panic was usually a short-lived pilot. I'd take this second-tour man, any day, over a first-tour FNG.

After forcing a few bites of our early morning breakfast, we went to the TOC (Tactical Operations Center) underground bunker for the day's mission briefing. I'd been flying Cobra helicopters in Vietnam for eleven months, which, when thought about, gave me my daily fix for extra courage. Finally, after all this time, I was actually seeing the glimmering light at the end of hell's tunnel. I could count my combat flying days left almost on my fingers and toes.

Never in my wildest dreams or futuristic fantasies could I have realized that this day was going to become a very memorable day, above all the other days, in my entire life span. This day would furnish me with a flight extraordinaire.

## Cobra Combat Mission

Cashon and I were assigned to a hunter killer mission. "Hunter killer" sounds primitive and evil but it boiled down to the following: The flight on this date would be inside the Song Be area up toward our farthest north, III Corps, operational area. We were lucky enough to be the only Cobra sent up there, from my unit, this day. Cashon and I were taking another small helicopter, a Hughes OH-6A Cayuse LOH, Light Observation Helicopter, pronounced "Loach," piloted by CW4 Rod Barber. Song Be was outside our usual AO (Area of Operations), so I felt uneasy about not knowing the area well.

The weather that day was an obstacle for us folks flying missions toward Song Be. They were calling for low ceilings and poor visibility up there. Bad weather was scattered throughout the high terrain in the region. Weather could make that type of terrain and its protruding hills near impossible to negotiate. Granite cliffs hid within the ground hugging cloud decks and if crashed into, the pilot kissed his "Alpha Hotel" (AH-1G) tail end, farewell.

I expected a long day of fighting the enemy and weather. My ability in handling these two conditions simultaneously would be tested, because when they worked together against me, they could sometimes unglue my emotional hinge. My gut feeling and expectations of bad things to come would not disappoint me. These acts would help explain, in my opinion, during future days, what made me aware of my psychic intuitions.

Cashon and I left our TOC and returned to our individual living areas to pick up our supply of personal equipment and weapons. I always carried the following: a six-shot .38 revolver, a Browning pump twelve-gauge shotgun with flechette darts inside the shotgun shells, plus a bag of thirty shotgun shells, along with an M-16 assault-rifle and ten taped-up clips of assault-rifle ammo and maps and code books. We pilots had learned the clip-taping trick from fighting grunts (infantrymen) who taped their clips together. In a firefight it was possible to extinguish a clip, pull out the one just emptied, flip it over handily and then push in the full one for immediate use.

The length of these assault rifles forced a serious problem upon Cobra pilots whenever we attempted to carry them inside our cockpits. The cockpit was so small, cramped, and filled with flight controls it allowed us to bring only our revolver inside. There was simply no room for long-barreled weapons inside that cockpit. The longer weapons were so unruly there; they got in the way in every way possible. My second-place choice for the weapons was to place them inside the ammo bay located down below. They could be stowed and locked away there below our cockpit.

If we went down, way out there in enemy country, my peers and I had to hurry outside and arm ourselves. This was of course after being shot down or mechanically grounded for some reason. That was if a pilot could get out of the cockpit successfully by locating the latches, and then open the ammo bay enough to reach inside and extract his weapons and ammo. That was a lot of "ifs."

Our cockpit doors opened on opposite sides, so that no matter which side our aircraft might end up lying on, one of us would be able to exit. So far, during my first combat tour in country, I hadn't been forced to use this option. I'd had some close calls so I always felt those weapons down below were too far away to ensure retrieval. To stand and fight with a six-shot .38 revolver wasn't my idea of an airtight defense.

We Cobra pilots had to try and stay near our downed aircraft whether or not we expected a rescue. A rescuer could find our aircraft much easier than two men fleeing into the jungle canopy. But staying near the crash might force us into having a firefight.

While I was inside my living area that morning I picked up my flight helmet. It was painted black in the upper front with a small white skull and cross bones. It seemed appropriate at the time. I had difficulty, from our ranking officers, in maintaining anything other than an Army-issued olive drab helmet. They didn't want us pilots killing with any kind of individual personality shown. They'd brought us to our units, in the war zone, alone, and they'd sent us away alone, but the brass wanted us to look and act as if we were an anonymous mass of army men in the war.

When we were ready for our day, Cashon and I went out to our "Smiling Tiger," D Company, 229th Helicopter Assault Battalion flight line to locate our assigned Cobra gunship for that day. Our aircraft wasn't the normally scheduled aircraft that I flew often and preferred. My favorite Cobra helicopter "340," with my name written boldly on its skin, was grounded for maintenance. Cashon and I checked our assigned aircraft 67-15458 carefully during preflight inspection. This bird had to take us into harm's way and back home again. I had done this so often, by now, it was just a routine. I felt I'd need a beer after this day was over.

Our Cobra was loaded down heavily with fifty-six warhead rockets measuring 2.75 inches in diameter and weighing seventeen pounds. A minigun with six barrels was located in the nose turret near a large supply of twelve-thousand rounds of 7.62 ammunition. The minigun alone could shoot 4,000 rounds each minute. She also had a grenade launcher located inside the nose turret that fired three hundred rounds of forty-millimeter grenades a minute. Each grenade had a ten-meter killing radius when exploded. The aircraft had 300 of these grenades stored in a large, round cylinder stowed just below my cockpit inside our ammo bay.

## Into the Weather

All seemed well with our aircraft, so we climbed in and cranked up its powerful turbine engine. Shortly after checking all the aircraft's many and varied systems, we flew off to join our Loach. Once that meeting was accomplished in the air, both helicopters headed north toward Song Be. It was a heading that would lead me toward a new experience and a totally new attitude about life itself.

I had difficulty with the weather on the way to Song Be, but low ceilings and drizzling rain wouldn't stop me. No, sir, I said to myself, Song Be must be in trouble if they were asking for help. That was my job: Go where the action was and help American soldiers.

Charlie, our enemy, preferred bad weather days to start combat. They attacked while our airplanes and helicopters couldn't fly to the rescue of American soldiers. Sure enough, in the early morning hours of this rainy day, a unit of ours was hit and men were wounded and bleeding. Medevac was called to get them out of their war zone. Medevac or DUSTOFF call signs were used in Vietnam often. Hospital Huey helicopters with big red and white crosses painted on them would launch to the rescue. Many of these aircraft were unarmed but there was a small number that had M-60 machine guns mounted on each side of their rear cabin doors for defense purposes.

We landed our Cobra at a place called Landing Zone Buttons adja-

This is a postwar view of an AH-1G Cobra identical to the aircraft flown in Vietnam by Ken Whitley.

*M. J. Kasiuba*

cent to the fixed-wing runway at Song Be. There, they were trying to figure out how to support the troops in the nearby battle. I was standing near my Cobra in the drizzling rain, trying hard to keep my fighting spirit from getting waterlogged. An operations officer ran up and asked me, "Would you consider covering a medevac helicopter that's going in after the wounded?"

He pointed north and said that all the other Cobra pilots on base had turned down this flight due to bad weather. I always felt that medevac flights were important missions. In my mind, these were the most important flights when compared to other missions flown. If I were out there fighting in rain and muck up to my bloody hips with Charlie I knew I'd want to be brought out quickly if wounded. I'd want to be picked up and taken to the closest hospital. Without that option being available, our fighting men wouldn't fight as well, and who could blame them?

So without knowing the region very well and despite the bad weather, I told the officer without hesitation, "I'll take the mission."

I felt much empathy for the guys on the ground. I still had that Hughes LOH, or Loach, with me, so I walked over to its pilot, Rod Barber, explained my intentions, and asked him, "Would you like to come along on this flight?" He readily agreed.

We took off. We headed north toward where the rendezvous would be made with the medevac. That meeting never took place. I heard later the medevac had completed its mission successfully without me.

In the meantime, the weather was worsening as we flew north. The rolling hills seemed to become part of the walls of wallowing clouds. We were forced to fly lower and slower until we finally began flying down inside a tree-filled valley. This valley was where we hoped to locate our medevac. It was while flying low level inside this valley that we were attacked.

## Cobra in the Crosshairs

The Hughes was a stone's throw out in front of me. We were flying at the same altitude of about 300 feet—much too low for my comfort. Suddenly and without warning something caught my eye toward my lower left, very close. I saw a .30-caliber machine gun firing at our aircraft. The enemy weapon was making large muzzle flashes and belching out smoke halos around itself. The rain hadn't dampened Charlie's spirit, it seemed. The machine gun was hiding behind its own smoke, while it threw red-hot projectiles towards us.

We were about 200 feet away from it. I could feel its closeness enormously. The enemy machine gunner could easily shoot us down. They had set up a convoy ambush along a small road. The trap was supposed to be tripped by surface vehicles on the road—not us flyboys. But since we were flying so low and slow we qualified as a target.

The gunner had let the little Hughes helicopter pass him by, hoping he might get the first shot at my gunship and put it out of commission quickly. He probably figured without my Cobra the LOH might flee in panic. His plan worked better than I would have liked. I had fallen into his trap perfectly.

My first response, upon seeing the danger, was to roll my ship hard right and dive. In this action I desired to get near those treetops below us. I knew if I could get low and near enough to those treetops I might easily evade the bullets. As instantly as I had moved my flight controls, the aircraft seemed to blow apart.

A tremendous explosion rocked the helicopter. All at once there was smoke, fire, dirt, and shrapnel about the cockpit. Both doors were blown ajar. Although I was strapped in, the force of the blast bounced my head against the top of the helicopter's cockpit.

**ROD BARBER** Ken doesn't remember this part, but that guy was a full-fledged NVA and he fired at me before he fired at the Cobra.

The weather was really crappy. Ceilings were low. We got a request to go out and assist some troops in contact. I was the Scout bird—the OH-6A Loach pilot—so I was basically the mission commander. On our way out from Song Be, we were doing a no-no, flying along a riverbed, down low. The weather didn't give us much choice.

We came around a bend, I saw an NVA in full uniform. He was not a black-pajama guy, a Viet Cong; he was a fully uniformed North Vietnamese regular soldier. I can still see the round canister on his .30-caliber machine gun.

He shoots at me. He misses me. He makes the mistake of not "leading" my helicopter with his gunsight, but he doesn't make that mistake twice.

About this time, Ken comes around the corner and he shoots out the underside of Ken's aircraft. His rounds went into the ammo bay of Ken's Cobra.

I took care of the guy on the edge of the riverbank. I had a door gunner with an M-60 machine gun on a bungee cord. I also had a minigun with a 4,000-round box. It shoots 4,000 rounds a minute, just like the gun on the Cobra. I wanted to eliminate that threat so future people passing through there would not be endangered, so I took care of that NVA—but that was only after Ken's Cobra was hit real bad.

**KEN WHITLEY** I knew my Cobra had been hit hard . . . very hard. Time slowed down and began to tick by as if what I was seeing around me was similar to some old black-and-white movie jumping from one frame to the other at slow hops and starts. Shock came over me quickly. My mind immediately began arguing with itself.

"I'm dead. I knew this was going to happen someday. I knew I'd never get out of Vietnam alive . . ." And then: "No, I'm immortal. I can live through anything. Haven't I always made it before?" Panic reigned. It was as if part of me had left the scene and a weird kind of peace came over me. "So this is what death feels like."

This may sound all too familiar now, but at that moment, I knew what people meant when they said, "Your life flashes before your eyes." Mine did. I saw my mother and father and women I had loved and women I wished I had loved. Hell, I even saw my second-grade teacher. This was it. Cashon and I were now mere prisoners heading straight down toward our certain death waiting below.

To my immense surprise, I felt little pain. Slowly, I looked down at myself through the smoke and dirt. I was still together with hardly a scratch. Suddenly, I realized I was just sitting there, in shock, looking at myself. I heard the warning horns blaring in my helmet. Overhead, I quickly observed rotor blades spinning. Through the smoke and dirt, to my front, I could make out numerous warning lights on the instrument panel, dim in their attempt to shine through all that smoke, blinking at me. Peering through that frightening haze, I discovered our engine was still running.

"Damn," I thought. How could I have an engine running and rotor blades turning after that huge explosion? With a reason of its own, my left hand darted out and began doing things as if it were a ghost limb, flipping switches and pulling circuit breakers. I pushed the transmitter switch on my cyclic stick with my right hand and yelled out into the air-waves, "I'm hit!"

A voice came back immediately and asked calmly, "Who's hit?" In my bewilderment I had neglected to tell anyone who I was. "Tiger 34 is hit," I yelled back.

I had maneuvered the aircraft at the beginning with a right turning dive just prior to the explosion. As low as our aircraft was, it wouldn't take us very long to get near those beautiful treetops and safety.

As I attempted to steer the ship out of its dive, a terribly sick feeling of dread overwhelmed me. It was at that moment when I discovered my cyclic—the main flight stick or the main flight control of my helicop-ter—wouldn't budge forward or backward any and it moved only slightly to the left or right. I couldn't pull her nose up. We were diving and I couldn't stop it.

## Coping with Crisis

My thoughts for a few more flash frames were, "My copilot must be responsible for this control problem. Cashon up there in the front seat must be frozen on my controls. Probably, he's in a state of panic." I had removed my flight gloves from my hands just prior to the explosion. During that event one of my gloves had blown up and over into his front cockpit. Cashon's first glance at my glove passing by him convinced him that one of my hands was blown off. He assumed I was severely injured. He grabbed his flight controls. He shouted, "I have the controls."

This was a normal reaction, from his point of view. Each and every time we exchanged the controls of the aircraft, the pilot being relieved would say, "You have the controls," and the one taking over would announce, "I have the controls." This was procedure. It eliminated cockpit confusion inside the ship about who was actually flying the chopper.

I quickly shouted back at him through the Cobra's intercom system, "Get off the controls." Being the appointed aircraft commander meant I was the boss. My copilot didn't have the authority to take the aircraft away from me unless I was endangering the aircraft or his life by some erratic behavior.

He shouted back, "You have the controls." I announced quickly, "I have the controls." This was a good sign because it meant he understood who was in charge. An emergency was no time for pilots to duel over the controls. That alone has caused many crashes in the past.

My cyclic stick was still stuck and it wouldn't budge aft. In my panic-filled mind, the problem still had to be with my copilot in the front seat. My controls had always moved before, so I felt as though they should move now. I shouted again at Cashon, "Get off the controls." He must have wondered why I had shouted this again. "I ain't on the controls," Cashon shouted back to me. Then, in a gesture of downright brilliance, he held both hands above his flight helmet. This simple act got my total attention. If his hands weren't on the controls, then why wouldn't our flight stick move?

I still couldn't move the thing. In a reversal of what I'd been saying

On his fateful Cobra flight in Vietnam, a Hughes OH-6 Cayuse like the one shown here, piloted by Rod Barber, accompanied Ken Whitley.

*U. S. Army*

up to now, I shouted at Cashon, "Get on the controls." I wanted to find out whether, with his different set of controls up front, he could fly this broken kite. He tried his cyclic stick, trying his best to pull us out of our turning dive and shouted hysterically, "I can't pull her head up."

Even though Cashon and I had different sets of controls, they combined into a single system as they left our cockpits for their journey toward our rotor head. If the push-pull control tubes were blocked in one place, they probably were blocked every place because they were all bolted solidly together from end to end. This wasn't pretty. Cashon was now fully aware of our impending doom. That earth down there was coming up fast and we were gaining speed in our dive. This might be our last meeting with Mother Earth because we were in nothing that resembled controlled flight. That earth down there was going to kill us.

# Chapter 15

## Cobra in the Crosshairs (II)

**KEN WHITLEY** No one had ever trained me to handle this kind of situation. I had to take responsibility for Cashon, the Cobra, and my life. It was "put up or shut up" time for this aircraft commander.

I was certain that when a control failure this catastrophic happened, pilots usually didn't get the chance to talk about it later. Still, I felt, if I could figure out how to fly this damn thing the terror would pass.

My left hand was still busy doing things, important things. It was as if this appendage of my body was deciding to go on automatic pilot. My left hand turned off that damn honking horn and the defective hydraulic system and the master arm switch and was fixing to turn off the rest of the rocket and gun systems. This was, of course, in case any of these systems had anything remotely to do with our problems at hand.

The trees were getting ready to eat the nose of our aircraft. That was when an old helicopter pilot adage came drifting out of the ether. Maybe it wasn't the best idea to bet our lives on, but I did. It was a simple old saying, "When things get tough, pull pitch."

Pulling pitch on a helicopter changes the angle of attack on all rotor blades at the same time. This is the action that causes the wind to blow downward from all the rotating rotor blades equally and simultaneously. When the wind blows hard enough the aircraft lifts off the ground and

CWO4 Ken Whitley
Bell AH-1G Cobra (HueyCobra)
67-15458
TIGER 34
October 14, 1969
D Company, "Smiling Tigers,"
229th Helicopter Assault
Battalion, First Cavalry
Division
Dau Teing, South Vietnam

Warrant Officer Kenneth Whitley looks out from the rear cockpit of his AH-1G Cobra gunship helicopter.

*Kenneth Whitley*

can then hover. Since we were diving toward our death with no other obvious control option left, what could it hurt?

"Left hand," I commanded, "quit whatever you're doing and pull some pitch. A bunch of pitch."

I was unprepared for what happened. The nose of our aircraft had the opposite reaction and dived even steeper toward the ground. This was the wrong reaction but it taught me that the pitch control (the collective) could change the attitude of the ship. I had never been trained to use the collective for attitude. Attitude is the angle that the nose is up or down in relation to the ground.

My left hand and my brain suddenly decided together I'd better try something in reverse. I bottomed the collective pitch full down as fast as I could. Then I waited to see the final result.

Suddenly the downward collective pitch action caused the Cobra's nose to start creeping upward. Then it kept right on moving until the aircraft nose passed through level and started upward toward a tail-low attitude.

Slowly, I added pitch back upward ever so slightly. It appeared this control was actually maneuvering the aircraft. It was doing things that were really helpful. Unbelievably, to me, as I inched the collective upward, the aircraft began to level out. We became perfectly level when the pitch pulled was approximately 50 percent of the normal power available for flight. Luckily for us, the helicopter could still maintain forward flight while staying level at a good twenty feet above the jungle.

We were no longer diving. But we were still turning right. I could jiggle the cycle stick ever so slightly from left to right but even when I pushed it "hard left" our aircraft kept turning right anyway. While we turned steadily around to the right I noticed the airframe was leaning over right as well.

The Hughes pilot, Rod Barber, came over the radio: "What's wrong with your aircraft, Tiger 34?"

I wasn't able to explain to Rod how I was controlling our AH-1G Cobra. I didn't know. Only seconds had passed since our helicopter had been in an explosion. Now Barber, in the Hughes, was shouting: "Taking fire." Charlie was shooting at him and he wasn't far from us. I couldn't hear well since the explosion. The enemy might have been shooting at us as well without my knowledge. I wouldn't know. Rod could have fled and left me there but he chose to return time and time again sticking his neck out for us by trying to draw enemy fire off us and our barely flying bird.

## On Fire in Midair

Cashon in the front tandem seat turned around and looked back toward the rear of our aircraft. His face was pale and tense. He said, "We're on fire!" I glanced behind my seat, trying to confirm any flames or smoke, but couldn't see behind us as well as Cashon could. Normally, if I didn't know one way or the other I could weave the aircraft from left to right to see whether the Cobra was trailing smoke—but without my main cyclic control, this weaving wasn't possible.

Fire in the air. That's one repulsive way of dying. I had often pondered my death while in Vietnam, but believed that fate and I had agreed on a deal. I could get shot, crash, or be blown to pieces but never, ever, would I be burned. Merely thinking about my helicopter burning back there as we flew along was absolutely overwhelming to my rational being.

I spotted a clearing in the jungle ahead of us but slightly over to the right. It looked as though our aircraft would curve round and enter that open area. There were no other clearings, so I figured it had to be land or burn up. I decided to plant this Cobra right in that jungle opening. I felt that landing this uncontrollable helicopter was nearly impossible but I knew the longer we flew, burning, the more that fire back there would grow. I feared my tail boom might soon fall off.

The enemy would be waiting down there. The Hughes wasn't well-enough armed to fight, land, pick us up, and climb back out of that clearing.

Ready to attempt a crash landing inside my enemy's backyard, I wondered if my firearms stowed in the fuselage had been destroyed in our "mother of all explosions." Charlie hated us Cobra pilots with a passion. Given the chance, they would take us out without hesitation, even if we were legally captured. The biggest thing to fear wasn't dying but how much torture they might apply prior to killing us. We had been taught within my unit that when downed we should expect the worst treatment and we might as well fight to our deaths. The policy was to save one bullet, using our .38 revolvers on ourselves as we ran out of fight.

If the enemy closed in tight, we might be able to fire a few .38 bullets at them, then we'd have to take ourselves out. That was, of course, depending on whether or not we could get out of this broken fireball we were riding in with an arm and eye left to shoot. From every angle, as I peered into our future, the vision came back, "You're going to be dead soon."

We were getting much nearer to the opening in that clearing. I lowered the pitch control, gently, and the helicopter's nose started rising. I had no realistic idea how to put the thing down. I called the Hughes pilot, Rod, on our radio and advised him, "I'm going to land in this clearing coming up." Rod asked, "Why are you landing?"

Shakily, I responded with, "I don't want us to burn up in this thing."

The Hughes pilot yelled back over the radio, "You're not on fire. You're not on fire. Fly it if you can. Fly it if you can."

## Helped by the Hughes

Rod Barber repeated those words to make damn sure I heard the message loud and clear. I did. He, from a close distance away, could tell that we were not trailing smoke. Therefore, I knew from his reaction, my Cobra wasn't burning.

"Damn," I thought. My copilot had totally misunderstood the fire issue. When the Hughes pilot had radioed us earlier about, "Taking fire," my copilot had mistakenly thought he'd meant, "We're on fire." As simple as this appears, I've heard about and known many a good chopper pilot who died from such misinterpretations.

I inched the pitch power back up but this was a difficult situation. Too much power would cause us to nose over into the field, while not enough power would settle us down into the clearing. My hope was that our Cobra might clear those trees on the far side of the clearing. The trees around it were tall indeed.

The aircraft had lost critical altitude. We flew forward and smacked into some small tree limbs near the treetops. A few of the smaller limbs broke off, and some took a ride as part of our now bushy rocket pods. We barely kept going on this wobbling flight. Those limbs had nearly stopped our flight completely and caused great grief to me inside the cockpit. We'd lost some of the ship's critical airspeed and altitude on impact.

The Cobra staggered forward and again started turning at a lower altitude off to her right. I was so relieved about our continued flight that I'd neglected to realize our crippled Cobra was completing a wide, 360-degree circle. This was taking us where we'd first been attacked. We were now heading straight, by ground path, toward the very same ambush position—now slower than before and without weapons or maneuverability.

The enemy had to have seen the explosion in the belly of our aircraft and had to know we were in big trouble. Maybe they thought I was going to crash and they all wanted to watch. Possibly they thought I was coming around to get a shot at them—so they all took cover. Maybe it was as simple as their machine gun jammed. Whatever the explanation, we passed over their position and were over heavy forest again.

Behind us, I heard some shooting from handheld AK-47 rifles. I heard them underneath us in the forest shooting upward. They missed, but this battered old Cobra was now running out of turbine fuel, so we'd be forced to crash land her one way or the other. If we continued in an uncontrolled, 360-degree arc, we were going to fly around and back over those bad guys again and in too short a time.

I figured, "They know, by now, that our aircraft is in trouble and we are up here without paddle, boat, or creek. If we go over that enemy position again we'll become a footnote in history, missing in action or killed in action. MIA or KIA. I felt strongly I was a warrior and should be given the opportunity to die as a warrior, fighting, and not inside some wounded duck flopping about.

That's when a new ideal sprang out of nowhere. "Pedals," I thought. "Maybe I can force this sucker's nose around to the left with our tail rotor." The foot pedals operated the tail rotor, the smaller of the helicopter's two fans located near the rear of the tail boom. It was the smaller spinning rotor back there that controlled the helicopter's yaw. Yaw is the rotation, from left to right, of the entire aircraft from nose to tail as the body of the aircraft hangs down from the rotor. When a person turns their head from left to right, motioning "no," that is yawing one's head.

## Controlling the Cobra

Slowly, I started pushing the left pedal down toward the bottom. The nose moved left as the Cobra's tail swung right. The Cobra ended up flying almost sideways, and this of course slowed her airspeed due to the increased drag caused by the sideways yawing. There had been some banging and clanging noises from her before outside the helicopter since her explosion, but as the ship leaned farther to the right and began flying sideways, the awful sounds outside our cockpit grew worse. There we were blown to hell, low, slow, and leaning far over to the right while the nose pointed off in a direction towards which we weren't traveling.

The Hughes aircraft flew up beside us and Rod gave our bird a look-see. What he said didn't help: "Your whole belly is gone."

I had no fore and aft cyclic and I had no idea how to land the aircraft. The weather had managed to get worse. Clouds and low visibility stayed with us through the whole flight, but now it was raining, hard. How were we going to find our base at Song Be when maneuvering was so difficult?

"Never give up," I said to myself. I cranked in the Guard frequency on our radio so I could transmit and start communicating better. That frequency that all pilots inside South Vietnam were supposed to monitor was available if we ever ran into big trouble. I radioed the following message, "Mayday, Mayday, does anyone flying in the Song Be area have a UHF (ultra-high frequency), or VHF (very-high frequency) air-to-air radio homer? If so, please come up on our frequency."

An Air Force OV-10 Bronco, a fixed-wing forward air control plane, came up on the frequency. "Tiger 34," he called, "this is Covey 29. I'll look for you over Song Be."

I told him, "Covey Two-Niner, this is Tiger Three-Four. I want you to locate us and help point our crippled bird back toward Song Be. We're real busy in the cockpit here and we don't have any extra time to be guessing at our true course." We exchanged more transmissions and within minutes, the OV-10 came busting out of the clouds. He'd tracked us by using my transmissions over the airway. There he was, in living color.

He flew away from us toward Song Be, disappeared, and returned. He repeated this while I flopped and banged along slowly toward the direction he indicated. Whoever that guy was I owe him big time. He was my lucky charm; may he always have luck on his side. I wish I knew who he was. I never found out.

As our broken ship crawled along in its leaning and banging fashion, Cashon and I discussed our soon-to-be attempted landing.

What to do? How? Cashon and I talked to each other as a team ought to, but we had no training for this unknown-type landing. We made a decision that was unheard of in routine flying. We would both try to land the ship.

During this time a parachute might have saved one of us. Jumping from a helicopter had its own danger though. I could have held the ship stable while Cashon jumped, but no one could have held it steady for me later. Parachutes were big and bulky things that we simply couldn't fit into our cramped cockpit. We didn't have one anyway.

I called the tower at Song Be and declared a "tactical emergency (Tac-E)." The tower closed the runway to other traffic. Soon we saw our goal, a long, north-south runway out there waiting for us with our nearly sideways approach. We tried hard to line up our ground track with the runway.

We came over the trees at the north end of the runway. We lowered our collective pitch together. The nose came up. The ground seemed as though it was in too big a hurry to greet us. Just before touching the runway, we both pulled our pitch control slightly upward to level the aircraft and to slow our descent.

Although neither of us knew it, the left door of our ammo bay compartment was hanging down lower than the aircraft skid. When we touched runway, that hanging door made contact first. The vector of force caused by the door, along with the helicopter's strong runway contact, made us bounce and threw us into a rolling, leaping bank to the right.

Time crawled in slow, long seconds. Watching our spinning rotor blades in apparent slow motion filled me with dread. They were just barely missing the ground on our right, by what appeared to be less than an inch. Meanwhile, my cyclic had for reasons unknown become totally loose in the left/right axis and was no use in controlling the helicopter. I pushed that cyclic stick as far over to the left as I could but the helicopter didn't comply.

I managed to pull the pitch. The overtaxed turbine engine cried out with a loud whistling moan. My Cobra's engine was bellowing like a dying calf. Never before, never since, have I heard a turbine engine make this sound. It made the hair on the back of my neck stand to attention. During our first impact with the runway the airframe started shuddering, a wave motion, as if it were a huge tuning fork. I was pushing the cyclic over to my left with every muscle in my body and was looking up through the top of the cockpit but it was really sideways in the direction we were going. I saw LZ Buttons spread out before us solidly along the right hand side of that runway. Tents and soldiers in large numbers were inside the base and toward that direction.

I thought, "I mustn't crash into our base camp." We were fixing to stop flying altogether one way or the other.

I bottomed the collective pitch, removing the request for power. I waited to see what would happen. Speed kills. Slowing down was a good thing. I also hoped to crash there, in that grassy area beside the runway proper. I expected the helicopter to plow into the mud and grass on its right side. I waited and watched for a long . . . long . . . minisecond.

Instead of plowing in on the chopper's right side, we were momentarily suspended a few feet off the ground. Nothing seemed to be holding us up. Suddenly, our right skid hit the soft, muddy ground and the aircraft slid and rocked wildly forward, now going straight in the direction the skids were pointing. We were just passengers now, sliding along rain-soaked grass and mud. Then, unexpectedly, our chopper stopped moving forward and came to rest.

## Tiger 34 at Song Be

She was sitting as she'd been designed to do, on her skids, in the grass, but with engine running and rotors turning at full rpm. It was raining on our canopy overhead. Water drops were sliding down the cockpit windows.

I rolled the engine throttle back to flight idle to slow the spinning rotor blades. Cashon opened his door, up front, got out quickly, and ran like a track runner to the left.

The control tower called me on the radio and asked forcefully, "Tiger three-four, please move that aircraft away from the side of the runway, we have landing traffic."

I explained, "Tower, I can't move it."

He called back and said again, "If you don't move that Cobra, I'll send some men down there with chains and a tug and we'll drag it off." I told him in a calm voice, "Go right ahead, I'm not moving this thing." After about five minutes, Cashon circled the nose of the aircraft, way out, at least fifty yards away, ran up to my side, and opened my cockpit door from the right hand side.

I couldn't believe we hadn't crashed. Cashon leaned inside and said quizzically to my helmet: "Why don't you shut her down?" I rolled off the throttle. The blades slowly came to a stop and then squeaked as they teeter-tottered in the breeze. I pulled myself out of the pilot's seat and started climbing down with great difficulty off the Cobra's steps.

The instant my feet touched the ground, my legs turned into wet noodles. I fell face-first into the mud. I had lost control of myself. My copilot pulled me up out of the muddy mess and helped me away from the damaged chopper.

I couldn't believe we were alive. The rain was hitting my face and fresh air was blowing on me. Cashon placed me in muddy green turf under a small bush and I had a cigarette, the best smoke of my life.

I sat there and peered at the piece of metal I'd just flown in and landed. It was a terrible yet lovely sight. Our own grenades and linked bullets were scattered along our flight path where I had first made contact with the runway. Some were hanging out of damaged areas on the craft below her belly line.

Later, investigators told me and Cashon that an estimated 9 of the 300 forty-millimeter grenades aboard our aircraft had gone off in flight. Out of all our miracles of life and death that day, the biggest one was . . . why only nine? My guess would be that the explosion itself must have blown the grenades away from the blast until they were no longer near enough to be detonated by one another. To us on board, at the time of the explosion, it had sounded as if one large grenade had exploded. On that day, the part inside my twenty-three-year-old self where I believed I was immortal died forever.

In Cobra class back in flight school, I had asked, "Can the ammo below our feet blow up and kill us?" Their answer was, "Never." The instructor added, "These grenades must be fired first and then spun rapidly before they become armed. They cannot be exploded accidentally inside the ammo bay." All the same, enemy bullets had struck our grenades and exploded them.

When the blast occurred, the hollow floor between our cockpit and the ammo bay was smashed. The fore and aft push-pull tubes were crushed beneath the floor. I luckily replaced the tubes' fore and aft control action by using the collective pitch control. I've learned since that many of today's helicopters with collective control are totally differently than our Cobra was back then. If our lateral controls had been made to lock up, totally solid, from left to right, I would have lost control of the whole shebang. I had just enough movement to survive but nothing else.

A combination of inexplicable events with the controls had enabled us to survive. Even at the final moment, we were lucky. The rain that day had softened the ground enough for the skids of the aircraft to plow through without turning us over or breaking the skids off. During Cobra training classes back stateside, before Vietnam, we'd never actually landed on the ground in a practice autorotation because of fear of breaking the skids. The Cobra's landing gear was lightly built because it didn't land on the gear very often. They were tiny compared to the much harder-worked Huey that carried heavy loads and landed repeatedly. The height of the tall, skinny, and top-heavy Cobra had made it prone to toppling over more easily than the Huey, even on flat smooth surfaces.

It was a miracle that our ship broke all the rules in our favor. Fate was my copilot during this flight. Even though I don't believe in an aircraft having soul, this Cobra seemed to have one—as if our aircraft wanted to survive. Fate seemed to be smiling that day as our Cobra sat out there on the muddy grass, all ripped open and soggy wet at Song Be. That seemed, at the time, appropriate—considering our company nickname, the "Smiling Tigers."

Soon a tug came driving down the runway after our helicopter. When they drew close, I called out to the men on it: "Before you move that ship, I think you should know, there are live grenades lying around it." They turned the tug around and left, fast-like. I reckoned that they went back down the runway and had informed that friendly tower operator that he could move our helicopter himself.

A week later, a high-ranking officer responsible for helicopter maintenance all over Vietnam called my company commander. "We know what went wrong with that Smiling Tiger Cobra, the one that exploded recently," he said, "and we also know exactly what caused the damage, but we've sat around here and talked about this incident until we've turned blue, and finally we decided to call and ask you just one question—How did that pilot of yours land that aircraft?" That question was and is still today very complicated. In my opinion it's closer to being a purely spiritual thing. Even the written words on the award I received were difficult for safety officials to write. How does one write on an official safety award document what appears to be nearly impossible to one's own peers and then have it read believable?

I received "The United States Army Aviation Safety Broken Wing Award" for bringing that aircraft back in one big broken chunk. I never really thought about saving that helicopter while I was trying to land it. I believe if I'd had a parachute with me I would have used it. Helicopter pilots within the Army, at that time and today as far as I know, never have worn parachutes. When I flew out of Song Be later that fateful day as a passenger on a Huey helicopter I mentally looked back at the day's events with new respect for the enemy, my aircraft, my copilot, and myself.

Cashon had hung in there. He had helped me as much as he could. I had other copilots freeze up or even cry out in terror during perilous flights. So thanks again, Cashon, I know you'll always remember that day, as I shall.

Some of my peers later advised that I should have jettisoned the rocket pods before attempting a landing. They figured this would reduce the size of any explosion during a crash landing. Maybe I should have, but since there was no crash, I'll take the results the way they turned out. After all, what if one of those fully loaded rocket pods had not jettisoned properly? That extra bit of weight might have thrown the aircraft into a fatal plunge.

For many years now I've flown and reflown that flight in my mind. The details are always the same in each event or flashback, except in my dreams, where I always crash and awaken sweating. After being awakened thusly, I can't return to sleep.

I will never have another rush of adrenaline as powerful as that flight gave me. I knew that night after the incident as I lay my twenty-

On his fateful Cobra flight in Vietnam, a Hughes OH-6 Cayuse like the one shown here, piloted by Rod Barber, accompanied Ken Whitley.

*U. S. Army*

three-year-old, combat-bruised body down on my bunk thinking over my day, I was no longer just an AH-1G Cobra pilot in the First Cavalry, D-229th Cobra Company. I was somebody different.

To this day, I love rainy days. The sound of water falling is truly my lifesaver. Rain had softened the ground and allowed us to land. Without soft ground that day, our aircraft would have surely rolled over and crashed into an exploding fireball.

If given the opportunity, I'd tell anybody and everybody that might listen, "That to be truly alive, one must know and understand death."

After a Huey dropped us off at Dau Teing base late that afternoon, I lugged the twisted ammo-bay door toward our warrant officers' hooch, When I arrived at the hooch, I walked in and threw that bent and distorted aircraft part down on the concrete floor. It hit with a loud bang in front of several Cobra pilots who had gathered to welcome us home. I said, "Gentleman, there is a chunk of 67-15458, the aircraft I took out of here this morning."

They stared. I went to get a beer.

## Bell AH-1G Cobra (HueyCobra)

The AH-1G was a sleek, narrow (thirty-eight-inch) battlefield helicopter that carried a machine gun and grenade launcher in the nose and rocket projectiles in pods on the fuselage.

An offspring of the UH-1 Huey helicopter, the AH-1G used a 1,100-shaft horsepower Lycoming T-53L-11 turboshaft engine and a forty-four-foot, two-bladed rotor. In 1967, the first ship in the series surprised observers by flying at 162 knots at the Bell Helicopter Co. factory in Dallas, Texas. The prototype also appeared at the Paris Air Show in June of that year, and still exists today—preserved at the George S. Patton Museum of Cavalry and Armor at Fort Knox, Kentucky.

The AH-1G accommodated a pilot in command in its rear seat and a gunner (who was also a pilot) in front. Documents from Bell credit the AH-1G with a maximum speed of 219 miles per hour.

The AH-1G was among the last Army aircraft to leave Vietnam be-

# Bell AH-1G Cobra (HueyCobra)

**Type:** Two-seat, single-rotor attack helicopter

**Powerplant:** One 1,400-shp (1070 kW) Avco Lycoming T53-L-13 turboshaft engine driving 44-ft 5-in (13.54-m), two-bladed main rotor

**Performance:** Maximum speed 200 mph (360 km/h); maximum diving speed, 219 mph (352 km/h); cruising speed, 166 mph (267 km/h); rate of climb at sea level, 1,680 ft (512 m) per min; hovering ceiling in ground effect, 10,800 ft (3290 m); range at 9,254 lb weight, 362 miles (582 km)

**Weights:** Empty, 5,500 lb (2491 kg); operating weight, 6,096 lb (2765 kg); maximum takeoff weight, 9,500 lb (4309 kg)

**Dimensions:** Main rotor diameter, 44 ft (13.41 m); fuselage length, 44 ft 5 in (13.54 m); height overall, 13 ft 5.5 in (4.10 m)

**Armament:** One M197 three-barrel 20-mm cannon (mounted under nose with 750 rounds in beltless container); four BGM-71 TOW (tube-launched, optically tracked, Wire-guided) air-to-ground missiles plus 2.75-in Zuni air-to-ground rocket projectiles

**Crew:** Pilot and gunner

**First flight:** September 7, 1965

fore the January 27, 1973, cease-fire that led to the United States withdrawal. Numerous post-Vietnam versions of the Cobra served with the Army and are still flying today with the Marine Corps (Chapter Twenty). Cobras are also flying today with the armies of Iran, Israel, Japan, Jordan, Pakistan, South Korea, Spain, Thailand, and Turkey.

# Chapter 16

## Aerial Ambulance

### What Happened

In Vietnam, one American soldier called them "beautiful angels." They were UH-1 Hueys adorned with the red cross that identified them as ambulances. The Army term for medical evacuation helicopters was DUSTOFF.

The term may have originated with a radio callsign that was assigned arbitrarily. "Or someone may have noticed that our helicopters kicked up a lot of dust when landing during the dry season," said former Warrant Officer Three Paul Mercandetti, fifty-seven, of Arlington, Massachusetts, who flew a Huey adorned with red crosses in Vietnam in 1968 and 1969.

Pilots like Mercandetti have received some notice for their service. They say, however, that the nation has largely overlooked the flight medics who served on DUSTOFF crews. In congressional testimony in 2004, DUSTOFF pilot retired Chief Warrant Officer Five John Travers, fifty-five, of Hershey, Pennsylvania, called medics "the bravest . . . men I have ever known." Travers said legislation is pending to make flight medics eligible for the combat medic badge and that, "This recognition is long overdue."

**CW3 Paul Mercandetti**
**Bell UH-1H Iroquois (Huey)**
**February 1969**
**283rd Medical Detachment**
**Pleiku, South Vietnam**

Chief Warrant Officer Three Paul Mercandetti fitted up for a DUSTOFF medical evacuation mission. Many Huey pilots carried a pistol or an M14 rifle. Mercandetti preferred the M79 grenade launcher clutched in his right hand.

*Paul Mercandetti*

Travers described one medic, Sgt. Kevin Donoghue, a medic who I personally watched jump from my aircraft, under extremely intense fire, and run through a minefield to retrieve a wounded soldier and bring him back to our aircraft, all while AK-47 rounds exploded around him. Travers said this kind of act "was . . . a daily ritual that gained the admiration and love of those on the ground."

Most DUSTOFF pilots were warrant officers who loved aviation. Mercandetti's experience was typical. After growing up in Boston, said Mercandetti, "I went to the Air Force wanting to fly, and they required four years of college. I went to the Navy wanting to fly, and they said they required two years. I had just one semester of college I went to the Army and they said, 'We'll train you to fly.' I'm glad my job was to save people, but my real goal was to fly."

On a February 1969 mission to haul out wounded troops, Mercandetti's UH-1 took fifty hits from small arms fire in the belly of the aircraft. "The following day, I was sent back to that same location to do a repeat of the same mission. That's the most scared I ever was in my life."

Mercandetti's late-model Huey helicopter, the UH-1H—newer and snappier than the UH-1Ds flown in the Ia Drang battle of 1965—could carry three stretcher patients and a medic inside the cabin. DUSTOFF helicopters sometimes dropped off supplies and even ammunition to troops in the field—what one pilot called "preventive medicine."

Under Geneva Convention rules, DUSTOFF helicopters were

supposed to be unarmed and the enemy was not supposed to shoot at them. "Our only protection was the red cross," said Mercandetti. "We were not allowed anything larger than weapons for personal defense. Once, I landed and saw a North Vietnamese soldier who could have shot at me, but didn't. Most of the time, however, they didn't hesitate to fire on us."

Mercandetti said the Huey was the best helicopter for DUSTOFF duty because its wide doors made it easy to load and unload casualties, and the Huey could get in and out of a landing zone quickly. Between 1963 and 1973, DUSTOFF crews flew 496,573 missions, evacuating over 900,000 casualties. Figures provided by Travers show 222 DUSTOFF pilots, crew chiefs, and medics killed in combat.

"This was strictly a humanitarian mission," said Mercandetti. "I spent thirteen months saving lives in Vietnam, got shot down once, and narrowly missed getting wounded or killed several times. It was all worth it."

Mercandetti flew about 1,000 sorties. "I pulled 1,600-plus people out of the woods," Mercandetti said. He left the Army in 1971. Today, he is a pilot for USAirways.

**PAUL MERCANDETTI** On one of my medevac flights, the medic on my helicopter had to perform a tracheotomy in flight. Right in the back of our shaking helicopter, he opened up a wounded soldier's throat and installed a tube. That was the sort of thing I experienced with the DUST-OFF mission, bringing wounded troops out of hot landing zones.

That wasn't what I expected to do in the Army. I joined up with a private pilot's license and forty-five to fifty hours in Cessna 150s and 172s. I wanted to fly fixed-wing airplanes because that was what I wanted to make my career. After I got into the warrant officer aviation program, they said I was going to fly helicopters. My first thought was, I was going to fly gunships. That was my objective, being brought up on *G.I. Joe* comic books and John Wayne. I didn't really know what DUSTOFF was.

Today, I get satisfaction from the DUSTOFF mission, knowing we brought out the wounded and saved their lives. In fact, I got satisfaction from it then. But I spent thirteen months over there saving people's lives and when I got home, people were spitting on my fellow soldiers. It never happened to me personally but I saw a member of the public run up to a soldier in uniform and call him a baby killer. That's what the Vietnam era was like.

How did I get into all this? I wanted to fly. I was taking flying lessons at home in Boston. I worked for RCA Burlington, building parts for the lunar excursion module and going to school part-time, but I wanted to fly and I was certain the military was the only way. Getting killed by bullets was the furthest thing from my mind. When you're eighteen or nineteen years old, you have a fatalistic view of life: "This can't happen to me. I'm not going to die in a war."

I went to the Air Force wanting to fly, and they said you needed four years of college. I went to the Navy wanting to fly, and they said they had a two-year program. I had just one semester of college.

The Army said, "We'll train you to fly." I joined the Army in April 1967. They put me into a program that would make me a warrant officer and a pilot at the same time. I went through basic training at Fort Polk, Louisiana. Under this program, we entered the Army as Private E-1s, and had our pay boosted up to Sergeant E-5 level when we entered flight school. If you didn't pass flying school, you were sent back to the regular Army to fulfill a two-year commitment. If you graduated from flight school and pinned on pilot wings, you owed them four years.

Right after basic and before flight school, some young, enterprising second lieutenant tried to give us the itch to go to Officer Candidate School to become commissioned officers. He said we could go to flight school after that.

We were all for this because an officer made more money. But we had questions. One guy said, "Excuse me, lieutenant, does this still mean we're guaranteed assignment to flying school afterward?" The lieutenant said, "I can assure you that for those of you who do well in OCS there is a probability that you'll get to fly." We said, "Excuse me, lieutenant, but a probability isn't a certainty. You need higher scores to go to flight school than to go to OCS. Is there a certainty that we could get flight school after OCS?" Not one person took the lieutenant up on his offer.

The Army has a different attitude than the other services. In the Army, you are a soldier first. Your secondary job is cook, truck driver, or helicopter pilot. Your first job is as a soldier.

In Vietnam, we had a commanding officer, a major bucking for lieutenant colonel, who had a dim view of warrant officers. We found this disturbing. Most commissioned officers had a lot of respect for warrant officers but this one didn't. He also thought we would probably prefer to become commissioned officers, and he kept urging us to apply. He said, "Wouldn't you rather be a commissioned officer than an enlisted man with a Club Card?" That was what he thought of warrant officers. Most in the Army, especially in Vietnam, had more respect for us. There were times when I was the aircraft commander as a lowly Warrant Officer One—we referred to ourselves as "Wobbly Ones"—and the guy sitting in the right seat was a colonel from division who had come down to get his four hours of flying so he could collect his flight pay. There was no argument about who was in charge.

So no commission for me, thank you. I went to Fort Wolters, Texas, for preflight training in the warrant officer candidate program.

## Flight Training at Fort Wolters

When I was in preflight training, they pulled us aside and asked, "How many here have any fixed wing flying experience?" Hands went up, including mine. They asked, "How many here have 200 flying hours?" I couldn't raise my hand for that. They asked, "How many have 100 hours?" I couldn't raise my hand for that, either. As it turned out, fixed-wing flying jobs in the Army were very coveted slots and very few people got them. So I went into helicopter training.

I started out on the little Hughes TH-55 at Wolters. There was a slogan from a toy company in those days: "If it's made by Mattel, it's swell." The Mattel Toy Company really did make the plastic parts on the TH-55, so we called it the Mattel Messerschmitt. We uttered that slogan to each other a lot: "If it's made by Mattel, it's swell."

Flight training was difficult but fun, too. Student pilots competed to get out to our staging area first so they could herd the farmers' cows out of the way. There's nothing funnier than a big, old bossy cow with a skid up her ass being pushed along by a helicopter.

In the TH-55, the student sat in the left seat with the instructor in the right. You soloed it from the left seat. My instructor was a civilian who'd been a B-52 pilot in the Air Force and had gotten rotary wing experience somewhere. He knew where I was going after training.

One of the procedures we do is autorotation. That's where you land an aircraft without power. At the time, we were trying to learn to land with little forward ground. We were doing 180-degree autorotations. After the simulated engine failure, you would have to turn 180 degrees and land in the dirt. I had done a couple of these with ground runs that were too long. This time when I landed too long, the instructor grabbed the stick out of my hand and it pulled the rotor blade down in the back and flexed it down so much that it chopped off our tail boom. He said, "Oh, my God, there goes 50,000 accident-free flying hours." As a result of that, I had to go before a Board and do a check ride. They made me do an autorotation, but straight ahead, not a 180. I did a beautiful autorotation with almost no forward ground run. The chief flight instructor repeated the process and we skidded ten or twenty skid lengths down the runway. The original instructor, to his credit, knew I was going to Vietnam and would need a zero-ground-run autorotation; the chief flight instructor was just thinking of keeping his flight safety hours up.

After primary training, I went to Fort Rucker, Alabama, for instrument training. In instrument training, we flew the Bell H-13. That was a different helicopter, a different rotor system, not as responsive. They had a screen they'd prop up so we could fly blind, on instruments. After that, we were granted a tactical instrument ticket. This was not a full instrument ticket because the H-13 was not fully instrumented. It didn't have an ILS [instrument landing system]. They said, "When you get back from Vietnam we'll give you a full instrument ticket." What they meant was, "If you get back . . ."

We stayed at Rucker for advanced tactical flying in the UH-1B Huey. We hauled troops around. We got to fly gunship models. We did low-level flying. The instructors at Rucker were Army and included Vietnam veterans. Our insignia read "WOC," since we were still warrant officer candidates.

I graduated in May 1966 and became an Army aviator and WO1. There was a parallel group who were lieutenants and captains who went through flight school with us. We did not hang around with each other.

In Vietnam, we flew with the aircraft commander in the left seat. Everything we flew in combat was VFR—that means visual flight rules, or flying without instruments. In the left seat, we didn't have an obstruction of view by an instrument panel in front of us.

## "In Country" Helicopter Flying

I arrived in Vietnam in June 1968 and was assigned to the 283rd Medical Detachment of the 498th Medical Co., 44th Medical Brigade, at Pleiku. My unit started out with UH-1D and UH-1H models, but all the Ds were replaced with H models while I was there.

During my time in Vietnam, we experimented with various ways to paint the red cross on our helicopters. This was an international signal meaning, "Don't shoot. I'm a medevac." At least some of the North Vietnamese respected it.

At first, we had just a red cross on a green helicopter. They shot at us. So we added a white border to make it more visible. They shot at us. So we added a white square to make it even more visible yet. And then we enlarged the square. Each time we lost an aircraft, they kept changing the cross to make it more visible. It worked sometimes: I have seen a North Vietnamese aim his weapon at me and not fire.

How do you fly a DUSTOFF mission? You do a lot of sitting around. We spent a lot of time sitting on call, waiting for the radio to light up. People would call in a mission. Of course, we didn't know when someone was going to be shot and need to be evacuated. Sometimes they alerted us in advance that there was going to be an operation, but mostly we waited for the radio call and they would assign us a set of coordinates.

When that happened, the aircraft commander would go off to the radio shack—the operations tent—and pick up the trip sheet that was being called in. There was an enlisted man who manned the radio. He takes down the information and puts it on the mission sheet and hands it to the aircraft commander.

While that's going on, the copilot, the crew chief and the medic get the aircraft cranked up and ready to go. The aircraft commander comes back out to the helipad and climbs in. Sometimes, depending on how critical it is, he's not even fully strapped in when the copilot is taking off and heading out. We often strapped in while under way.

Things seemed very rushed. We never performed preflight on the machine, which sounds awkward, but whenever we came back from a mission we did a postflight evaluation and got it ready to go again. That way, when a mission came in, all we had to do was run to the helicopter, turn battery on, hit the switch, and start the thing up. This was contrary to most aircraft operations where you're required to do a preflight before you take off.

What happens after takeoff depends on the experience level of the copilot and what the aircraft commander wants to do. The aircraft commander may sit there and navigate and let the copilot fly. Or he may take over the controls. Because the aircraft is set up in such a way that all of the instruments are on the right-hand side, the copilot generally sat on the right and the aircraft commander on the left, which is contrary to what we do today in helicopters where we put the aircraft commander in front of the instruments.

We wanted the copilot to fly as much as possible to build up experience. When we first got in country as copilots, most of us had only 200 or 250 hours from flight school. It really was a baptism by fire. You were thrown into a combat situation with a very low experience level.

There were a couple of missions that were my hairiest or scariest. In February 1969, as a UH-1H aircraft commander, I took over fifty hits in the belly of the aircraft on a hoist mission. The following day, I was given another aircraft to back out to that exact same area and do another mission. I've never been so scared in my life as I was that day. I had been out there once and had gotten shot up really bad, so bad we lost the helicopter, and when I got called back out again that's the most scared I ever was in my life.

When you're being hit, you hear it. It sounds like popcorn. That

Paul Mercandetti at the controls of his Huey helicopter. In the Army in Vietnam, contrary to usual helicopter practice, the pilot-in-command usually flew in the left seat.

*Paul Mercandetti*

first day, I was called up to do a hoist mission. I had to extract wounded American soldiers from two different locations, sitting on top of the trees and dropping a cable down through the trees. There was a jungle penetrator on the end of the cable. This is like a grappling hook arrangement, where you unfold these paddles and the patient would sit on this hook and hold on for dear life. You would haul him back up into the aircraft.

This was how you did it when there was no place to land. We were operating in a triple-canopy, jungle-type setting in the mountains. You would do this when time was critical. Either the ground troops can't take the time to open up a landing zone or the patient is so critical that he needs to be extracted immediately.

How did we find the spot to make the rescue? The ground people would give us a set of coordinates on a regular map—not an aviation map, but a regular terrain map. After you've been in country for a while, you get to know where the general coordinates are. You head for that direction. When you get close to the pickup point, you get on the radio. They can hear you and they can direct you toward the spot. It's a combination of what we call FM homing and very crude visual operation. With FM homing, you have a needle on your instrument panel and you zigzag back and forth trying to pick up the signal and find the location that way. Or, you could have them pop a smoke grenade. Popping smoke only worked out in the open or in a low-canopy situation.

But in a triple-canopy situation, the smoke would filter through the trees and it would come up in another area. It would not always indicate exactly where the people were. If you were relying on smoke it became problematic. It was just a matter of hovering over the trees until you could find them. Also, sometimes the enemy had smoke, too, and they would use it to lure us into a position where they could shoot at us.

## Under Fire

The first of those two missions in late January 1969 did not begin as a scary situation, at least initially, except that the unit I was supporting was in contact with the enemy. I knew there was a high probability of taking fire.

On the first pull, I didn't take any hits. We got that patient up on board the helicopter, and then we flew over to another location where we repeated the process and pulled the second patient. Both times there was no landing zone carved out for us: We used the hoist to raise the wounded soldiers into the helicopter.

On the second pickup of the mission, the ground unit was on top of a knoll, kind of a high point—not quite a peak, but a rising slope on a hill—and they had just broken contact with the enemy and had not had time to open up an LZ. They would not move down off the knoll. So I had to hop, hop, hop over the trees—about 150- to 175-foot trees—to hoist down to them.

Because it was up on this knoll, it exposed me to a wide area of enemy fire. The enemy held off, and held off, until I had the patient on the hoist, and when I began the extraction, all hell broke loose and we took hits from all over the place.

Most of the hits went right through the belly of the aircraft, which meant that the enemy was in direct contact, right in the next tree over from the friendlies. They were actually too close for me to see. I could not see them because I was hovering right over them. My crew chief and medic could see them.

My copilot that day was John Connors. He was relatively new. It was a new awakening for him.

We took multiple hits in the belly of the aircraft. The instrument panel exploded on me and the shrapnel from the instrument panel flew up into my face. John took control of the airplane because he thought I was hit.

I cleared the debris from around me. I took control of the aircraft again. We had already started to pull the aircraft up.

Because the hoist had jammed, we could no longer reel the hoist in. So we had to go straight up to pull our survivor out. And, of course, the higher we went up from the trees the more we exposed ourselves to a wider angle of fire from the enemy—and the more hits we took.

We kept pulling and pulling. We finally got high enough that the jungle penetrator was almost clear of the trees before we started moving forward. But at this time, we had no oil pressure, no fuel pressure, no hydraulic pressure. All the gauges were shot up. The helicopter was still producing power. The hydraulics were still functioning; we just had no indication of how much fluid we had left or how much longer we could function.

The crew chief was asking to cut the cable because we couldn't reel it in and it made us like a sitting duck. I denied that request to cut the cable because we were still pulling power and I still thought we could make the save. The survivor was hanging from the cable.

As long as the aircraft was still pulling power, I was going to keep trying to fly it—and get out of there. I wanted to take the patient with me, so I left him on the cable. I had no choice but to drag him through the trees, and I possibly injured him more, dragging him through the treetops—until I could get more altitude—than he was initially injured from his bullet wound. The alternative would have been to drop him in the enemy's lap and he would have been dead for sure.

### Havoc Aboard a Huey

That first patient was right in the path of the rounds pumping into our fuselage. Bullets came up through the floorboard of the helicopter and took his testicles off.

We had no intercom. We were yelling at each other, trying to hear each other, because all the radios were shot out. In the heat of battle, if you speak loud enough, you can force yourself to be heard, even above the din of the rotor blades. I was also gesturing, trying to urge everybody to settle down. It was a moment of chaos.

I reiterated that I was okay. They thought I was hit and it looked like it, but I wasn't. I had an emergency handheld radio on my survival vest that I handed to the copilot and he used it to communicate to the other aircraft. They were two C-model gunships and two Cobras circling around near us putting down suppressing fire.

We struggled to traverse the three or four kilometers to an Army firebase. Fuel was pouring from under the belly of the aircraft. It had soaked the patient in jet fuel. We had fuel, oil, and hydraulics pouring out of the bottom of the aircraft.

We reached the firebase and I was able to go into a shaky hover, long enough to lower the patient down to the ground. Then, I nosed the helicopter down and landed next to him.

That was the end of that aircraft. That aircraft was shot. We junked it after we were through with it.

We counted over fifty direct hits in the belly of the aircraft.

We sat there on that firebase for about three or four hours until we were pulled out. Another of our ships came in and pulled out the patient and got him to a hospital, but we had to stay there for a while longer until they pulled us out.

The next day, we were called up for another mission in the same area. We went out there and took fire once again, and were hit once again. We made the extraction, but only with a lot of metal flying around. That evening, they gave me yet another mission into the same area. I went to the operations shack and picked up the mission sheet. I came out to the helipad and the helicopter was already running. I got in it and my copilot flew out to the pickup area.

I just sat there. I was never so scared in my life. I was almost paralyzed. I knew that my number was up, that this would be the last mission. I just sat there and gave the copilot the coordinates and told him where to go. And I just sat there. I could not function. I was shaking, sitting there.

We continued on. By the time we got out there, the patient had died. I came back without the patient, without making the pickup. I would not risk my crew and aircraft by going in there to pick up a dead man. We hated it when anybody died, but there was plenty of time for him to come out the next day on a supply ship, and there was no point in subjecting us to enemy fire with night coming on. And I did not feel I could function at that point.

Our frequency on the FM radio was 46.9. This was the universal frequency for DUSTOFF in Vietnam. We would often write radio frequencies and mission coordinates in grease pencil on the windshield. Anybody that needed to be extracted could come up on 46.9, and if there was a bird there that could relay the information to us, we could go and get him. When we got into the area where the extraction was to be made, we would initially contact him on that frequency, 46.9, and we would stay on that frequency or be given a discrete frequency to use in carrying out the mission. So we were usually in contact with the ground unit on the radio.

As for the UH-1H Huey, we thought it was a fabulous machine. It was state of the art for its day. We had just come out of flight school where we had flown TH-55s and Bell OH-13s and others. With the Huey, we first encountered a governor on the throttle that kept us from overspeeding the engine, which is a critical thing in a helicopter. This was a feature not found in the smaller, earlier helicopters. It was hydraulic assisted. But it was vulnerable because the fuel cells were in the belly of the aircraft, and if you were doing a hoist mission, that was where you were going to take the hits, in the belly. One of our pilots around the same time took a B-40 rocket in the belly of the aircraft and it exploded his fuel cells. That blew his Huey out of the sky completely.

You could hit the Huey elsewhere and not much would happen. We had a titanium leading edge on the rotor blade. Sometimes we'd take bullet holes through the blade and all it would do is whistle.

## Our Outfit in Vietnam

We had a small detachment. We had six aircraft and twelve pilots. Two of the pilots were the CO and the XO of the company, and although they did fly nearly a full schedule, they were also busy running the company.

UH-1H Huey helicopters of Paul Mercandetti's medical evacuation unit wait for action on an overcast morning.

*Paul Mercandetti*

For six aircraft, we had probably the largest area of operation in the country. We operated from the Mang Yang Pass in the east all the way to the border with Laos and Cambodia on the west, from Ban My Thuet in the south all the way up to Dak Tek. Of the six aircraft, most of the time, two or three were in for maintenance. So we really only had three or four aircraft at any one time. We lost six or eight ships while I was there. When I left, we didn't have any of the original aircraft that were there when I started. They had all been lost to enemy fire. Three out of twelve of our pilots had been killed. Three or four of our enlisted men were killed as well.

When I finished my tour in Vietnam, I went back to the States and trained pilots at Fort Wolters. I got out of the Army in 1971. Today, I'm an airline captain for USAirways and I own a Globe Swift aircraft that I fly at air shows.

# Chapter Seventeen

## "We're Shutting Down the War to Get Roger Locher"

### What Happened

"There's nothing to compare in satisfaction to a successful combat rescue of a fellow airman," said Dale Stovall.

Stovall piloted the HH-53C helicopter that went deep inside North Vietnam on June 2, 1972, to try to pick up Capt. Roger Locher, a downed F-4 Phantom weapons officer.

Locher had been on the ground for twenty-three days, struggling to evade capture only a few miles from a huge MiG base. No other airman downed in North Vietnam had ever avoided capture longer than three days.

When the 1973 Jabara Award for Airmanship was presented to Stovall, the citation accompanying the award referred to "the deepest rescue mission ever into North Vietnam to pick up a downed U. S. Air Force [flight crew member] 60 miles northwest of Hanoi."

Stovall, the citation said, "repeatedly and successfully penetrated extremely hostile and heavily defended areas of North Vietnam to arrive at the downed [airman's] location five miles northeast of Yen Bai airfield, one of the most active enemy MiG airfields."

A native of Toppenish, Washington, Stovall attended the Air Force

**Captain Dale Stovall**
**June 2, 1972**
**Sikorsky HH-53B/C Super Jolly Green**
**JOLLY 30**
**40th Aerospace Rescue and Recovery**
**Squadron**
**Nakhon Phanom Air Base, Thailand**

Dale Stovall as a captain in January 1973, seven months after he earned the Air Force Cross for the rescue of Roger Locher far behind enemy lines in North Vietnam.

*U. S. Air Force*

Academy, where he was a three-year letterman in track. He qualified for the 1966 All-America Indoor Track Team. He graduated in 1967 and completed fixed-wing pilot training with Flying Class 69-02, pinning on his wings in 1969.

Stovall's first assignment was flying the C-141A Starlifter on long-range transport missions. He was selected for helicopter training in 1970 and flew the HH-53C at Patrick Air Force Base, Florida, as part of the recovery team for the Apollo 14 and 15 lunar spaceflights. Then, he joined the 40th Aerospace Rescue and Recovery Squadron at Nakhon Phanom Air Base, Thailand.

The base, known as "Naked Fanny" to some and simply NKP to most, was a springboard for special operations missions into North Vietnam. NKP's flight line bristled with H-3 Jolly Green and H-53 Super Jolly Green Rescue helicopters, with propeller-driven A-1 Skyraider and B-26 Invader bombers that looked like throwbacks to the past, and with forward air control planes that were painted all black for clandestine flights behind enemy lines.

NKP was the focal point for rescues in the most heavily defended parts of North Vietnam, where missiles, MiGs, and antiaircraft guns

This is Stovall's aircraft: A Sikorsky HH-53B/C Super Jolly Green of the 40th Aerospace Rescue and Recovery Squadron in flight over Southeast Asia, 1972.

*U. S. Air Force*

were everywhere. The airmen at NKP had an irreverent look about them—mavericks, looking like a posse from the Wild West. Like the World War II 1st Air Commando Group from which they descended, the flyers at NKP weren't much for spit and polish, but they would fly into the jaws of hell.

"In my squadron, four out of forty pilots were killed in combat, a loss of 10 percent, something most units wouldn't be able to handle," Stovall said. "Our rescue missions were very much combat first, rescue second. And our successes were very much the work of many people, from the maintainers who worked on our aircraft at night to the pararescuemen who helped with rescues."

May 10, 1972, was the date of the biggest air battles ever fought over North Vietnam. Air Force and Navy F-4 Phantoms, operating in different parts of the country, shot down more than a dozen MiGs in a day of furious fighting.

When F-4 back-seater Locher came up on the radio three weeks after being shot down, rescue experts initially did not believe an Ameri-

Super Jolly Green combat pilot Capt. Dale Stovall gives the re-enlistment oath to flight engineer Technical Sgt. James Duarte at the height of combat operations against North Vietnam in 1972. The python was a fixture at Nakhon Phanom Air Base, Thailand, but the base newspaper refused to publish this photo.

*U. S. Air Force*

can could have survived that long without being rounded up by enemy troops.

## Lodge and Locher

By 1972, after a bombing halt of four years when no air battles were fought over North Vietnam, Hanoi had built up its defenses with Soviet SA-2 Guideline surface-to-air missiles and MiG-17, MiG-19, and MiG-21 fighters. When the bombing halt ended and fighting resumed, their nemesis was the F-4 Phantom.

On a mission up north, the Phantom flew to an anchor orbit, refueled from a KC-135 tanker, and then punched into enemy air space at medium-to-high altitude. When configured for air-to-air combat, a Phantom carried four Sparrow radar-guided missiles, four Sidewinder heat-seeking missiles—and no gun. As surface-to-air missiles proliferated, tactics shifted to lower altitude where fuel burned more quickly, and KC-135 anchors moved closer to the combat zone.

One of the Air Force's top fighter tacticians was Major Robert Lodge, an F-4 Phantom pilot of the 555th Tactical Fighter Squadron, the "Triple Nickel," at Udorn, Thailand. On February 21, 1972, Lodge and back-seater Capt. Roger Locher, flying an F-4D Phantom, chased a MiG-21 up a narrow Laotian valley at night and shot it down. It was a feat of extraordinary daring, handled with businesslike precision. If any

## Who's Who

**The crew of HH-53C callsign JOLLY 30:**

Capt. Dale Stovall, HH-53C aircraft commander (JOLLY 30)

Capt. John Gillespie II, copilot

Airman 1st Class Jim Walsh, flight engineer

Sgt. Chuck McQuoid II, pararescue jumper (PJ)

Airman 1st Class Henry Cakebread, PJ

Tech. Sgt. Bobbie Welborn, gunner

**The crew of HH-53C callsign JOLLY 60:**

Capt. Jerry Shipman, HH-53C aircraft commander (JOLLY 60)

Capt. Stan Zielinski, copilot

Sgt. Bill Liles, flight engineer

Sgt. Dennis Williamson, PJ

Staff Sgt. Don Goodlett, PJ

Staff Sgt. Hal Smith, combat photographer

**Others:**

Capt. Roger Locher, F-4 Phantom weapons officer (OYSTER 01-B)

Major Jim Harding, A-1 Skyraider pilot (SANDY 01)

Capt. Darrel Whitcomb, an OV-10A Bronco pilot

Phantom crew could achieve the feat of shooting down five enemy aircraft to become aces, Lodge and Locher were expected to be the ones. A few days later, they downed a second MiG.

A bombing halt, years of diplomacy, every effort to find some solution in Vietnam—all of it had failed. On April 2, 1972, invading North Vietnamese forces launched a spring offensive and captured the provincial capital of Quang Tri. On April 6, President Nixon resumed limited bombing of North Vietnam for the first time since 1968. The new campaign became known as Linebacker.

Joining many dozens of U.S. warplanes over the North on May 10, 1972, Lodge led four F-4s northwest from Hanoi at low altitude and high speed toward Yen Bai airfield. No U.S. aircraft were north of Lodge, meaning that he could fire his Sparrow radar missiles head-on without visual confirmation of the MiGs. Warnings from DISCO (the EC-121 radar plane off the coast), from RED CROWN (the U.S. Navy's radar picket ship), and from backseater Locher told Lodge that plenty of MiGs were coming up to fight.

Lodge's OYSTER flight engaged a formation of MiG-21s and fired Sparrows from almost the limits of visual range. OYSTER 2, the Phantom piloted by Lt. John Markle, brought down a MiG-21.

Lodge wanted to prevent MiGs from reaching U.S. strike forces in the Hanoi-Haiphong region. He succeeded, but OYSTER flight was suddenly engulfed in MiGs.

Lodge blasted a MiG-21 out of the sky, the third aerial kill for him and his back-seater. Another MiG-21 popped in front of him and would have been a perfect target—if only the Phantom had had a gun. Meanwhile, four MiG-19s dropped out of the clouds behind them and worked into Lodge's six o'clock position. Lodge was still chasing the MiG-21 and may not have heard Markle's voice shouting that he was being tailed. Lodge's Phantom was now an inviting target for the MiG-19s as they closed to within 1,500 ft (460 m) and opened fire with their cannons. "Break right!" boomed Markle's voice in Lodge's ears. "Break right, now! They are firing at you!"

Cannon shells pierced the Phantom's thin metal skin, rupturing its hydraulic and electrical lines, exploding with a furious noise and setting the F-4 afire.

Lodge had been exposed to sensitive classified information on a previous tour of duty. His buddies believe he made a personal decision not to become a North Vietnamese captive. Lodge ordered Locher to eject. Lodge was still in the Phantom, in its final seconds, boring to the ground when Locher watched a good parachute canopy fill with air above his head and saw the green-brown terrain of North Vietnam coming up to meet him.

**DALE STOVALL** On June 1, 1972, I was flying the lead helicopter on a precautionary rescue orbit in northern Laos when I received word that Locher had radioed from deep inside North Vietnam that he had been on the ground since May 10 and was still evading capture. We were sure this was a ploy to lure our slow-moving helicopters into a trap, but we made the decision to go in. Escorted by two A-1H Skyraider, or SANDY, prop-driven attack planes, we took two helicopters 110 miles (175 km) into North Vietnam. We halted just eight miles short of North Vietnam's Yen Bai airfield where about seventy MiGs were stationed.

That's when they started shooting surface-to-air missiles, or SAMs, in our direction. Small-arms and antiaircraft fire also came up at us.

The view from the tanker: This is Dale Stovall's pilot's view of the C-130 tanker aircraft used to refuel his Super Jolly Green helicopter en route to North Vietnam.

*U. S. Air Force*

The enemy reaction, coupled with confusing directions on the radio, made it impossible to locate the man on the ground—who might have been Locher, we thought, though we were still very skeptical and worried. We searched for forty-five minutes, using up precious fuel and daylight. We couldn't find him. And just when we needed something good to happen, a MiG-21 came after us.

This was not a pretty picture—a pair of Super Jolly Greens breaking from each other, going nose-down, diving into a narrow valley and weaving in the shadows with a cannon-armed supersonic fighter stalking us.

I had my squadron commander in the right seat. It was his first and only combat mission. He was a poor commander and nobody respected him. I had just told him to take the aircraft while I reached for a map. That's when the MiG-21 appeared.

I heard Smith in the SANDY yelling, "MiGs! Get down, Jollys! A MiG!" One of my guys in the back yelled out, "A MiG at six o'clock!" I took control of the helicopter back. I decided to do a split-S. I turned us upside down, but we were only 700 feet off the ground and there wasn't space to complete the maneuver I'd begun. I realized it wasn't going to work. That's when the whole world stopped. You've heard the image of the baseball player when he's going for the ball, time stops for him, and he can actually see the stitches? Time came to such a halt for me that I could actually see our rotors, as if they were in slow motion.

I found a way to pull out us out of that maneuver—but just barely. Now we were hopping over the ground. I looked out forward and saw the MiG-21 going by us. I saw his tail pipe. He was heading up the Red River, going upstream. If he had fired on us, he had missed. Both HH-53Cs had split and now we had to find each other.

Then, I heard SANDY pilot Smith yelling, "MiG! MiG! Get the hell out of here! I've been hit." I said, "What's your position?" He said, "Don't ask about me. Get the hell out of here!" There was indeed another MiG behind us and our HH-53C was diving toward a village below us. I figured, "If he shoots at us, he's going to shoot into this village. I can't stop him from shooting but I can take some of them with us." So I headed down main street in this village with the MiG behind us, the helicopter and MiG each trying to outguess the other.

It turned out the A-1 hadn't been hit, after all. Trying to outmaneuver the MiG, he had gone into a spin and heard a horrible noise when his airplane objected, but he had not actually been hit.

The number-two A-1 pilot got this MiG in his sight. But he hesitated. He wasn't certain. He wasn't sure it wasn't one of our F-4s. During that split second when he paused, the MiG pulled out of his gunsight and was gone, and that pilot has kicked himself in the butt about it ever since. In the entire war, an Air Force A-1 never shot down a MiG: He had had a chance and blown it.

With all this maneuvering, we would have run out of fuel and gone down in North Vietnam had it not been for a brave HC-130 crew that came fifty miles inside the border and refueled us over the Black River. The A-1s had to leave us because they were low on fuel. We worked our way out of North Vietnam without our escort.

We were heading for NKP when my wingman's bird had a power transmission problem. They performed an autorotation and set down in a rice paddy just after dark. This was a serious blow because we needed that particular HH-53C: It was the only one available to us that was equipped with a device called ELF (electronic location finder)—a primitive first attempt to marry low-light-level television and night-vision goggles, making it possible to pinpoint the location of the survivor. This was far more effective than the direction-finding method known as ADF. We looked at each other and said, "We have to have that helicopter."

Our maintenance guys worked all night in waist-deep water to fix the transmission on the HH-53C. Next morning, it was sitting on the ramp, sparkling like new.

We had to sleep, of course, if we were going to go back after Locher. You might ask, how could we sleep, knowing we were going back there, where we'd been chased by a MiG-21? Well, when you're young and in combat, you're fatalistic. You see harm and injury happen to others but you're sure it isn't going to happen to you.

## Going in Again: June 2, 1972

There was activity all night long at NKP as plans were put together for a more robust rescue attempt. The commander of Seventh Air Force in Saigon called us up and said, "Do you think you can go get Roger Locher?" He had made a big decision. This was the first time in the war that we bombed a MiG airfield. We had sixteen F-4 Phantoms assigned to drop bombs on the runway at Yen Bai. Afterward, Capt. Ron Smith was going to fly over in his A-1 Skyraider to make sure the runway was cratered and then he was going to cover us while we went for Locher. We also put some extra H-53s on the ground in northern Laos on standby alert in case anybody in our rescue force went down.

We got up at what the troops called "oh dark thirty"—that's military for "early"—and got ready to go. On our missions into North Vietnam, I was determined that if I ever got shot down, I was going to fight and my crew felt the same way. I carried a Walther PPK with 200 rounds of .22 ammo, a .38 revolver with fifty rounds, a folding-stock AR-15 rifle with three thirty-shot clips (ninety rounds), and a bandolier with more rounds. I looked like Pancho Villa. If they thought they were going to get me, I was going to shoot it out. Our crew had a plan that we all agreed to: If we went down in Bad Guy Land, we would set up a

"I looked like Pancho Villa," said Capt. Dale Stovall, seen here at a briefing before a combat mission into North Vietnam.

*U. S. Air Force*

perimeter around the helicopter, use our M-60 machine gun and our miniguns and whatever else we had, and defend ourselves. We looked at each other that morning and everybody knew we were ready.

The next morning, we launched at 5:39 a.m. Our plan was to launch all of our helicopters in waves of two so we would be available all day and be on the tanker at different times. Right after takeoff, my wingman had a failure in his flight control system and aborted. So my roommate Jerry Shipman became my wingman and caught up with me in a different HH-53C. We were accompanied by A-1 Skyraiders, which were limited to six hours of flight, not by fuel but by oil.

This was very different from the previous day. This time, there was an armada going into North Vietnam—tankers, fighters, forward air controllers, SANDYs, and helicopters. We shut down the war to go get Roger Locher. There were 119 aircraft over North Vietnam supporting us one way or another. Hundreds of Americans contributed to this effort and my crew just happened to be lucky to be the one on the end point.

There were two conflicting forces at work as we headed into North Vietnam. On one hand, the entire United States command in Southeast

Asia was stirred up at the prospect that we might be able to save a guy who had dodged the enemy and stayed alive for three weeks. Locher's fighter wing was stationed at Udorn, Thailand, and the brass there were extremely interested in what was going on, but we learned later that the interest went much higher. A couple of top generals in Saigon were traveling up to Udorn to monitor the situation.

The other conflicting force was skepticism. Was this really Locher and, if so, was he broadcasting with a North Vietnamese AK-47 up against his head? We knew that the North Vietnamese used various tricks to try to lure us—especially our very vulnerable helicopters—into places where they could blast away at us.

The attack on Yen Bai proceeded and the A-1s moved in ahead of us to the location where we believed Locher—if it was Locher—was located. As we went in over rolling foothills, there were two A-1s putting down phosphorus smoke so the North Vietnamese wouldn't be able to see us to shoot when we went into the hover.

After we began our run-in, somebody pointed out that we didn't have MiGCAP—the MiG Combat Air Patrol of friendly fighters that would keep the bad guys off our backs. We knew the airfield at Yen Bai was supposed to be neutralized now, but without CAP there could still be MiGs coming after us from some other location. They said, "You still want to go in?" I said, "We came this far and we may not be able to create a chance like this again."

As we moved in, automatic weapons fire erupted from a Vietnamese hut nearby. Sgt. Charles B. McQuoid and Airman Kenneth W. Cakebread, my PJs, silenced the ground fire with miniguns.

My wingman Jerry said, "Okay, he's over the top this next ridgeline." I came over the top of the ridgeline. They told him to pop his smoke. That means igniting a colored-smoke canister to mark your location. At this point we had authenticated his identity using the procedures we had in place in Southeast Asia—we still don't discuss those—but we were still not 100 percent certain that this was our American survivor. I told my gunners, "If you see more than one person down there, shoot them all."

I held our HH-53C, JOLLY 30, in a slightly nose-high attitude and an eighty-foot hover and moved to the slope where he was supposed to be. I was right on top of him now. I couldn't see his smoke, but I saw his mirror flash. I said, "Okay, I've got a good mirror flash. I'm going over him and putting down the hoist." The hill had a decent amount of smoke on it and we had to stay probably eighty feet off the slope while lowering the penetrator. My gunners were bent over their weapons, looking for trouble—but the gunners and the PJs were telling me over the intercom that they saw only one man standing below us.

When we arrived overhead and saw only one guy on the ground I was pretty relieved. Later, I learned a lot about the survival saga of Roger Locher, who consumed mostly rainwater, leafy foliage, and small nibbles of some kind of sparse, unripe jungle fruit. He scrambled around near a huge MiG base with enemy troops often within a few hundred feet of him. It rained every day, and he took special care not to let his boots or socks rot. He could hear the MiGs at nearby Yen Bai. He lost fifteen pounds.

At the moment of the pickup, though, my relief that it really was Locher was tempered by the knowledge that we really had to get the hell out of there, fast. Now my gunners were laying down fire in a direction behind the survivor where it appeared there were some bad guys.

We weren't in a hover more than three or four minutes at most. I didn't have to lower a PJ to the ground. Roger was able to grab the hoist penetrator by himself, so my PJ stayed on board and hoisted him up. For a moment there, he was just dangling in space, and for a moment after that he seemed to be jammed in the doorway. But we pulled him in—this rail-thin, emaciated figure in a tattered American flight suit—and I started to get us out of there. On the radio, we passed along the news that it really was Locher and that we had him, but that we weren't safely out of the critical area.

I had time for only a quick greeting with Locher. He came up to the cockpit to thank me. In my pocket, I had a package of cookies from my mother. I knew he hadn't eaten in a long time, so I gave him the cook-

F-4 Phantom back-seater Capt. Roger Locher, otherwise known as OYSTER 01 BRAVO, safe inside Stovall's helicopter after being rescued following three weeks on the ground in North Vietnam.

*U. S. Air Force*

ies. He stuffed them in his pockets and said, "If we get shot down, this time I'll have something to eat with me." One of my crewmembers also handed Roger his first cigarette in twenty-three days.

That's when we started taking ground fire—and soon afterward, a MiG attack.

## Getting Home from Yen Bai

We crossed the river at a place called the Thumb in the River. There was a train from China coming toward us on the northwest rail line. It was a supply train. I saw this steam engine right below us. Yes, it was one of those ancient steam engines letting out a white trail of smoke. It had sandbagged gun cars and wooden rail cars.

Everything was happening quickly. We were taking ground fire from somewhere along the rail tracks. My minigunners were trying to shoot at the train. The gunners on the train were all looking downriver at the smoke from our rescue site and never had a chance to get a shot off at us. We went right over the train at 200 feet. I was jinking furiously from left to right, so my minigunners probably weren't able to hit anything.

Behind us came the A-1s, the SANDY rescue escorts, led by their squadron commander, Major Jim Harding, who was an unbelievably brave guy. He was also our friend. If anybody took a shot at a helicopter, he killed them. Jim made a pass on the train. Here you had a World War II propeller airplane attacking a World War II train.

A moment later, a MiG-19 attacked us.

Now I'm thinking both of getting killed and of suffering the embarrassment of losing our valuable survivor after we've rescued him. Jerry calls out, "MiG! Level, at nine o'clock!" I look out at this MiG-19 coming at us from ninety degrees. He must have been really focusing on our helicopters because he turned belly-up to Jim Harding, giving Jim a perfect target. Harding let loose with four 20-milimeters and with the white phosphorus rockets he had on board. Harding led the MiG by too much, missed him, and went past him. But he must have put an awful fear into that MiG pilot because the MiG pulled up into a chandelle and departed. Now I had seen two incidents in which A-1 pilots had had a chance to get a MiG and didn't. Believe me, the A-1 guys were grumpy at the NKP bar that night.

We didn't go straight back to NKP. The word came that we were to take Roger to Udorn. When we landed at his base, there were probably 5,000 people waiting for him. I'm looking out my window and there are two four-star generals in front of the crowd. I'm thinking, "Hey, I need a haircut." With some fanfare, we deposited Roger Locher among the waiting dignitaries—he came up to visit us at NKP a couple of weeks later—and we said, "Well, at least we're finished for the day." So we headed for the bar at NKP. We were just getting real comfortable when they told us we would have to fly our helicopters back to NKP that night.

**DARREL WHITCOMB** Roger Locher later became a pilot, flew F-4 Phantoms in Alaska, and had a key role in the early days of the supersecret "black program" that produced the F-117 Nighthawk stealth fighter (Chapter Eighteen). He retired as a colonel and lives in Kansas.

Dale Stovall credits his training at the Air Force Academy (class of 1967) for helping him when he became a helicopter pilot in combat in Southeast Asia. He said, "The leadership experience you get as a cadet was very valuable to me as a young officer when I had to work with troops of different ranks, ages, and motivations. There are two basic elements, responsibility and authority. You are responsible for the crew and mission and all the things that can go wrong. But you cannot

The two helicopter crews that pulled off the Locher rescue. In the top row is the crew of JOLLY 60: (left to right), Capt. Jerry Shipman, pilot; Capt. Stan Zielinski, copilot; Sgt. Bill Liles, engineer; Sgt. Dennis Williamson, pararescue jumper (PJ); Staff Sgt. Don Goodlett, PJ; Staff Sgt. Hal Smith, combat photographer. In the bottom row is the crew of JOLLY 30: Capt. Dale Stovall, pilot; Capt. John Gillespie II, copilot; Airman 1st Class Jim Walsh, engineer; Sgt. Chuck McQuoid II, PJ; Airman 1st Class Henry Cakebread, PJ; Tech Sgt. Bobbie Welborn, gunner.

*U. S. Air Force*

overstep your bounds of authority—becoming that little Napoleon. You need to understand the hierarchy of authority—try to give the lower ranking guys the proper amount of authority and responsibility."

Stovall repeatedly makes the point that he couldn't have done it alone. As a young HH-53C aircraft commander, he commanded young men of various ranks, ages, and motivations who rescued downed airmen from Laos and North Vietnam. Later, he would command squadrons and wings that carried out combat search-and-rescue missions in other wars.

Stovall was awarded the Air Force Cross for that mission. He received two Silver Star awards for other rescues among the twelve he accomplished in Southeast Asia. Stovall flew seventy-nine combat missions and logged 267.7 combat hours. Crews like Stovall's saved 2,624 lives under hostile conditions and another 1,231 lives between December 1, 1964, and March 29, 1973.

Stovall continued from Southeast Asia to a full Air Force career in rescue and special operations. He commanded the 1st Special Operations Wing at Hurlburt Field, Florida, from 1987 to 1989.

In his final two assignments between 1990 and 1993, Stovall was vice commander of Air Force Special Operations Command and deputy commanding general of Joint Special Operations Command at Fort Bragg, North Carolina.

Stovall lives today in Montana and is a commercial pilot. He and his wife Carol have three children.

# Sikorsky HH-53C Super Jolly Green Giant

The HH-53C was the biggest U.S. helicopter of the Vietnam era. It was developed after the Marine Corps introduced the first version, the CH-53A, as a cargo hauler in Vietnam. Development of an Air Force combat rescue model began in November 1966 when two Marine CH-53As

## Sikorsky HH-53C Super Jolly Green (S-65)

**Type:** Four-place combat rescue helicopter

**Powerplant:** Two 3,925-shp (2927-kW) General Electric T64-GE-7 turbo-shaft engines driving a 72 ft 3 in (22.02-m), six-bladed main rotor

**Performance:** Maximum level speed at sea level, 196 mph (315 km/h); cruising speed, 173 mph (278 km/h); maximum rate of climb at sea level, 2,070 ft (631 m) per minute; service ceiling, 20,400 ft (6220 m); hovering ceiling in ground effect, 11,700 ft (3565 m); range with two 450 U.S.-gal (1073-liter) auxiliary tanks and 10 percent reserves, 540 miles (869 km)

**Weights:** Empty, 23,569 lb (10690 kg); mission takeoff weight, 38,238 lb (17344 kg); maximum takeoff weight, 42,000 lb (19050 kg)

**Dimensions:** Main rotor diameter, 72 ft 3 in (22.02 m); fuselage length, excluding refueling probe, 67 ft 2 in (20.47 m); height overall, 24 ft 11 in (7.60 m); tail rotor diameter, 16 ft (4.88 m); main rotor disc area, 4,070 sq ft (378.10 sq m)

**Payload:** 38 troops; 24 stretchers and 4 attendants; or 7,000 lb (3,629 kg) of cargo loaded through full section rear ramp/doors

**Armament:** Up to three 7.62-mm miniguns

**Dimensions:** Main rotor diameter, 72 ft 2-3/4 in (22.02 m)

**Armament:** Door-mounted 7.62-mm minigun

**First flight:** March 15, 1967 (HH-53B)

A formation of HH-53B/C Super Jolly Green helicopters escorted by A-1 Skyraiders over North Vietnam.

*U. S. Air Force*

were loaned to the Air Force. Eight USAF combat-rescue HH-53Bs followed. One of these was tested in 1969 with a night/all-weather rescue system known as Pave Low I, which did not prove successful. By the time of the Roger Locher rescue in North Vietnam, the HH-53B models had been relegated to training squadrons.

The Air Force also acquired twenty CH-53C cargo haulers, six VH-53F VIP transports, and forty-four improved HH-53C combat-rescue helicopters that served in Vietnam beginning in 1969. These helicopters participated in the attempt to rescue American prisoners of war in the celebrated Son Tay raid of November 1970. During that mission, Special Forces troops were taken to a site hundreds of miles behind enemy lines, where they fought successfully against superior numbers, but discovered in the end that no prisoners were at Son Tay to be rescued. The HH-53C remained in service into the late 1980s and supported Apollo space missions: The HH-53C's external cargo hook of 20,000 lb (9,072 kg) capacity would have enabled it to retrieve the manned lunar capsule in the event of an abort just after launch.

In the years since Vietnam, the Air Force's HH-53C fleet has evolved into the subsequent MH-53H, MH-53J, and MH-53M Pave Low helicopters—Vietnam-era fuselages, now with modernized interiors, used in later conflicts like the one in Kosovo (Chapter Eighteen). Less directly, the twin-engined HH-53C series led to today's three-engined Marine Corps CH-53A Super Sea Stallion, used in Afghanistan and Iraq (Chapter Nineteen).

# Chapter 18

---

# Stealth Fighter Down in Serbia

## What Happened

When the Air Force's F-117 stealth fighter, the supersecret "Black Jet," was shot down by a Serbian surface-to-air missile on March 27, 1999, a radio call went into the night: "Mayday, Mayday, Mayday. I'm VEGA 31, on the way down."

That call came from the stealth fighter's pilot, dangling beneath a parachute, scanning the bare Serbian farmscape, and talking into a PRC-112A, handheld, line-of-sight survival radio. The radar-evading stealth fighter was the newest thing in the sky, a high-tech marvel never before touched by any enemy. The handheld survival radio was one of the oldest in inventory. The F-117 pilot, whose name is withheld at his request, was parachuting into enemy territory with an obsolete radio that might or might not reach friendly forces. Smack in the middle of the information age, the age of instant communication, the age of satellites and global positioning systems, the United States was sending its elite aerial warriors into battle with survival equipment that hadn't changed since Vietnam.

Operation Allied Force, the 1999 battle for Kosovo—like wars before it—brought together the new and the old. While the pilot of the

Captain James Cardoso
March 27, 1999
Sikorsky MH-53J/M Enhanced
     Pave Low III-E (MOCCASIN
     60)
Sikorsky MH-60G Pave Hawk
     (GATOR 67)
Lockheed F-117A Nighthawk
     (82-806/VEGA 31)
55th Special Operations
     Squadron
20th/21st Special Operations
     Squadron
Budjanovci, Serbia

Capt. James Cardoso (far right) with
his MH-53H crew at the time of the
rescue of the F-117 pilot.

*Jim Cardoso*

high-tech stealth descended in his chute using a low-tech radio, Capt. Jim Cardoso was preparing to lead a rescue force of three helicopters standing on alert to fly a combat rescue if needed. The two larger helicopters were Pave Lows, an MH-53M and a similar MH-53J model. One was the very same airframe Dale Stovall had flown in combat twenty-seven years earlier (Chapter Seventeen), but modified many times since then. The Pave Low was a Vietnam-era airframe packed full of new equipment for night- and low-level operations, even in bad weather, but it was still very old. The third helicopter, an MH-60G, was smaller and newer, but some crew members considered it inadequate. The Air Force had considered buying a version with terrain-following radar but had purchased a no-frills model instead. Fighting a modern war against a modern Serbian army with modern radar, missiles, and guns, the Air Force was flying helicopters that weren't good enough and would now use them in an attempt to rescue a pilot with a handheld radio that wasn't good enough, either.

MOCCASIN 60, a Sikorsky MH-53H Enhanced Pave Low III piloted by Capt. James Cardoso, led the rescue force that went into Serbia to attempt to save the pilot of the downed F-117 stealth fighter.

*Robert F. Dorr*

**F-117 PILOT (NAME WITHHELD)** I ate a bowl of Grape Nuts before I went on my flight that night. Before I even stepped into the aircraft, I was well acquainted with my risks and vulnerabilities. I had flown in Operation Desert Storm in 1991—twenty combat sorties, about the average for guys who were there for the whole war—so I had combat experience.

I took off from Aviano Air Base, Italy. I flew the F-117 to the target and dropped two 2,000-lb laser-guided weapons on a very specific target in the Belgrade area. I can't say exactly what the target was, but I can say we were spot on.

Bad weather is nothing unusual in the Balkans. Because of the weather, only 50 percent of us got our targets that night. Those who did not get their targets did not drop their weapons. The rules of engagement were pretty strict.

I came off the target twenty nautical miles northwest of Belgrade when it happened. I saw it coming. It didn't surprise me. I thought the possibility of something like that happening was very great. [Author's note: The F-117 pilot, callsign VEGA 31, is referring to an enemy surface-to-air missile being fired at his aircraft. Neither the Air Force nor the pilot will discuss the details of the shootdown, but the Air Force acknowledges than "an enemy missile system" was the culprit. Other sources say an SA-6 missile shot down VEGA 31. During Operation Allied Force, pilots reported almost 700 missile shots: 266 from SA-6s; 174 from SA-3s; 106 from shoulder-mounted, portable missiles; and another

## Who's Who

### Aboard the first Pave Low (MOCCASIN 60):

Capt. James Cardoso, aircraft commander and helicopter flight commander

Lt. Col. Steve Laushine, aboard Cardoso's aircraft as rescue mission commander

Capt. John Glass, copilot

And others

### Aboard the second Pave Low (MOCCASIN 61):

Capt. Shawn Cameron, aircraft commander

Major Mark Daley, copilot

And others

### Aboard the MH-60G Pave Hawk (GATOR 67):

Capt. Chad P. Franks, aircraft commander

Capt. Matt Glover, copilot

Staff Sgt. Shawn Swift, flight engineer/right door gunner

Staff Sgt. Joe Kirsch, door gunner

Staff Sgt. Eric "Chino" Giacchino, pararescue jumper (PJ)

And others

### Aboard other aircraft:

Capt. John A. Cherrey, A-10 Warthog "Sandy" pilot (SANDY 01)

(Name Withheld), F-117 stealth fighter pilot (VEGA 31)

126 from unidentified weapons. Two aircraft were shot down during the Kosovo campaign: The other was an F-16 Fighting Falcon, callsign HAMMER 34.]

It was extremely violent. The aircraft went into a left roll and a negative G tuck, meaning I was getting negative gravity forces of seven Gs or more. The physiology folks say that three-and-a-half negative Gs is the point of total incapacitation, so I was literally pinned inside my straps. Folks were surprised that I lived through that and did not sustain any debilitating injuries.

I ejected.

My first thing to do was to inventory the condition of my parachute and my equipment. It was a 90 percent almost-full-moon night. We were receiving a lot of illumination. I looked up at the canopy and thought it was great, perfect—a fully inflated parachute. And my second thought was, "You gotta be kidding me," because it was an orange and white parachute glowing like a Chinese lantern out there in the middle of the night. When I looked up and noticed the canopy, I thought in a humorous way, "You gotta be kidding me." I tapped my left bottom vest pocket that had two signal flares in

The helicopter that went down to pick up the F-117 pilot was a Sikorsky MH-60G Pave Low, similar to this one.

*Geoff LeBaron*

it, I thought, "Why don't I just pull out a flare and light it, too?" Anybody down on the ground was certain to see me and track me visually as I floated downward, surrounded by all that light.

A lot of thoughts went through my mind. In our SERE (survival, evasion, resistance, and escape) training we'd been taught, "Don't do anything while you're still under the parachute other than basic survival stuff: Focus on your breathing and on being intact. Treat yourself for shock. Get on the ground and get into an established hole-up site *before* you get on the radio." That's the way they taught it, but it didn't take into account a lot of things, including the fact that any radio call would reach a lot farther if I made it while still up in the sky.

I was thinking, "I'm alone out here. I'm single-ship. There has been no talking, no squawking. I have no wingman. If I don't get things going now, it may take hours before they know I'm out here. So I'd better get on the radio and get something started right now." The JPRA, the Joint Personnel Recovery Agency, says chances of a combat rescue go way down after two hours.

I had a basic, handheld PRC-112A ("prick 112") radio—essentially a walkie-talkie with very limited line-of-sight capability. No over-the-horizon capability. No secure voice capability. So I figured while under the parachute, long before hitting the ground, was the best time to make that radio work. I figured my chances of being captured once I hit the ground were pretty good. I wanted the Serbs not to capture an F-117 pilot—the ultimate prize—without our side knowing I was alive.

If captured, the Serbs would know I had communicated with our side and that might encourage them to keep me alive. It was contrary to our training but when I was debriefed later, they said that my rescue would have been almost impossible without that radio call right after ejecting.

"I'm out of the aircraft," I said. We have some procedures that help our side know this is the real thing. I said the right words, carefully.

**JIM CARDOSO** Our helicopter force that night consisted of two Pave Lows, the Air Force's largest special-operations helicopters, plus a single MH-60G Pave Hawk, a smaller craft that would go in and make the pickup if we were able to rescue VEGA 31.

Air Force Special Operations Command, or AFSOC, was the "owner" of the helicopters. The Pave Low community had been operating in that part of the world for many years, and our Pave Low detachment was a mixture of aircraft and people from the 20th and 21st Special Operations Squadrons. The solo MH-60G belonged to the 55th Special Operations Squadron. All three of the helicopter units were home-based at Hurlburt Field, Florida, which is also where AFSOC is headquartered.

Our helicopters were deployed to Brindisi, Italy, but we took off that night from an FOL, or forward operating location, at Tusla in eastern Croatia. It was the fourth night of the war.

There were, of course, a lot of other people in the air. Most important were the A-10 Warthog, or SANDY aircraft, that controlled the rescue scene, but there were also a tanker, an airborne control ship, and several other aircraft in the area.

The command arrangements that night were a little complicated. Lt. Col. Steve Laushine (pronounced *la-sheen*), the 55th SOS commander, was aboard my Pave Low, not in his usual capacity as a pilot but as the commander of the rescue helicopter force. I was the helicopter flight commander, which meant I was responsible for the actual flying of the three helicopters. Capt. John Cherrey, pilot of the A-10, the SANDY, was the OSC, or on-scene commander, meaning he would survey the site of the possible rescue and determine what actions to take.

When we learned that a friendly aircraft was down, we realized that a lot of things could happen. The Serbs could even capture the pilot and try to use him to lure us into their gunsights.

The weather started out to be not too bad when we departed. As the night progressed, it got progressively worse. By the time we were proceeding inbound from the border (Bosnia to Serbia), it dropped to 3,000 feet overcast, solid—and below that it was intermittent rain showers with areas of low visibility. It is not a big deal for us to be limited to flying below 3,000 feet but it was difficult for the other aircraft, like the A-10s. The weather made it impossible for them to try to visually identify the survivor on the ground. They functioned more as command-and-control platforms than as conventional warplanes. The OSC, again, was Capt. John Cherrey, piloting an A-10 with the callsign SANDY 01. I think there was a brief period when John was somewhere else. Someone else took over for a short time.

It became a night of attempting to communicate with VEGA 31 and trying to achieve a successful rescue despite repeated obstacles posed by communication, the weather, and the Serbs. A definite concern the entire night was that we might be lured in. The Sandys couldn't see. VEGA 31 knew only what was in his immediate vicinity. We had been briefed that Serbs had countertactics specifically aimed at rescue forces. A lot of folks think, "Serbs? Aha! Dumb guys!" But the Serbs had access to all the intelligence techniques and electronic capabilities of the former Soviet Union. They knew electronic deception. They were definitely not dumb guys.

## What Happened

When the MH-53M, MH-53J, and MH-60G took off to attempt the pickup, everyone in the rescue force knew the United States had lost an F-117 stealth fighter in combat for the first time. Developed in a super-secret "black program" in the 1980s and revealed to the public only in 1989 after almost fifty were already flying, the "Black Jet" was the silver bullet of the U.S. war arsenal. It had been developed to attack high-value targets in a Soviet Union that no longer existed. Used in combat

Until one was shot down over Serbia by a surface-to-air missile in 1999, no F-117 stealth fighter had ever been touched by enemy action. The F-117 pilot, known by the call-sign VEGA 31, ejected over Serbia and hoped for rescue.

*Joseph G. Handelman*

in Panama in 1989 and in Operation Desert Storm in 1991, the "Black Jet" had seemed to many to be invulnerable. "When our helicopters launched, we knew exactly what kind of aircraft had gone down," said a helicopter crewmember who, like the F-117 pilot, requested not to be named. Much later, the F-117 pilot himself described the stakes: "Allowing the Serbs to have a senior officer, an F-117 pilot, to parade around in front of the world like a trophy would have changed the whole feeling and attitude and complexion for everyone."

The F-117 was shot down at 8:38 p.m. By 1:00 a.m., Serbian television was showing footage of civilians dancing around the burning, crumpled wreckage of the stealth fighter, with its serial number (82-806) and other markings plainly visible. Serbian radio and television said that, "Certain electronic equipment was recovered from wreckage and stored for further investigation." In fact, the only stealth aircraft ever shot down was probably of interest not only to the Serbs but to the Russians, who were nominally on the other side. For days afterward, commentators asked why the United States didn't bomb the wreckage to make it useless to hostile intelligence. There really wasn't time to mount a bombing mission for that purpose.

The three rescue helicopters led by Capt. Jim Cardoso's MH-53M Pave Low were airborne quickly but ran into an expected problem when they reached the Serbian border: Fighters, command-and-control airplanes, and other assets needed for the rescue weren't yet ready for the push into Serbian airspace. Cardoso's helicopters hovered for awhile at the edge of Serbian territory, then landed with engines running—and gunners on high alert—to conserve fuel.

**F-117 PILOT (NAME WITHHELD)** Still hanging from my chute, I established contact with FRANK 36, a tanker that was refueling F-16s over Bosnia. Isn't it funny that with all the assets out there, it was a tanker doing his little thing over there that answered my transmission?

That got everything going. Nobody was aware that this had happened, believe it or not, until they heard me talking.

I came down through several layers of clouds. I broke through clouds at 2,000 feet. The ground was well illuminated. I scoped out the terrain and picked out an initial hole-up site. I was able to steer and crab into the wind with the parachute on my way down and get myself to touch down in a better area than I otherwise would have, which helped my not getting captured right off the bat.

I landed in a meticulously plowed farm field. It was very flat and there was no cover. People were amazed later that I evaded as well as I did. I was near a north-south, two-lane road that had a lot of activity on it. I was certain someone would have seen me coming down. So I wanted to clear my landing site as rapidly as possible. I tried to minimize movement and sound and to not use my flashlight.

Now I'm no longer a high-speed jet pilot. Now I'm a special ops, special tactics kind of guy on a covert mission. I made my way to my initial hole-up sight, a shallow irrigation ditch. As it ended up, that was where I stayed the whole time. I figured it was foolish to travel across that open farm field in the middle of the night.

I was in great shape. I was well hydrated. I had a lot of extra water I'd brought with me. I'd had a meal, so I had some good complex carbohydrates inside me. I didn't have any serious injuries.

Once in my hole-up site, I jumped back up on the radio. That was one hour and 20 minutes into the event [9:58 p.m.] and the first folks I talked to were in the ABCCC [airborne command and control center, an aircraft orbiting on the other side of the border]. Before that, I tried to establish exactly where I was, coordinate-wise.

My squadron's life-support shop had just purchased a $100 KMart special Garman-40 handheld GPS [global positioning system, for navigation]. Before the war started, I grabbed my intelligence officer, looked at a huge map of the AOR [area of responsibility, meaning the combat theater], oriented myself on where the country borders were, and where the SAR dot was. [The SAR dot, for search and rescue, is a point on a map picked at random and briefed to everyone on a combat mission, to be used as a point of reference without need to mention geographic names.]

I had an idea geographically where SAR dot was. I made a guess and when I checked my GPS—it took awhile for that sucker to connect to the satellite—and the SAR dot was in the GPS. It told me I was thirty-nine degrees and 101 miles from the SAR dot. So when I came up, I said, "Hey, I'm oh-thirty-nine degrees and 101 miles from the SAR dot." This made a big difference because the rescue people had a lot of ideas as to where I was. The actual set of coordinates that got the helicopters into the area came from me.

I've been asked why some of us didn't have survival radios. I wish I had had an STU-3 [a secure telephone used in ground communications]. It would have been nice to have secure voice and over-the-horizon capability and to say, "Hey, do you guys know what happened?"

As a survivor and an evader, it was important to me to have situational awareness. Unfortunately, I had extremely limited situational awareness—namely, only as far as I could see or hear from my ditch. Without secure communication, you want minimize radio contact. If I could have picked the equipment I'd have in that ditch with me, I might have chosen a better radio, but I had other wants besides the radio. I would have loved a full-day shopping spree at L.L.Bean, including some sort of night vision device, perhaps a monocular. After the moon set there was no illumination whatsoever. There was a thick, low cloud deck that rolled in with heavy rain.

Throughout the night, I stayed very busy. I thought, what will my initial reaction be if I'm captured? What's my plan if I don't get rescued tonight? Do I go back to my landing site and bury my parachute harness and helmet to make it harder to find me? I spent a lot of time in-

The F-117 stealth fighter is sometimes called "the Black Jet" because of the paint scheme it wears for night operations.

*Robert F. Dorr*

ventorying my survival equipment. I knew I did not want to make noise or use a flashlight. I arranged to be able to find my equipment anytime just by feel.

At the three-hour point [11:38 p.m.], I first made contact with the SANDYs. It had taken them awhile to get on scene. We established good radio contact—again, in the clear, no secure voice capability. They authenticated me multiple times throughout the event. That means we used a technique that enabled me to confirm that I was not an imposter. I won't discuss how we do it, beyond that.

We knew that the Serbs had very good tactical radio reception and were almost certainly listening. The SANDYs [Capt Cherrey in his A-10] wanted to know if I'd been captured, if this was an ambush. The helicopters were approaching me now, and they were ready to execute, but they were called off because they feared I'd been captured. JPRA guys are still shaking their heads in disbelief that we pulled that off.

**JIM CARDOSO** We were heading toward VEGA 31 in the middle of the night and were almost called off once or twice. We didn't know what to expect when we got there. It was a prebriefed tactic that the MH-6G would make the pickup. It was a little smaller than our Pave Lows and could fit into a smaller space. We had two pararescue jumpers, or PJs, on the MH-60G. If we needed to land in the larger helicopters, we had a site security team in the back of mine: five Army Special Forces guys.

There could be bad guys in the general area. There could be all kinds of possibilities. So we wanted to carry a little extra firepower.

**F-117 PILOT (NAME WITHHELD)** At the three-and-a-half hour point or so [about 11:30 p.m.], I had a visitor—a dog. It was evident there was quite a bit of search activity very near me. I had a nine millimeter with two extra clips but had no intention of using it in any combat role. There was some pretty good rain, so I fashioned an awning with one of my waterproof maps and huddled under it. This was very effective.

The most difficult thing for me was that my situational awareness was very limited. We had not been made aware of what kind of rescue task force would be assembled or what to expect. They said if you went down near the Bulgarian border, you might see as Bulgarian Hip helicopter coming to get you. If you came down in some other place, you might see a French helicopter.

The hours went on. We were coming near the end of the night, which was bad for me because our forces are trained to fight at night.

Because of the weather, the SANDYs were frustrated because they were not able to do their rescue escort job very well. Normally, they expect the survivor, that's me, to be clueless, so they train not to have to rely on the survivor at all. But because the SANDYs were hindered by the weather and couldn't drop down below the weather, they had to rely on me for a great deal of their situational awareness, including whether it was safe to come in. They apologized to me later because shortly before pickup, they authenticated me again. Over and over again, they questioned whether it was really me, and whether this was a Serb trap.

Maybe I had a gun to my head. Maybe I was under duress. They asked, "VEGA 31, is it okay to come in there?" I thought, "Don't ask me that. I don't want that to be my decision." I did not know what assets were out there. I didn't know it was high-speed helicopters with trained special-weapons guys. I couldn't answer them. At least a minute went by. I'm still thinking, *I can't answer them*. There was definitely enemy right there, no kidding, 100 yards from me, but the extent of the enemy and their capability I didn't know.

After about a minute, SANDY said, "VEGA 31, if you don't answer we're going to have to not do this now but come back later." I paused and said, "Yeah. Let's go for it." I felt I would know if capture was imminent. If I learned I was about to be captured, I felt I would have time to make a radio call, starting with authentication information, and saying, "Knock it off. Don't come in here."

They were pressing on in. I could hear them as they approached. It wasn't until the very end game that I could get two-way communication with the MH-60G. Now the challenge for them was, how do we get eyes on the survivor? I had an infrared strobe, a covert device. But I had no other backup covert signaling devices. We agreed on the radio that when I got the signal I would activate the strobe. When it came time for that, I turned it on and it didn't work. We learned later that it wasn't a mistake by me: It really, no kidding, wasn't working.

**JIM CARDOSO** We had spent the whole night trying to get to this point—the pickup. We came in to the area where the pilot was. We were unable to spot him. It was an extremely dark night. We were expecting an infrared strobe. We couldn't see that. We were talking to him. We knew he was close. We made a couple of passes trying to find him, our three helicopters spread out in a loose formation so we could maneuver as necessary, and could not see him. We saw some trucks near him. But we could not see the strobe, and we had no way to know that it wasn't working.

**F-117 PILOT (NAME WITHHELD)** Still on the radio with them using my VEGA 31 callsign, I communicated that my strobe wasn't working. The SANDYs asked for a pen-gun flare. I had one of those but I hadn't prepared it for use. God bless our life support people, that device was all wrapped in duct tape, meaning there was no way I could prepare it for use. I thought, *It's going to take me minutes to prep this sucker. Besides, there's no way I want to shoot this a thousand feet into the air because it's going to compromise my position to everybody for miles around.*

Jim Cardoso's copilot, John Glass, came on the radio—of course, I didn't know their names then, but this was my first contact with the Pave Low—and "If we're this close . . ." I came back with, "How about a regular flare?" They said, "Go for it."

So I pulled out my regular road flare and decided to use the night end of it. I was very uncomfortable with them exposed in the area. I thought, *We either need to make this happen right now or tell them to go away and try again at a later time.* We all knew that lighting the road flare ended my prospects of staying hidden. I was going to get rescued or captured—one or the other.

I lit that flare for just two seconds and then put it out. They told me later this got their attention immediately. They had been on night vision for hours and a signal like that is going to burn. I think they were about a mile from me at that point and decided the MH-60G would make a quick grab and go. They were very anxious about the Serbian vehicular activity around me.

**JIM CARDOSO** He lit a regular flare, an overt flare, which obviously was very visible on night-vision goggles. When he lit that, we knew we were only a half a mile away from him. We turned and my aircraft and the number two Pave Low flew over top of him. Our intention was we would circle and provide fire support as necessary. The MH-60G came behind us and made a very aggressive approach in basically black-hole conditions, working on the goggles. He put the aircraft down and had VEGA 31 virtually almost at the rotor tips.

**CHAD FRANKS** We landed at about 3:38 a.m., or seven hours after the pilot bailed out. That was the longest thirty seconds I ever spent on the ground. We finally found him when he lit off his flare. We were right on top of him, so we did an autorotation down on top of him. Then, we came into a hover because we'd made a deal with our pararescue jumpers that we would always keep the survivor out at the one o'clock position. By this time, we were sure, this was our F-117 pilot but going on in the back of my mind was the idea that it might have been him, but he might have been in a Serb trap.

He stood up and I saw him alone. He was on the radio and asked permission to come aboard the copilot. My PJs and the combat controller went out and grabbed him and brought him back in. We weren't on the ground very long at all.

**JIM CARDOSO** VEGA 31 got up, kept his hands behind his head in a nonthreatening manner. He came over the radio and said, "Can I approach?" We said, "Granted." The PJs were getting out and were going to him when they met right at the rotor arc. They ensured that he wasn't injured and that he fit the profile, the size, and shape of the guy we were looking for. They visually IDed him and basically tossed him in the back of the MH-60G, jumped in after him, and away they went. In our Pave Lows, we were in the process of a slow turn to come in and cover him, but we had a call from the MH-60G: "Thirty seconds to liftoff!" So as we came inbound again, we didn't need to cover him. We headed west and the 60 joined up behind us.

**F-117 PILOT (NAME WITHHELD)** Until the PJ was close to me, breathing on my face, they still were not certain whether this was an ambush.

It was so dark that when the MH-60G landed, it landed one rotor arc from me and I could not see it. Jim Cardoso later talked about how challenging conditions were. I finally saw the top part of the helicopter, which began to glow because it was illuminated by dust in the air creating static electricity from the leading edge of the rotors.

From the moment they spotted me, said Chad Franks—the MH-60G pilot—there was no time to set up a typical pattern, so he autorotated into a black hole of nothing with no horizon, no feel for closure rate to the ground. Crew members on the MH-60G later told me they thought they were going to crash.

The helicopters hauled me to Tusla. There, I was ordered to change immediately to a C-130 and continue on to my base at Aviano.

We pulled off my rescue with a walkie-talkie, a road flare, and a $100 GPS: our success was a testimony to the human spirit—and a wake-up call.

On the C-130 flying to Aviano, relaxing, in a high state of intensity after being rescued, I had a plastic bag next to me with all my gear in it, and I started hearing this ticking noise. It was my infrared strobe, the one that hadn't worked when I needed it to save my life. I thought to myself, *"You've got to be kidding me."*

# Chapter 19

## Assault Landing in Afghanistan

## What Happened

Aboard Capt. Allison Thompson's CH-53E helicopter, the tension was thick enough to cut with a knife.

"We knew there was no going back," said Thompson's air observer/gunner, Sgt. David L. McMichael. Three of the United States Marine Corps' heftiest, heavy-lift helicopters were carrying troops to seize a Taliban airfield in Afghanistan. The date was November 25, 2001, and it was one of the first actions of Operation Ending Freedom. There was expected to be no resistance to the Marine assault on the airfield (which would later be called Camp Rhino when in American hands), but intelligence had been wrong before. These Marines were going in prepared to fight.

The helicopters were plowing through the night, assailed by wind gusts, spattered with intermittent sprinkles of rain, while pilots peered into their night-vision goggles, worked their instruments, and maintained formation only by concentrating every instant.

Thompson was working overtime at the controls. It was night. There were brownout conditions. She was on night-vision goggles. One of the Marine Corps' most experienced CH-53E pilots, Thompson was

Captain Jacob M. "Cajun" Matt
November 25, 2001
Operation Enduring Freedom
Sikorsky CH-53E Super Sea Stallion (S-80)
Marine Heavy Helicopter Squadron 464,
   the "Condors"
BIG IRON
Camp Rhino, Afghanistan

Capt. Jacob M. "Cajun" Matt was a pilot in
squadron HMH-365 "Blue Knights" when he flew
the airfield seizure mission to Camp Rhino,
Afghanistan, on November 25, 2001. Today, he be-
longs to HMH-464 "Condors" at New River, N. C.

*Robert F. Dorr*

struggling with multiple issues on the longest flight she had ever made, which was also her first in combat. Thompson's CH-53E, belonging to squadron HMH-365 "Blue Knights," had lost one of its three engines to a compressor stall and had a misbehaving gyro compass. During the grueling flight from the USS *Bataan* (LHD 5), with a stopover aboard the USS *Peleliu* (LHA 5) to pick up thirty-six Marines per helicopter, a mechanical glitch had prevented the other two CH-53Es in the formation from refueling in flight. The only one of the trio to gulp gas from the KC-130F Hercules tanker plane, Thompson was working not merely to keep the mission on track, but to maintain her assigned position relative to the rest of the formation.

"We were at a crossroads," said McMichael, referring to the moment when this mission was going to succeed or fail.

But McMichael might as easily have been referring to the Marine Corps' experience with the Sikorsky CH-53E Super Sea Stallion and its need for a heavy-lift helicopter for 21st century wars. The CH-53E fleet has reached the point where the Marines need to make a decision about modernizing it—and there are no easy solutions. Unlike other aging helicopters in Marine inventory, the CH-53E has never been through an upgrade or modernization program. In terms of technology, the big, bulky helicopter is a creature of the 1970s, older now than the Marines

The Sikorsky CH-53E Super Sea Stallion is the heavy lifter of the Marine Corps, and was the star of the airfield assault mission flown during the first hours of combat in Iraq in October 2001.

*Sikorsky*

who fly it. It's a robust machine—going into Afghanistan, the squadron was using the radio callsign BIG IRON, which describes the CH-53E aptly—but it needs to be updated.

To understand why the CH-53E is approaching a pivotal juncture in its career, it helps to realize that the airfield seizure mission in Afghanistan wasn't supposed to happen that way at all.

"The CH-53E was supposed to carry *things*, not *people*," said Capt. Jacob M. "Cajun" Matt, another CH-53E pilot who flew in Afghanistan. "That's what we were taught in the Marine Corps from day one. The CH-46E Sea Knight, which we call the 'Frog,' would carry the troops on any air assault mission and the CH-53E would carry their equipment and supplies. It was always that way, but it hasn't been that way recently."

The CH-46E fleet, which was once scheduled to be replaced by the

Sgt. David L. McMichael was air observer/gunner aboard the Thompson CH-53E during the airfield seizure mission to Camp Rhino, Afghanistan. McMichael has been a CH-53E maintainer for more than a decade.

*Robert F. Dorr*

MV-22 Osprey tilt-rotor in 1994 (yes, in 1994!), is overworked and stretched too thin. Even on its best day, the Vietnam-era CH-46E never had the very-long-range capability needed for operations like those in Afghanistan—to which this narrative will return momentarily.

## The Marines' Heavy "Echo"

Pulled through the sky by three 3,696-shp (2756-kW) General Electric T64-GE-416 turboshaft engines driving a seven-bladed, 79-ft (24.08-m) diameter rotor, the CH-53E Super Sea Stallion is usually called, simply, the "Echo" by Marines. It's a new-generation, three-engine development of the twin-engine, Vietnam-era CH-53A aircraft. Forty-three of those earlier twin-engine versions, now upgraded to CH-53D, or "Delta," status, are still stationed today at Marine Base Kaneohe Bay, Hawaii. They have plenty of airframe life left, but critics argue in favor of scrapping them as an economy move since they use parts incompatible with any other U.S. helicopter. The CH-53E is 20 percent bigger and has 1.8 percent the lifting capacity of the earlier versions. It is the largest helicopter in the world except for some built in Russia. It is also the heavy-lift champion of the Marine Corps in an era when Marines fight wars in remote locations at very long range.

Apart from the third engine, features of the CH-53E include a dual-point cargo hook system, improved main-rotor blades, and composite tail-rotor blades. A dual digital automatic flight-control system and engine anti-ice system give the aircraft an all-weather capability.

In a perfect world, if plans from long ago had materialized, the Marines today would have 360 MV-22B Osprey tilt-rotor aircraft to carry troops and about 180 CH-53Es to haul artillery, ammunition, fuel, and supplies, leaving the CH-46E Sea Knight, the "Frog," to entertain children in museums. The airfield assault in Afghanistan, in darkness and bad weather, would have been flown by a fleet of Ospreys with that new-car smell and the CH-53E freighter would have been relegated to heavy-hauling duty, bringing in the Marines; supplies behind them.

But the Osprey program came to a halt—almost—when Defense Secretary Dick Cheney cancelled it in 1991. Later, as vice president, Cheney did a turnaround and supported the tilt-rotor, but meanwhile, the Osprey suffered several long periods of grounding as a result of fatal crashes. Today, the number of MV-22Bs planned for long-delayed purchase has dropped to 348 and the fleet of 248 CH-46Es has undergone a SLEP (service life extension program), a much-needed modernization effort that hasn't been tried for the CH-53E. Marines still go into battle when they can aboard the Frog, but for high-altitude, long-distance fighting in Afghanistan the Echo proved more suitable for hauling both people and things. The result is a CH-53E fleet that is overworked, running hard, and stretched thin.

From the standpoint of a Marine going into combat and burdened down with gear, the interior of the CH-53E is all that matters. The Echo's cargo or troop compartment measures 30 ft (9.14 m) long by 7 ft 2 in (2.19 m) wide and 6 ft 2 in (1.88 m) high, and has a rear door and loading ramp. A remotely controlled winch is located at the forward end of the compartment and can be used for cargo handling. The original requirement for the helicopter's spacious interior called for accommodating systems that are no longer in service today, including a Jeep with trailer, a 105 mm howitzer and a Hawk surface-to-air missile system. When transporting Marines, the CH-53E seats thirty-six troops in its normal configuration and has provisions to carry fifty-five passengers with centerline seats installed. It can also be configured to carry twenty-four litter patients.

It takes a cup of alphabet soup, maybe even a bowl, to describe how Marines use the CH-53E. When deployed aboard ship or to a remote base, CH-53Es may join an ACE (Aviation Combat Element) of an MAGTF (Marine Air-Ground Task Force) that can include conventional assault support tasks and special operations. The ACE is a Marine medium helicopter squadron (CH-46Es) augmented by additional types of aircraft into a composite squadron. These detachments include equipment and personnel to support CH-53Es, UH-1N Twin Hueys, and AH-1W Super Cobras. The ACE may also be equipped with fixed-wing aircraft such as the AV-8B Harrier, and support by a KC-130F Hercules squadron. The ACE is structured to fit the tactical situation, the MAGTF's mission and size, and space limitations within the ARG (Amphibious Ready Group) and is capable of conducting the full range of Marine air operations.

To translate this military jargon into real life, the author visited HMH-464 "Condors" at MCAS New River, North Carolina, at the end of 2003, just after the squadron's return from combat in the now-legendary march north that led to the fall of Baghdad. Lt. Col. Joaquin "Keen" Malavet commanded the squadron.

Marines are not introspective. They do not spend a lot of time

Capt. Andrew H. "Silkie" Mills of squadron HMH-464 "Condors" flew the CH-53E on combat missions in Iraq during Operation Iraqi Freedom.

*Robert F. Dorr*

thinking about who they are and what they do. Interviewed for this book, CH-53E pilots and crew members seemed more interested in talking about practical matters—the heavy maintenance demands of their helicopter are a constant gripe—than in waxing philosophic, even about the terrible pace they pay as a result of high-tempo operations in a global war on terrorism. Capt. Andrew H. "Silkie" Mills, a veteran of Iraq but not the earlier operations in Afghanistan, commented that the CH-53E is especially vulnerable and that "survivability is based on denying the aircraft to the enemy rather than trying to dodge bullets." Marine CH-53E pilots and crew members would like very much to achieve their difficult job, hauling people and things, often in difficult weather and terrain, without being shot at.

Jumping ahead for just a moment from Afghanistan to Iraq, Mills was copilot with Major Van Tran on a mission to haul external fuel bladders into the combat zone during the battle for An Nasiriyah in March 2003—a battle recounted by Cobra attack helicopter pilots in the next chapter. Mills had to fly at 200 ft (61 m) altitude in a region dotted with wires and towers—those brooding, silent enemies of the low-level helicopter pilot—with the prospect of Saddam Fedayeen guerillas possibly spotting and firing on the Echo. Mills' helicopter hauled fifteen of the big fuel bladders, one at a time, as external loads. "The CH-53E has a lot of power," Mills said, but noted that the engines have reliability issues. "The performance of the engine is under a lot of scrutiny," he added. Mills seemed to feel that the CH-53E force is stretched too thin, a situation he attributes to "the sluggishness of the Osprey program." Another Marine commented that the CH-53E "is a great helicopter but it's a lot like my ex-wife—very high maintenance." The CH-53E requires forty-one maintenance hours per flight hour, the highest of any Marine aircraft.

The need for a service-life extension program for the CH-53E arises in any conversation with Marines. Most want practical improvements to their helicopter, not a costly glass cockpit that they say isn't necessary. Mills said he wants "better motors and better filters, not cosmetic stuff like a digital cockpit." He noted that you can sometimes hate the CH-53E when it "breaks" but that the situation is always a love-hate relationship. "I love flying it. It has unusual hovering characteristics. You worry about banging the tail into the ground."

## Assault on Camp Rhino

The airfield seizure mission flown by Marine CH-53Es on November 25, 2001, was subtitled Operation Swift Freedom and was part of the larger effort against Taliban and al-Qaeda infrastructure known as Operation Enduring Freedom. The purpose was to fly a long-range, air-refueled sortie at night, from ships in the North Arabian Sea, deep into Afghanistan to take the Taliban airfield that later became known as Camp Rhino.

In the number one CH-53E on this mission were pilot Major Mitch Rios, copilot Major Pete Gadd, main crew chief Sgt. Keith Gilliland, crew chief Sgt. Mark Ulsh, and aerial observer/gunner Sgt. Roger Frese. Flying the number two aircraft were Major Allison Thompson and Capt. Mac Ward, plus their enlisted crew. In the number three helicopter were pilot Capt. Craig LeFlore and copilot Capt. Jacob M. "Cajun" Matt ("my name rhymes with 'hot'"). The three helicopters were carrying a BLT (battalion landing team) commanded by a lieutenant colonel and consisting of about 108 men of the 2nd Battalion, 8th Marines.

This kind of operation is known in Marine talk as vertical envelopment. When the nuclear age arrived in 1945, Marines realized that their very reason for existence—amphibious warfare—was threatened by a quantum leap in the effectiveness of a potential enemy's weapons. Just after World War II, Marines took to the idea of using a new vehicle—the helicopter—to establish "beachheads" not on the beach but deep inside an enemy's territory. The concept was supposed to enable Marines to take the offensive in an atomic war with the Soviet Union. In a new century, with a new threat from terrorism, the concept of vertical envelopment and the capabilities offered by the helicopter became just what the Marines needed when waging war at long distance, far from home.

**JACOB MATT** L-hour was at dusk. We took off from USS *Bataan* (LHD-5) about sixty miles (97 km) offshore and flew to the USS *Peleliu* (LHA 5). There, we picked up our troops, about thirty-six Marines per helicopter. We took off again, departing from the ship under emcon (emissions control, meaning radio silence), using night vision goggles. We flew at 1,000 to 1,500 ft (457 m) AGL (above ground level). My callsign was BIG IRON, which is an appropriate name for the CH-53E helicopter. Despite the emcon condition, we did do some communicating with the *Bataan*, which was using the callsign GLORY.

We were carrying a BLT, or battalion landing team of the 2nd Battalion, 8th Marines, commanded by a lieutenant colonel. Ours was the first of what would eventually be three 3-ship formations. Our route was to take us 425 miles (680 km) through Pakistan with air refueling from KC-130F Hercules tankers of the 2nd Marine Aircraft Wing that were deployed in the Persian Gulf region. Almost from the moment we launched from Peleliu and went under our ANVIS-9 night vision goggles, our CH-53E aircraft commanders—Rios, Thompson, and LeFlore—ran into technical and mechanical glitches of the kind you have to expect in any operational situation.

Thompson's problems began with the bum engine and renegade gyrocompass, but Thompson, at least, was able to take on fuel from the KC-130Fs. The other two helicopters made the link-up and started to gulp down gas, but were able to receive only a little fuel. Approaching the objective nearly five hours after takeoff, they were down to a minimum fuel load of 2,000 lb (907 kg). The CH-53Es had launched with a maximum internal fuel load of 1,017 U.S. gal (3,849 liters) plus two 650 U.S. gal (2,421 liters) drop tanks.

**DAVID McMICHAEL** Before I flew that mission in Capt. Thompson's CH-53E, I worked as a crew chief and maintainer with a four-plane detachment in Kosovo from April to August 1997 with squadron HMM-365, the "Blue Knights." I had long ago experienced the best moments you can experience in the Marine Corps—when they pull you aside and say, "How'd you like to have your name stenciled on this helicopter?" When you're the crew chief and it's your aircraft, it had your name right on it, that means a lot.

So I was at the right window of Capt. Thompson's, ready for this one, when we became the only helicopter in our formation that was able to take on fuel. They had said the weather was going to be clear. It wasn't. It was cold in the back, let me tell you that. We were carrying Marines who were cold, sick, and nervous, and this was an unusually long mission, but they were prepped up, too, and they were ready.

The CH-53E might be a better aircraft with a different engine, maybe the same engine that's on the V-22 Osprey. It's a very tough and dependable bird but it has a lot of quirks. For example, we need to get rid of a lot of old, brittle wire in the aircraft and replace it with new wire. That would mean a lot more to us than a digital, glass cockpit, which would be mostly cosmetic. Still, this is a very tough aircraft and it can be very flexible. One of the qualities of the CH-53E is that you can lose an engine and still go in.

Capt. Thompson was coping with an avionics problem. The gyro was off twenty degrees. She thought we were straight when we weren't. She got vertigo. She pulled the collective up, and sorted it out, and we pressed on.

**JACOB MATT** Marine Corps doctrine calls for never exposing the CH-53E to enemy fire. As the night wore on for us and as we drew closer, we continued to believe our intelligence experts, who had said the Taliban airfield was unmanned. We were not supposed to be greeted by enemy fire. As it turned out, of course, we were not, but those final moments were interesting.

When our three helicopters approached the Afghan airfield after that marathon trip, my adrenaline was pumping. Our LZ, or landing zone, was not a concrete runway. It was a dry, lake-bed plain. There were very few visual cues. I had to rely on my crew chief to scan visually as we tried to let down in darkness and brownout conditions. To be honest, the CH-53E is difficult to handle under the best of circumstances—no one ever called it a forgiving aircraft—and this was not the best. After the crew chief told us over the intercom that he had the ground in sight, we made the worst landing of my career that night. The helicopter just smacked itself into the ground. We dropped the ramp and the troops poured out.

## What Happened

With rotors thrashing, dust rising in clouds, and pebbles ricocheting around them in the half light, the first 104 Marines of the assault team charged out of the trio of CH-53Es, fanned out, and began to secure abandoned buildings and to set up communications. Matt peered out from his copilot's seat, looking into the mixed high and low light ahead of him on the lake bed, wondering if there would be hostile fire. There was none.

The battalion landing team had rehearsed the airfield seizure while still aboard ship. Now Marines secured the airfield in a series of fast, systematic moves that they'd had plenty of time to remember during the five-hour trip. It was the kind of anticlimax that every helicopter pilot would want in this situation. The pilots of the BIG IRON flight never saw muzzle flashes, never heard the impact of rounds. Within hours, a second wave of Marines would be arriving, and light-armored vehicles would be on Afghan soil. New waves of CH-53E helicopters would be bringing in fuel bladders, MREs, drinking water, and vehicle parts.

The job of the CH-53E pilots was done. They did, however, face new issues, not so dramatic but probably more typical of the vagaries of helicopter warfare.

The BIG IRON formation had one CH-53E that was operating on only two of its three engines (Thompson's), and two others that had insufficient fuel to return to the ships offshore. Instead of the 425-mile (680-km) journey back to the *Bataan* and the *Peleliu*, the trio of CH-53Es would have to make the 222-mile (357-km) flight to a FARC, a forward arming and refueling point, at Shamsi, Pakistan, where special-operations troops were standing watch over prepositioned fuel bladders, supplies, and communications. The light had changed and it was now pitch black as the three CH-53Es lifted off again, departing just as subsequent helicopters began to arrive.

"We were tired aviators," said Matt. The flight was as eventless as it could be, given the glitches and the weather. Still, "When we got to Shamsi we had been flying for eight hours."

Three weeks later on December 16, 2001, Marines used vertical envelopment to leapfrog another sixty miles to seize the airfield outside Kandahar. The city quickly fell. Now Marines had a commanding position, with their air squadrons taking up residence in the enemy's rear at Camp Rhino. Later in the war, Capt. Jacob M. "Cajun" Matt was called upon to extract special operations troops at high altitude in cold, gusty conditions, while being shot at north of Kandahar. Later in the war, too, Taliban gunfire claimed a CH-53E was near Baghran, along with two of its crew members, a victim of Taliban gunfire.

Those who questioned the Afghanistan campaign had said that it would take many months and require a million troops to dislodge the Taliban regime and destroy al-Qaeda forces in Afghanistan. Some warned that U.S. troops would get bogged down in Afghanistan, just as the Soviet Union's forces had done more than a decade earlier. They were all wrong. They were wrong because of vertical envelopment and helicopters. They were wrong, in part, because of the CH-53E.

As the United States approaches new challenges in the war on terrorism, some Marines are mystified that plans to for a state-of-the-art, heavy-lift helicopter seem to keep changing and being postponed. "A new version of the CH-53E is like a mirage in the desert," one Marine

This is a Marine CH-53E as seen from above.

*U. S. Marine Corps*

said. "You can see it out there. You keep getting closer to it. It keeps growing larger. But you never seem to reach it."

In 2000, the Marine Corps announced a plan to remanufacture its CH-53Es. Four years later, a contract had not yet been issued. Thereafter, Marine Corps spent four years refining a plan to upgrade 111 of its 165 Echos to like-new standard. The plan took shape on paper and looked good to those familiar with it, but no one ever cut metal.

In December 2003, during the visit to New River, North Carolina, made in the preparation of this volume, Marines said they didn't know what was happening with the plan or when they would put their hands on more modern equipment.

In March 2004, the Marine Corps announced that it was scrapping the upgrade program and, instead, would reopen the Sikorsky production line and purchase a redesigned version of the CH-53E. The Corps would purchase 154 new helicopters to replace the oldest and most exhausted ships in the fleet. The new craft would look like the current Echo but would be almost entirely a new aircraft.

The new ship is tentatively being called the CH-53X, and would be a direct descendant of a long line of helicopters that date to the Vietnam era (see p. 291). According to Marine officers, the CH-53X will use the Allison/Rolls-Royce AE1107C turbine engine, the very engine favored by

Sgt. McMichael. The new helicopter will have an all-composite rotor blade based on the blade used by a newer Sikorsky model, the S-92 blade. It will also have an improved cargo hook system and a common "glass" (digital) cockpit identical to either that of the MV-22B Osprey. The load capacity will be increased: The CH-53X will have a payload three times that of the CH-53E over a 200-nautical-mile radius and will reduce operational costs by 25 percent, or roughly $30 million per year.

That sounds like good news. But a lot of time was lost delaying and then canceling the upgrade program. So far, the new-build CH-53X exists only on paper. Marines are being told they now may have to wait until 2010 before they will see even a test model of the CH-53X. The future of all Marine aircraft is inextricably linked to the future of the MV-22B Osprey, which has first priority—but after more than twenty years of developmental work the Corps does not have a single Osprey ready to carry Marines into battle.

Meanwhile, the CH-53E—the oldest aircraft in service never to have been put through a service-life extension program—continues to serve the Marine Corps. The Echo has strong points and flaws, but in a pinch it almost always performs. Most Marines probably have the same overall opinion of the aircraft as Sgt. McMichael, who remembers the subzero cold of high-altitude operations in Afghanistan. "This aircraft," said McMichael, "has never let me down."

## Sikorsky CH-53E Super Sea Stallion

The CH-53E is the muscle of the Marine Corps.

The "Echo," which is called the Super Sea Stallion in official jargon, is a three-engine version of a twin-engine, heavy-lift helicopter operated by the Marines as a cargo-hauler in Vietnam and by the Air Force for combat rescue duty in Vietnam (Chapter Seventeen) and later conflicts (Chapter Eighteen). In addition to the extra engine, the Echo has an additional main rotor blade for a total of seven, and is heavier and more robust than twin-engine versions. The CH-53E also has a slightly increased main rotor diameter compared to earlier versions.

This is another view of a CH-53E on the ground.

*John Gourley*

Building on Vietnam experience with the Marines' twin-engine CH-53A and CH-53D, Sikorsky designed the bigger CH-53E in the 1970s.

Known to its manufacturer as the Sikorsky S-80, the CH-53E, or Echo, began as a YCH-53E service-test helicopter that made its initial flight at the manufacturer's Stratford, Connecticut, plant on March 1, 1974. After the first prototype burned into oblivion during a ground taxi run, a second prototype resumed flying with a revised tail design: The upright was canted twenty degrees to the left and fitted with a gull-winged tailplane cantilevered to the right.

The first preproduction CH-53E took to the air on December 8, 1975. The first production aircraft flew in December 1980 and was delivered to Marine squadron HMH-464, the "Condors," shortly after the squadron's activation on May 1, 1981. The United States Navy also employs the CH-53E for heavy lift and vertical onboard delivery (VOD) to haul supplies to warships in the Mediterranean. Another Navy version, the MH-53E, is used for minesweeping duties.

By the early 1980s, five Marine squadrons were flying the CH-53E. Most participated in Operation Desert Storm in 1991. The weight-lifting prowess of the CH-53E is a big boost to Marine commanders seeking to get troops and equipment to the battlefield, but mechanics say the Echo is also a challenge, requiring long maintenance hours, and it is tough to maintain amid desert sand storms.

A Marine Corps document lists the official tasks of the CH-53E as follows:

- Providing combat assault transport of heavy weapons, equipment, and supplies.

- Providing combat assault transport of troops.

- Conducting TRAP (tactical retrieval and recovery) operations for downed aircraft. (This happened on June 8, 1995, when CH-53Es spearheaded the rescue of Capt. Scott O'Grady, callsign

## Sikorsky MH-53E Super Sea Stallion (S-80)

**Type:** Two-pilot, four-crew heavy transport helicopter

**Powerplant:** Three 3,696-shp (2,756-kW) General Electric T64-GE-416 turboshaft engines driving seven-bladed, 79-ft (24.08-m) main rotors

**Performance:** Maximum speed, 196 mph (315 km/h) at sea level; cruising speed, 173 mph (278 km/h) at sea level; ferry range 1,290 miles (2075 km); operational radius 575 miles (925 km) with a 20,000-lb (9072-kg) external cargo; maximum rate of climb, 2,500 ft (762 m) per minute from sea level with a 25,000-lb (11340-kg) cargo; service ceiling, 18,500 ft (5640 m); hovering ceiling, 11,550 ft (3520 m) in-ground effect and 9,500 ft (2895 m) out-of-ground effect

**Weights:** Empty, 33,326 lb (15,061 kg); maximum takeoff, 69,750 lb (31,640 kg) with an internal payload or 73,500 lb (33340 kg) with an external payload

**Dimensions:** Main rotor diameter, 79 ft 0 in (24.08 m); length, rotors turning, 99 ft 0.5 in (30.19 m); fuselage length 73 ft 4 in (22.35 m); tail rotor diameter 20 ft 0 in (6/10 m); main rotor disc area, 4,901.67 sq ft (455.38 sq m); tail rotor disc area, 314.16 sq ft (29.19 sq m)

**Armament:** None; can be equipped with 7.62-mm or .50-cal door guns

**First flight:** March 1, 1974 (YCH-53E); December 1980 (production CH-53E)

BASHER 52, an F-16C Fighting Falcon pilot of the U.S. Air Force's 555th Fighter Squadron, "Triple Nickel," shot down in Bosnia.)

- Conducting assault support for evacuation operations and other maritime special operations.

- Providing support for mobile FARPs (forward arming and refueling points).

- Maintaining the capability to operate from amphibious shipping, other floating bases, and austere shore bases.

- Maintaining the capability to operate at night, in adverse weather conditions, and under instrument flight conditions at extended ranges.

- Maintaining the capability to deploy and conduct extended range operations by employing aerial refueling.

# Chapter 20

## Snake Drivers Versus Saddam

## What Happened

The place is Iraq. The helicopter is the AH-1W Super Cobra, also called the "Snake." The pilots are Marines like Major Craig Streeter, who has the square-jawed look of a recruiting-poster Marine. One of Streeter's buddies referred to the thin, fast, heavily armed Super Cobra as "the F-16 of helicopters." Streeter himself, as we'll see, wanted to fly fighters—until he decided that the AH-1W is one.

The outfit is Marine attack squadron HMLA-269, the "Gun Runners," commanded in Iraq by Lt. Col. Jeffrey M. "Huey" Hewlett. When not at war, these Marines and their helicopters reside at New River near Jacksonville, North Carolina.

Some of the heaviest fighting kicked off on March 23, 2003, with the battle of An Nasiriyah. "We were actually flying under power lines at one point," said Hewlett. "We were taking heavy fire from 37-millimeter RPGs [rocket-propelled grenades] and manpads [man-portable air defense systems, or shoulder-mounted surface-to-air missiles]."

Amid high winds, fog, and flooding, Super Cobra pilots shot up tanks, armored vehicles, and Saddam Fedayeen guerrillas. Cobra support helped ground Marines to charge into An Nasiriyah.

**Major Craig H. Streeter**
**January 13–June 22, 2003**
**Operation Iraqi Freedom**
**Bell AH-1W Super Cobra**
**Marine Light Attack Utility Squadron 269,**
**"Gun Runners"**
**GUN RUNNER 22**
**An Nasiriyah, Iraq (RIVERFRONT)**

Major Craig H. Streeter stands in front of his AH-1W Super Cobra of squadron HMLA-269, the "Gun Runners," in October 2003 after returning from Iraq.

After that battle, the Cobras moved north and fought at Baghdad and Tikrit. Altogether, Hewlett's AH-1Ws destroyed 697 targets, including ninety tanks. Of fifty-four Cobras in Iraq, forty-four were hit by enemy gunfire at least once.

Describing the fighting for An Nasiriyah, Baghdad, and Tikrit, Major Craig Streeter talks about the Cobra weapons in Marine shorthand. The Cobra carries a cannon, unguided rocket projectiles, and "TOW" and "Hellfire" guided missiles.

When Streeter talks about "the gun," he means the M197 20-millimeter cannon hanging in the Cobra's chin turret. The "rockets" are 2.75-inch, folding-fin, unguided projectiles that are launched from canisters, each holding nineteen rockets. The TOW is the BGM-71A (tube-mounted, optically tracked, wire-guided) missile that Marines love because it's a line-of-sight weapon that's easy to use visually. The Hellfire is the sophisticated AGM-114 missile that often heads straight up when fired, gets into a proper trajectory, and comes down on its target. Rockets, TOW, and Hellfire are mounted on tiny stub wings astride the Cobra's fuselage. When Streeter talks about whether they "come off" his aircraft, he is referring to whether they launch properly. Another Marine shorthand term is *manpad*, for man-portable air defense system, meaning a shoulder-mounted, surface-to-air missile fired at the

The Marine Corps' AH-1W Super Cobra fought in Operation Iraqi Freedom in 2003 after fighting earlier in the 1991 Persian Gulf War. Marine helicopter pilots like the mission because the AH-1W does its job in close coordination with Marine combat units on the ground.

*John Gourley*

Cobra from the ground. When Streeter talks about *flares* and *chaff*, he refers to devices dropped by the Cobra to decoy enemy missiles. Like all helicopter pilots, Streeter sometimes uses the word *airplane* to refer to his helicopter. In Marine parlance, a *section* is a formation of two aircraft; a *division* is a formation of four.

**CRAIG STREETER** I'll tell you straight up. I wanted to fly jets. I saw myself as an F/A-18 Hornet jock flying around, winning a dogfight.

I ended up flying Cobras, and now I think that's what God wanted me to do. I think I'm a better pilot for the Marine Corps because I'm a Cobra pilot. I'm more closely attuned to the grunts. I understand the whole fire support coordination thing, the ballet that takes place between helicopters and Marines on the ground. A Cobra pilot eats and breathes that stuff.

In Iraq, we flew with so much gear that it was always crowded inside. Visibility wasn't great. The Cobra cockpit is small, anyway. I mean, it's really tight. You have just enough room to slide a publication or a map into the cockpit before your hips rub up against the plate. To add to that, you've got NBC protective clothing—nuclear, biological, chemical. You've got a map, a copy of all the freqs [radio frequencies] of everybody in theater. You've got your survival maps, your 1:50,000 maps, and your NVGs if you're flying with night vision goggles. You've got your pistol, your body armor, your backup set of goggles, chem

The author photographed this AH-1W Super Cobra of squadron HMLA-269, the "Gun Runners," in October 2003, just weeks after the squadron's return to New River, N. C., following combat in Operation Iraqi Freedom. The Cobra in the photo is being piloted by Lt. Col. Jeffrey "Huey" Hewlett, squadron commander.

*Robert F. Dorr*

sticks, you name it, and all this stuff is going into the aircraft before you climb in. You've got your "hit-and-run bag" in case the aircraft gets shot down. You've got your survival pack filled up with a space blanket, extra ammo, and water, and you just rapidly run out of room. Every inch of space is used. It got extremely small in there, very quickly.

In the Cobra, the pilot in command sits in the back seat. The copilot, who is also the gunner, sits up front. In Iraq, I was a senior pilot and was teamed up with the most junior copilot in our squadron. First Lt. Steve Feher had been in -269 for all of a week and a half. He's a very good guy but he had almost no experience.

Usually we flew with a good mix of Hellfire and TOW missiles. There's a safety limit on aircraft weight, and we flew above that weight in Iraq all the time. I hate spilling the beans, but we went well above the helicopter gross weight limit of 14,750 pounds.

We routinely carried four TOW or four Hellfires, plus seven 2.75-inch HE [high-explosive] rockets, seven flechette rockets, and maybe 300 rounds of 20-milimeter [ammunition]. Sometimes we'd take all HE, or vary the ordnance mix in some other way. So we flew above 15,000 pounds gross weight, which is hard on the airframe, but you need the bullets and you need the rockets.

We had a heavy fight at An Nasiriyah on March 23, 2003. We linked up with Task Force Tarawa on the southern reaches of the city limit, pushing north into the city.

## Going into Combat

The adrenaline is rushing. Your pulse rate is going up. For me, it took a conscious effort to keep pulling the collective, to keep the power up, because your adrenaline was going like, "Oh, my God, this is it, and I'm going to get into a shooting match."

Before you found out what was really going on, that's when you feared the worst. Usually, as soon as you got someone on the radio, you felt better. You knew, "Okay, this is something similar to what I trained for. I can do this."

The communication back and forth with the FAC [forward air controller, a Marine aviator working on the ground] was essential. We always asked him to fill us in on the enemy situation right off the bat. Until you know that, you get this unnatural fear, you fear they're everywhere, you fear the absolute worst. Then you get a call from the FAC like, "We got bad guys on the treeline 3,000 meters away." He'll paint the picture for you.

On March 23, Task Force Tarawa had just started into An Nasiriyah. They were pausing before they made the push over the southern bridge.

We were at our primitive new base at Jalibah, also called RIVERFRONT, which had belonged to the Iraqi Army until a few days earlier. We were fifteen minutes flight time or twenty-five miles from An Nasiriyah.

This particular day was unusual because I was a division leader. I had a flight of three aircraft.

Our comm (communication) structure hadn't been fully developed, as far as how to tell us to launch. Normally, someone would go, "Hey, launch!" The only people who had comm with the outside were the refuelers and air traffic control guys in the support squadron on the other side of the base. We were in sleeping bags next to a fuel truck. So I go, "Hey, I'm going to get up in the morning. I'm going to go talk to the air

The Marine Corps AH-1W Super Cobra had a simple, two-bladed main rotor, twin engines, a three-barrel cannon in a chin turret beneath the front cockpit, and a stub wing that can carry ordnance.

*Norman Taylor*

traffic controllers and see if they have word on what the higher ups want us to do."

So I left the guys in my division. I told them, "I will call you and tell you what the situation is." Then I got into a Humvee, took off for the other side of the base, and got in touch with somebody who had access to the tactical situation. He said, "Yeah, we want you to launch and go to An Nasiriyah. Contact the FAC, whose callsign is MOUTH." He gave me the frequency. This was 6 or 6:30 in the morning and we were told to go ahead and launch.

So I called back from the other side of the base to my waiting pilots and said, "Hey, you guys! Hit starters now! I I'll catch up with you. Soon as I get back in this Humvee." I wanted to get them going quick.

So when I got the word to launch from the ATO [air tasking order], I called back and said, "Launch." I jumped back in the Humvee and I drove to my aircraft. By the time I got there, those guys were already turning rotors. I told them I would catch up.

So by the time I turned rotors and contacted them on the radio, I found . . . nobody. "Hello? You guys? Hello?" Two of the three AH-1W Cobras in my division were out there somewhere but I couldn't reach them. I'd lost them. All I knew was, I'd told them An Nasiriyah was where the action was going on.

I went up to the [dispatcher] and said, "Hey, I'm launching as a single. I'm looking for my wingmen." This was biggest day of the war, and I couldn't find them. I took off as a single, looking for my Dash Two and Dash Three. All I knew was, there was a fight going on in An Nasiriyah, so that's why I went as a single. Bad, bad, bad. You never want to do that.

## Alone at An Nasiriyah

I went north trying to feel my way up, calling on the radio, trying to catch up. The next thing I knew, I'm talking to the FAC, callsign MOUTH, saying, "I'm a single Cobra. I'm looking for my wingmen." Then the FAC says, "We need help."

They had already gotten into a firefight. Some west coast Cobras had already been working with them. Those Cobras were low on gas and ready to leave. Now the Marines were getting ready to push into the city and didn't have any Cobras on station. There were bad guys on the treeline. The west coast Cobras had been engaging these Iraqis on the treeline all morning.

MOUTH asked me, "Are you a FAC-A?" meaning, "Are you forward air controller, airborne? Can you control other aircraft or artillery?" I said, "Yes, I am." And I said, "Yes, I will."

So here I am with a brand-new lieutenant in my front seat, single ship, without my wingmen, going to control a section of F-18 Deltas [F/A-18D Hornet strike fighters] to drop bombs on these bad guys on the treeline.

Steve was supporting me in the front seat and doing a great job. But I was the one who held the FAC-A qual, so I started talking to these Hornets who were on the same net as MOUTH.

Actually, the FAC had just changed his callsign from MOUTH to HAWK. I talked to him and to the F-18s, who were using the callsigns NAIL 53 and NAIL 54.

We picked up some targets, a tank and an armored personnel carrier. HAWK helped us pinpoint them by saying, "We've been taking fire from personnel in the treeline. We're taking fire from a tank and an armored vehicle." We saw a tank on the treeline and attempted to shoot it with a Hellfire [from our helicopter] but our laser boresight was off and we didn't hit it.

So here we are. My heart is in my throat. I've got no Dash Two [wingman]. I've got no Dash Three. I've just gotten into the fight. I've got a section of F-18s on station. I've got bad guys in the treeline.

I said, "I'm ready when you're ready." NAIL 24 said, "I'm in." I said, "My laser's on. I have a good spot. Put it hot."

He came in and dropped. Boom. A 2,000 pounder penetrated the treeline. Ka-boom. He dropped number two. He took out the treeline and there were no more enemy personnel. There was still a tank, or we thought it could be a truck; it was hard to tell in the trees. Afterward we said, "Yeah, I think we got him." I would never have seen these bad guys initially if HAWK hadn't told me where they were. Initially, it had been a warning: "They're right off your nose. Recommend you stay away from them."

This was the same treeline where later on in this day there was a manpad [i.e., a shoulder-mounted surface-to-air missile], like an SA-7 or some sort of shoulder-launched, heat-seeking missile that shot out of the treeline at one of our helicopters.

So that was our mission engagement—boom, boom, two 2,000 pounders on the bad guys, and the Marines were loving it.

Now we're going low on gas. And at about this time, lo and behold, well guess who shows up? My Dash Two and my Dash Three. They'd gone off and gotten separate tasking, came back, refueled, and wanted to get into the fight.

They showed up with a full bag of gas. It was an interesting conversation. I said, "What were you guys doing?" So now we're all on the same frequency and right behind my Dash Two and my Dash Three, flying in a section, and then the CO [commanding officer, Lt. Col. Jeffrey "Huey" Hewlett] shows up with his wingman and I'm alone but I'm going back to get gas.

Lt. Col. Jeffrey "Huey" Hewlett (left, with author Robert F. Dorr) took squadron HMLA-269 to war in Iraq and returned without losing a single Marine. The "plane captain" identified on the AH-1W Super Cobra is the Marine enlisted crew chief responsible for the aircraft.

*Robert F. Dorr*

## *"Round Two" of Fighting*

So Round Two starts. Now it's forty-five minutes later. Now I'm back in the fight with fresh fuel. Now my old Dash Two and Dash Three are the ones running low on gas and they're heading back. I'm still a single but I jump onto the Lt. Col. Hewlett's section. I say, "Hey, sir, can I get in? Can I get in?" And he says, "Yes," so we become a three-ship section. Hewlett is in the middle of shooting up this treeline that I'd just dropped the two 2,000 pounders on. So now I become his Dash Three.

Hewlett was flying with Capt. John Ginn. His wingman was Capt. Doug Sanders, who was flying with Lt. Pound. For about five minutes, we had five Snakes engaging that treeline; then my Dash Two and Dash Three left, and three of us were engaging. I brought TOW and Hellfire to the fight, and of course 20-milimeter, so we were using all of our weapons.

This Round Two was before lunch, maybe 10:30 a.m., so I'd been flying for just a few hours at that point. Most days, we flew much longer.

We never ran into a tank or any other target we couldn't shoot with a TOW. We were shooting things with TOWs inside of 500 meters. They say the minimum range of a TOW is 500 meters but we were shooting as close as 150 or even 100 meters. The TOW is also effective all the way out to 3,000 meters. During Round Two that day at An Nasiriyah, I chose Hellfire because my TOW wasn't working.

The Hellfire was working. We squirted the laser. We got a nice laser spot, shot the Hellfire. Feher was like, "Okay, looking good, looking good, looking good." Often, when we engaged targets, boresighting was a problem. It's a very sensitive piece of equipment. You boresight it one time and it's perfect. Other days you have to boresight it six or seven times, and still it isn't right. It was a constant challenge to get a tight boresight for the laser.

During Round Two, two T-55 tanks showed up by the bridge up the way from us, though I wasn't involved in that melee.

There was just a lot of shooting going on. The FAC we were working with called a manpad in the air [meaning we were being fired at by a shoulder-mounted surface to air missile]. "SAM in the air, SAM in the air!" he called. "Flares, flares, flares!" telling us to dispense flares to decoy the missile.

Here's this treeline. There's two racetracks of Cobras flying around, three Cobras on one track, two on another, and they're all attacking the same target. I'm on the far side of the racetrack about to turn inbound when he calls, "SAM in the air!" So, again, I looked towards the treeline and every single Cobra in my field of view had flares popping out of the back. It was pretty amazing. It was a remarkable sight. And it was evidence of good training.

We continued to shoot at that treeline for thirty or forty minutes before coming back to get more gas. And by the time we flew back for Round Three, we now started working on the eastern side of An Nasiriyah. It was now early afternoon, maybe 1300 or 1400 hours. We were flying about two hours at a stretch and it took about forty-five minutes to go back, refuel, and return each time.

There was not as much shooting in Round Three. It was constant on the eastern side of the city, but not as intense as before. My role now was to let Hewlett's section get into the fight—and while they were doing that I was covering them the entire time. I was checking their six, making sure nothing was sneaking behind them. I was constantly checking the treelines for the bad guys. I was looking for a triple-A piece [antiaircraft artillery] or any other threat that might be pointed at Hewlett's section.

This was the time they had the fratricide incident where the Air Force A-10 ran down some Marines, so things were pretty nutty. A lot of people were getting emotional because they'd just had an AAV that had just gotten destroyed. [Author's note: A Marine armored assault vehicle, or AAV, was destroyed in a "friendly fire" mishap by an A-10 Thunderbolt II which opened up with its cannon on members of Charlie Company, 1st Battalion, 2nd Marines, killing as many as nine of the fourteen Americans who died in fighting at An Nasiriyah that afternoon.]

There was a lot of confusion. The FAC was talking to the A-10, and there was a lot of activity. I think I have pretty good SA [situational awareness] and I can do a pretty good job of keeping track of the fight, but this was a confusing battle with a lot of chatter going on. The A-10s weren't there very long. They ran their missions and were gone. We made comments like, "Holy shit, we had A-10s in the area and never saw them." I wasn't privy to the A-10 attacks. I didn't see the effects of the attacks. At the time it happened, I don't think anyone there that day believed the AAV got hit by anything other than enemy fire.

This was the most weird and wily day I ever had. On this particular day, there was no Round Four. The CO [Lt. Col. Hewlett] was spent. Ironically, my Dash Two and Dash Three—Capt. Matt Schindberger and 1st Lt. Travis Richie in one helicopter, Capt. Brian Bruggeman and 1st Lt. John Parker in the other—did go out one last time.

Altogether, in Operation Iraqi Freedom, I logged over 100 hours of combat time.

## AH-1W Pilot Background

There's nothing remarkable about how I became an AH-1W Super Cobra pilot. I went to the Virginia Military Institute and graduated in 1991 on an ROTC scholarship. I went to Officer Candidate School, the officers' boot camp, after my junior year in college and got commissioned as a second lieutenant on my graduation. I went to flight school in 1992 and was winged in July 1993. We flew the T-34C Turbo Mentor basic trainer and the TH-57 training helicopter. I went off to squadron HMT-303 at Camp Pendleton, California, from summer 1993 to May 1994. My first squadron was HMLA-269, so I came right here [New River, North Carolina]. I checked in in June of 1995. I went off to Haiti when the Haiti thing went down in October.

I married Chris-Ann in 1995. We have a little girl, Jaden, and a son, Nathaniel.

I've been asked for a description of how you fly the "Snake" in combat. For example, how do you organize a Cobra attack? Here are some observations on how things work:

You show up to work with one guy and they say, "Go check that out." It's the FAC, an aviator attached to a ground unit who tells you what to do. For example, that day at An Nasiriyah, it was MOUTH and HAWK who were steering us to our targets. They talk to the company or battalion commander about what the Marines are doing that day.

When we enter the combat area, we call the FAC. "Hey MOUTH, this is DEADLY 41." "Hey, DEADLY, what are you?" they ask, because they may not know what type of aircraft are coming. So we say, "We're a section of Snakes [Cobras]." They'll respond, "Hey, great, how much time you got? How much gas you got? What kind of ordnance you got? Here's what we need." And the FAC is literally claiming us. He'll say, "I need you to check out this little town over here. We got suspected enemy fire coming from this little town." Or, "Can you check out this bridge?" Or, "We're taking fire from this building. Can you shoot it with a TOW?" Or, "We got bad guys shooting us right now and we need you to get in here, fast."

About the AH-1W Cobra aircraft: It's a great weapon. The Cobra is nasty. I like the weapons mix. The ability to shoot TOW if you need it gives you a line-of-sight capability you don't have with the Hellfire. You can shoot something up close and get warm and fuzzy. It's got 20-millimeter, rockets, TOW, Hellfire. I mean, it is one versatile mix of weapons.

It's a lot of fun to fly, too. It's awesome. It's got a lot of power.

So what's wrong with the AH-1W Cobra? Well, it has poor human engineering. It's hard to get weapons off that airplane. You need to be a contortionist to get some of the switches in the proper position in order to be ready to go into the fight. To get our chaff and flares ready, you've got to get a switch that's behind your right shoulder. So you've literally got to reach way back here to flip this toggle switch—you can't see it;

you have to feel for it. Then there's the cockpit design in the back seat. Everything was designed in the 1960s and 1970s. Everything consists of old-generation up/down switches, which are prone to making a mistake if you're in a rush or not well trained. It's very easy to flip a switch [thinking you're firing] and have the weapon fail to come off the helicopter because you forgot to flip one circuit breaker.

I wish visibility in the back seat were better. We've got so many black boxes on the dashboard of the Cobra. There are multiple black boxes that have just been added onto the airframe throughout the years. For example, in '99 we picked up the capability to shoot the Sidewinder [air-to-air missile]. Some of our radar warning gear has taken up new space on the dash. The HUD [head-up display] is a great piece of gear but unfortunately that, too, takes up space. And what it amounts to is, in the back seat your forward visibility is impaired. There's no way to get around it. We compensate instead of flying nose-up by flying side-to-side until we see what's ahead.

Other than the engineering of the back seat, the AH-1W Super Cobra is a good platform. It really is.

How do you decide what mix of weapons to carry? As we went farther north in Iraq there were just as many targets for our precision-guided munitions. I found I did more and more PGM shooting as the war went on. Here's why: Initially we were moving fast and furious. You go in, you aim, and you're out. It was like hip shots, you know? "Here I am!" Very quick reaction—rocket, rocket, rocket, 20-millimeter and you're out of there. A lot of the Iraqis were abandoning their gear—just taking off and leaving it. For example, I stumbled on a field that was full of, like, twenty to thirty T-72 tanks, armored vehicles, and stuff. They were abandoned. But the Iraqis also had this trick of leaving their equipment, then coming back and using it again, then leaving it again. So the message to us was, "Destroy it, destroy it," and that's exactly what we did. But we made less use of precision weapons in the early days.

Now we're outside of Baghdad. We're saying, "Okay, let's find the juiciest targets. Let's start getting these guys." We did a lot of shooting and went through a lot of Hellfires and TOWs in one day outside Baghdad.

Sometimes you'd go out and try to shoot the gun and it wouldn't work. So you go out. You come back for your next tank of gas. You talk to your ordnance personnel and say, "Hey, look, my gun doesn't work. I need you to troubleshoot it." We had some reliability problems with the cannon. It jammed, not half of the time maybe, but more than 35 percent of the time. The gun is pretty reliable on the whole, but over time as we continued shooting a lot in all that dirt and dust we had problems. You'd go in and shoot a few rounds and then it wouldn't shoot any more.

Looking back at Iraq, I've been asked for an overall assessment: What worked and what didn't in the Cobra in Iraq? I'll make a blanket statement about that. I think the way we're training right now is right on the money. I think we fought exactly how we trained. There was no radical change in tactics when we got to Iraq and said, "This is for real." We actually fought the way we trained.

I've been asked about being taken under fire by the enemy. The thing that caught me off guard, thank God, is that I thought the Iraqis would put up a stiffer resistance than I experienced. I did a lot of shooting and took a lot of enemy fire at An Nasiriyah, but I don't think it was ever intense, you know? The enemy fire was sporadic. I brought my wingman home on two separate occasions with bullet holes in his airplane. By the grace of God, I never got touched. You'd be shooting targets and it seemed like you were shooting guys who were shooting back, but you didn't always know where their rounds were going. I expected a lot of flak, triple-A, dodging, planes falling, you know? Compared to that mental image, my stuff was pretty benign, if you can call combat benign. It wasn't like the stuff you might see in a *Flash Gordon* comic book, or *Sergeant*. You just went out and did a good job and tried to stay safe.

The Iraqis that I came across, other than in An Nasiriyah, didn't much want to fight. There was one small fight at a time where some Iraqis were in a bunker and I put some rockets into that bunker. I know I got those guys. They were shooting at me before I took them out, but that was the exception. My war experience was exciting enough, thank you very much.

As a "Snake driver," I was proud of what we did every day. I was very proud that all of us, to a man, did what we were supposed to do: We sometimes would fight for eight hours and you didn't see anybody getting sick or dodging responsibility. Morale was very good and very strong. I don't want to say people enjoyed the combat experience but there was job satisfaction when it was all said and done. The Cobra is absolutely a good aircraft to go to war in. This whole Marine air-ground team works out fantastic.

# Bell AH-1W Super Cobra

The AH-1W Super Cobra is the 21st-century version of the Vietnam-era AH-1G (Chapter 15). Today, the Army is retiring its last Cobras but the Marines are forging ahead with today's AH-1W model and the more advanced AH-1Z planned for the near future.

## AH-1W Super Cobra Specifications

**Type:** Two-seat attack helicopter

**Power:** Two 1,690-shaft horsepower General Electric T700-GE-401 Turboshaft engines

**Performance:** Maximum speed 170 knots (195 mph/313 km/h); cruising speed 152 knots (173 mph/278 km/h), service ceiling 14,750 ft (4558 m); range 256 nautical miles (294 miles/473 km) in basic attack configuration

**Weights:** Maximum takeoff weight 14,750 lb (6696 m)

**Dimensions:** Rotor diameter: 48 ft (14.62 m); length: 58 ft (17.67 m), height: 13.7 feet (4.17 meters)

**Armament:** One M197 three-barrel 20-mm cannon (mounted under nose with 750 rounds in beltless container); four BGM-71 TOW (tube-launched, optically tracked, wire-guided) air-to-ground missiles or four AGM-114K/M/N Hellfire missiles plus 2.75-in Zuni air-to-ground rocket projectiles or AIM-9L Sidewinder air-to-air missile; AN/ALE-39 chaff system; SUU-4/1 flare dispenser

**Crew:** Two seats, in tandem (pilot in rear, copilot/gunner in front)

**First flight:** November 16, 1983

# Index

Page numbers in *italic* indicate photographs.